Diary of a Wimpy Eventer

The Wimpy Trilogy

For Patrick, my shining star in the most wonderful sky.
I loved you more than any words could ever say.
Rest easy my sweet boy.

© 2023 Victoria Brant – Diary of a Wimpy Eventer
www.wimpyeventer.com

The moral right of the author has been asserted.
Printed in Great Britain.

Written, designed and published by Victoria Brant.

Reworked Edition 2023
ISBN: 9798322500889
Imprint: Independently published

The advice and strategies found within may not be suitable for every situation. This work is sold with the understanding that the author is not held responsible for the results accrued from the advice in this book.

Part One
How to get your leg over

The reader of this book,
must only pick it up
if, you've got an open mind
and aren't too posh or too refined.

GLOSSARY

If you're sat in someone's downstairs loo reading this and having 16 hands between your thighs seems a little… risk*é*, there are probably a few terms within this book that might also need further explanation. I have used my own terminology to help you to understand those phrases in the glossary over leaf, these may or may not be factually correct. Throughout the book, the first time they are used will be marked with an asterisk*.

Affiliated: Namely, British Eventing, British Dressage, British Show Jumping, etc. A governing organisation providing an exemplary standard of sport, facilities, results documentation, and archive. You pay handsomely to be a member of these organisations, but it usually means that things run much more smoothly on the day resulting in less chance of death.

Arena: An area of land that has a rubber or sand floor and a gate that closes so that when you fall off, the horse can't escape. Also known as a menage.

Bloodstock Auctions: An occasion that sees the auctioning of horses that aren't very good at racing or that are being sold off to pay their training/livery bills.

Bravery Vest: an inflatable body warmer that is clipped to your saddle which will inflate in less than a second if the cord is pulled. I wear the brand Point Two who were brave enough to sponsor me when I was just an unsuccessful amateur without a massive social media following. From experience, wearing it will make you braver and safer.

Breakers and Youngsters: Young horses that you shouldn't ever get on unless you are very experienced or very foolish, or both.

British Eventing (also referred to as BE): The affiliated society that I pay vast amounts of money to each year. They govern the sport of eventing. Also, the name written on my car window sticker – I think it makes me look more professional when I'm out and about (it does not).

Calming Cookies: A nugget of joy containing a herbal blend that makes my horse less frisky – could also be a placebo but I don't really care much for that theory.

Chip Pisser: Someone that frequently sprays their metaphorical urine all over your good day/first place/clear round/bag of celebratory chips. They are people that indirectly say negative comments and make you feel like smearing faeces in their eyeballs.

Clear round: When you don't knock any of the coloured poles down (or have refusals, fall off or die) whilst practicing the art of show jumping.

Clinic: Organised training sessions, usually in groups of 3 or 4 where an instructor tells you how to be less shit at riding your horse.

Combined Training: This is a competition involving a dressage test and a show jumping round. Like eventing but with less death potential.

Cross-country (also; death phase or XC): The third phase of eventing in which you cover yourself and your horse in layers of protective clothing and gallop as fast as at obstacles that are solid, unforgiving and might well kill you.

Dressage: The first phase of eventing which is also a standalone sport. You and your horse perform a sequence of movements inside an enclosed area having memorised and practiced the moves in the run up to the event (or the night before, in the pub, on the back of a beer mat). You have the least chance of dying in this part.

Eventing: Something that you should not do unless you are mad or rich, or both. You will become obsessed with its intricacies; you will have a lot less money and your chances of fatality will increase considerably.

Field Master: Someone that is in charge of how fast and how far you gallop when you go out hunting.

Gelding: a male horse that has been removed of his testicles in order to prevent him from lustfully chasing the opposite sex.

Hacking: Riding your horse in any area that isn't an arena (e.g. roads, fields, paths, to the pub)

Hunter Trial/Team Chase: Competitive cross-country riding, solo or in a team, for the truly unhinged.

Hunting: A group of people and a pack of hounds run across the countryside chasing after the etiquette and morals of the 1940s. – They NEVER find them and usually return home pissed and covered in mud.

Livery yard: a house share arrangement for horses that people pay generously for the use of. Usually a place of rivalry, one-upmanship, sneaking a pee in your stable and occasional rare friendships.

Long Reining and Lunging: something you do when you are training horses or when you are too scared to ride them.

Mare: a female horse over 4 years old. A force to be reckoned with.

Master Imp: the Father (sire) of my beloved horse Patrick. His semen has produced some of the best (and notoriously some of the trickiest) event horses of all time.

Medium Trot: like regular trot (the up/down pace) only the horse stretches more and the rider loses more balance.

Minky: Vagina/general lady crotch area.

Neck Strap: a band of leather secured around the horses neck that you can grab hold of if you feel like you might wobble off.

Oxer: a type of jump that is wider than just a single pole, also known as a parallel or spread.

Prelim, Novice and Elementary: Levels in dressage competitions – prelim being the easiest, elementary being the one I'm not that good at.

Rearing, Napping, Bucking and Bolting: Things that horses do that terrify their riders. These things are usually caused by humans and their lack of understanding.

Riding Club: a group of middle-aged women that enjoy wine, low key horse shows and horse chatter.

Rosette: The Holy Grail of competitive riding, a large frilly badge that symbolises sweating, HOURS of practice and successful non-death.

Schooling: Teaching your horse to behave in a respectable manner so that when you finally make it out in public, you don't get asked to leave.

Schoolmaster: a horse that has been 'schooled' so much it has given up the need to disagree with its rider. This type of horse may even be safe for a non-rider/husband to hack to the pub on.

Sedalin Gel/dope: a syringe full of gel that you must get prescribed from the vet for sedating your horse.

Show Jumping: The sport of jumping over obstacles that will fall if you breathe on them the wrong way. Four penalties are issued if you knock one down, several penalties are issued if you stop to catch your breath and go too slow!

Showing: Pruning your horse until it is almost bald for a judge to assess its suitability for a particular job.

Spooking – The reaction a horse gives when he sees something that might well jump out and slit his throat, usually an upturned leaf, wheelie bin or crisp packet.

Start box (of doom) the area that you are imprisoned into whilst you are counted down to ride the cross country phase of eventing.

Stock: a type of tie that hides a double chin very nicely indeed.

Tack: a collective word for all of the things I buy and hide from my husband, namely saddles, bridles etc.

Trakehner: (track-ay-ner) a type of cross country jump that looks okay from a distance but when you get nearer it has a huge gaping hole under it that might well swallow you up.

Vetting: the process you can choose to go through when buying a horse to see how many legs it is lame on.

Wasurk: A Lincolnshirse term for a horse or human whose behaviour is less than ideal.

Wither: A part of the horse that when you ride without a saddle hurts your minky* (see above).

INTRODUCTION

Ever wondered what it takes to over-come fear, to grab hold of something with both hands and never let go? Read on my dear friend; read on.

I sit here and write this having come through the darkest of tunnels, knowing full well what it takes to keep lifting your feet, even through the deepest clay. You don't even need to have touched a horse to know what it's like to feel consumed by self-doubt.

Let go of everything just for a while, give yourself to this book and I guarantee that you will feel less alone, more capable and laugh with me as I share my journey with you.

You are more capable than you realise, trust me.

IN THE BEGINNING

Growing up in rural Lincolnshire in the arse end of nowhere there wasn't a lot else going on other than field sports and farming, this meant that my equestrian fate was almost inevitable. Neither of my parents encouraged the habit, none of my siblings appreciated the scent of horse urine either but it had me hooked from a very young age.

My father worked long hours as a farm worker on a large arable estate in south Lincolnshire and my mother was the housekeeper for the estate owners. Unfortunately for their pony-mad daughter, their salaries combined definitely couldn't fund a pony. I begged and borrowed for any opportunity to stroke one, to ride a Skegness beach donkey and stole e very spare moment to gallop around the garden on Dobbin. Dobbin was my first pony. I was 5 years old, and an early morning mystery tour of our farm workers cottage led me to him. Hidden under a blanket behind the living room door, as black as the night with a very rare white mane was the most beautiful horse I had ever seen. He was a little stiff to ride and rather narrow through the wither*, but I rode him every day for at least 4 years. Dobbin and I would go out jumping over buckets and vegetable canes for hours each day until sadly I grew too big for him. His wooden pole was replaced, and his paintwork touched up and he was handed down to other children for them to create their own magical memories on. My father had handmade Dobbin after work in the run up to my birthday. I can still remember the smell of varnish on my pillow after I had tucked him up in my bed, my first horse – one I will never forget.

At 7 years old my best school friend Lindsey had started horse riding lessons at a local riding school. I remember sobbing endlessly for what felt like forever (probably a few hours), begging for my chance to go with her to the next lesson. It worked! I took my £6.50 and my smelly old wax coat to the next Saturday pony day, and that was that - I was hooked. Though, nothing could have prepared my parents for just how hooked I was going to be. They probably hoped I would find the mud and the wind and rain a bit tedious, or perhaps after I had fallen off a few times, they might have hoped I would get frightened into never returning. Sadly, for them, nothing could put me off. I was very regularly wet through to my knickers and trodden on by a runaway Shetland, to this day I love every memory of my first equestrian experiences at those smelly wet riding stables.

Let's skip on a few years, we can come back to those later.

At 16 after spending much of my youth hunting*, showing* and pony clubbing on borrowed ponies and horses, I dabbled in the sport of eventing*. I followed my heart to a small, private yard that offered me the opportunity to compete two wonderful horses. I wasn't technically skilled in the dressage* arena or correctly positioned over a show-jump but I was brave as a lion going cross-country*. I was fearless, I would jump any fence, hedge, or ditch from any stride, on any angle and love every single second of flying through the air. That feeling of soaring over a huge log pile, landing with a thump, and galloping away was what my dreams were made of. I was of course only 18 and full of life. Hunting had made me a plucky rider, throwing my heart over every jump and feeling my horse follow, I hated standing around at the coverts getting cold, but I loved the chase. The sound of the horn and the cry of the hounds. Once it's in your blood, once you have breathed the scent of a frosty hunt meet, you will never let it go; it consumes you. This, it turns out, was to be a pivotal point in my journey.

After a few wonderful years riding for the Crockers at Tollbar, I decided to broaden my skills and set out on a career path as a polo groom. I applied for a position advertised in the back of Horse and Hound magazine, three months of bunking out of university and a hastily passed driving test later, I had moved 200 miles south. A big step at such a young age, I moved to a sleepy little village called Chiddingfold in Surrey. I arrived at Stonehurst to work for the Roberts family aged 18, I knew absolutely no-one but it didn't matter one bit. I fell in love with the sport. Polo taught me balance, bravery and added strings to my bow that I never knew existed. Managing this high calibre of performance horse taught me so much and I am so glad I took the gamble – it paid off for sure.

The polo social is unlike any other I have experienced. The sport and the ponies came first, Monday was rest day so, on a Sunday evening, sleeping in my car in a field and cheeky kisses behind stable blocks were what stick in my memory most. And how could I forget, the best meat I've ever eaten, cooked on an Asado by the Argentine contingent, are still some of my fondest memories of this time.

I was one of the luckier grooms that got to regularly 'stick and ball' which is a term for practice chukkas in a field at home. I LOVED those days, which now looking back, were mainly getting pelted by polo balls for not keeping my eyes up or fracturing my wrist mis-hitting the floor instead of the ball!

It wasn't for long though – 2 seasons in and I met my first husband, a soldier. Following a whirlwind engagement after his tours of Iraq, we got married. I was far too young, just 19 when we met, 22 when we married, and I left behind everything once again but for life as an army wife. Suddenly, I felt very alone. I had no one for miles that I could call on, no-one to talk to or ponies to whisper my secrets to. I had ridden all my life, it was all I knew, so I saved up £500 and went to Ascot Bloodstock Auctions* to find myself a friend of the four-legged kind.

Buying my first horse was one of the most exciting things I have ever encountered. I borrowed one of my husband's friends, hired a trailer and trundled off to a racehorse auction. Here I was, walking up and down lines and lines of thoroughbred horses that I couldn't even get out of the stables and watch them move let alone 'test ride'. I'll be honest, I had absolutely no clue what I was looking for! A horse that looked kind and non-bitey was high on the list, preferably one that wasn't angrily gnawing on the door or kicking the crap out of the stable was also okay too. I chose a few geldings* that looked nice, marked them in my catalogue and went into the bidding ring.

I was terrified of the actual bidding, the commitment and pressure of raising my number amongst people who were more experienced was very scary. Incidentally, the horse I was looking at all sold for a lot more than my measly budget, after all I only had £500. It was raining outside, miserable, grey and I just wanted to go home, but I wasn't going home without a pony. In she came; the sorry looking 4 year old mare*. She had no name;

she had no life in her eyes. The bidding dropped to a starting price of £350 and I couldn't believe my ears. I had to have her, so in went my bid for £400. SOLD. Down went the gavel, a 16hh mare, fit and ready to ride - I called her India.

The next 2 hours were spent getting that previously lifeless looking beast into the hired trailer. No longer a sorry looking pauper, she was a little testing to say the least, and wasn't grateful for being saved at all. The next 18 months were much the same; spirited, but fun. India was a challenge to retrain but she was so bold and confident going cross-country that all was forgiven. Hunting my very own horse on Boxing Day was the best day of my life and because of her, I met some lovely friends on my first livery yard – these friends moulded my beginnings of horse ownership and are now life-long ones. The funny thing was, I never really fell in love with that funny little mare. I just couldn't put my finger on it. I actually think the expectation was too great for this first pony, it meant that reality only ever had one way to go.

As time with India slipped through my fingers, so did my marriage. I felt totally lost. Getting married before I had worked out who I was, before I grew into my own character, turned out to be a terrible mistake. The huge age difference between us became a bigger deal than it once was and the army lifestyle was taking its toll. I wasn't in a safe place sometimes and I felt scared on more than one occasion. I was totally dependent on my husband financially and after a while, I felt totally trapped. My unhappiness at home was rubbing off onto my horse. She was getting quite tricky to bring in from the field and the ridden work just wasn't making any progress thanks to my stinky attitude. I felt totally out of my depth with her, I felt like a giant sack of shit if I'm totally honest.

I made the decision to sell her.

It wasn't at all as tough as it could have been. The most wonderful person turned up and took her away that same day. I knew my first horse child would be very loved by her new mother and so I rested easy on that.

A BROKEN HOME, A BROKEN HEART

A few horseless months passed, and I was growing increasingly fed up. Still treading the rocky road of my marriage, I needed a getaway, a distraction… I went looking for another horse, this time in the shape of a 4 year old warmblood*.

I remember the day I bought Freckles like it was yesterday, I was so desperately excited, and I couldn't wait to get him home, even before I'd seen him. He looked like a rocking horse in the photos, perfectly dappled with the prettiest face. Who could have predicted what the day would turn into? On arrival, the grey lump was strolling around a muddy field, a field which then became a schooling* paddock. He was so calm and quiet in nature, a touch wobbly to ride (I liken it to the first time you take the stabilisers off a push bike) and it felt as though he was going to fall over at every turn, but what a soft look he had in his eye. I handed over the £1200 and loaded him up, just like that! He was the most money I had ever spent on anything in my whole life.

We got 15 minutes into our 2 hour trip home on a dual-carriage way when the trailer threw us sideways into the other lane. Our Land Rover Discovery was being tugged and tossed about the road like a cat with a ball of wool. Never have I experienced anything quite so gut wrenching. What could have been going on in that trailer to cause such a jolt? We pulled onto the verge, and I climbed out. All was still inside. Weird. I unbolted the small jockey door at the front left of the trailer and my heart jumped out of my throat. Out of the tiny door burst the blood-stained grey fur of my new horse's head. He had severely sliced an ear, but this was the least of my troubles. On second glance, not a single hoof was on the floor of the trailer. The poor thing had jumped over the breast bar and was suspended from it like a pendulum, crushing his head and neck against the front of the box. He was still (for now) but that look in his eye was sheer terror, one I hadn't seen for many years. I very quickly pushed the bleeding head back in and closed the door to seek assistance.

The British Army spend millions of pounds training soldiers to remain calm and methodical in times of crisis – this was particularly useful that day, my then Sgt. husband climbed into the trailer and levered the poor horse upwards attempting to rock him backwards and free the breast bar that he was hanging from. It seemed like it was the best and only option until the poor frightened horse panicked. Suddenly, he had flipped, attempted to stand bolt upright, thrashing and banging with both of us still inside the trailer. He came crashing down onto his back, squashed this time between the back ramp and the separating partition. Everything went silent for what felt like an eternity. Was he dead? Unconscious? Could a horse lose consciousness? We left the trailer in the nick of time because the silence didn't last long. He was soon thrashing violently again trying to free himself from the metal bars of the partition that had enclosed his limbs. He was trapped.

On the grass verge, panic, fear and overwhelming emotion caused vomit to shoot up into my throat. I found the nearest motorway marker and called 999. Within 10 minutes, all lanes in both directions of the dual carriage way were empty. It was like a scene from a zombie apocalypse. Blue lights surrounded us very soon after.

The fire brigade was amazing that day. A calm and confident chap jumped in with my petrified horse, chopped out the partition and soon Freckles was standing, his bleeding head hanging over the back door. We were escorted off the motorway and they cordoned off a pristine area of turf and opened the ramp. I glanced over at the entrance sign welcoming people into the Olympic Turf Centre. I winced as the flying, blood-stained lump churned up what was intended to be the London 2012 shot put field! He limped about and stood looking into the distance, wired to the moon. How the bloody hell was I going to get him home now? I called a vet and they found me a professional transporter who, ever so coolly loaded him onto a 3.5t lorry and safely got us home.

For days I couldn't face handling him, it took every ounce of my being to even check he had everything he needed. I felt emotionally wrecked. This was supposed to be exciting, that 'getting to know you' week was stained with blood and tears. I had to find some light from somewhere, but where? Lord only knew!

ONE STEP FORWARD... 6 STEPS BACK

Months of rehabilitation, the purchase of a big ancient 7.5t horse lorry and some serious soul searching ensued. I gave his wounds time to heal and started long reining and lunging* to get some strength into his weak muscles. My first ride was just the same as I had that first day of trying him; slow, unbalanced and VERY wobbly. 6 months passed and we were given the all clear by vet and physio to resume 'business as usual'. I jumped a few cross poles and started hacking* a bit with friends, that's when it became very clear that our trust issues were much deeper rooted than the injuries sustained in the accident.

Hacking* was a huge issue for us, in the arena* he was willing to learn and be educated, out in a field, on a bridle path or the lanes; he was severely lacking in confidence. His default behaviour was rearing, the further we got from home, the more he did it and the higher they got. After a couple of months, it definitely started chipping away at my confidence. The sweet, young horse should have had guidance, boundaries, everything I knew I had to give him, but somehow managed to fail at. He needed showing that it was okay, I didn't believe that it was myself so I couldn't tell him that. The experience I had from riding anything I could get my grubby, child size mitts for all of those years that led up to this were lost. All of those 'lost causes' that I had helped train and compete for years, where was that experience now? I had ridden so many breakers*, youngsters and project horses, I knew the drill. I knew what was required, I just couldn't supply it to poor Freckles, and I didn't know why. Those 'Over Horsing' alarm bells that I had seen so often in other people were sounding in my head...

Ring A Ding 1 - Doubting yourself.

I began doubting whether I had the capabilities to help him develop and progress. Maybe the problems in my home life were to blame, maybe a combination of things but I was a trembling mess in all areas of my life.

Doubting yourself when dealing with horses, especially young horses that need defined instruction, is only ever going to end in confusion.

Alarm Bell 2 – 'Ding – Dong' there it is … Confusion.

Rearing, napping, bolting*, his way of telling me he was confused. Every time I attempted to leave the yard it ended in tears. I was in way too deep now and every inch of confidence was draining from my trembling body. 8 months passed; I wasn't sure I knew what I was doing anymore. Maybe I should get a hamster, might be safer.

Alarm Bell 3 – Outside influencers

The imaginary pressure from people around me wasn't helping and I felt required to take the lump cross-country schooling to prove I still had 'it'. The biggest bell of all…The pressure of external influencers; you do stupid things to prove you're not a giant sack of rotting fruit.

The day started badly because he still wasn't overly confident in loading onto the lorry so when we pulled up to the course, I was white with fear. I rode around for a while (just re-living this moment makes my palms sweat) and decided to attempt a small log. We scrambled over a few tiny jumps, but I was having no fun at all. I wanted to cry. Until the point where he simply had

had enough, he threw in the towel, shut his eyes and bolted*. I tried everything to pull him up, he ran through two lines of stock fencing, and I bailed out into a hedge. No surprises that we parted company, it was a stupid thing to have taken him to before he was ready. But that day, shattered, beaten and terrified - I waved the white flag.

Alarm Bell 4 - Sweating palms? Racing heart? Making excuses not to ride?

If I have learnt one thing (and most certainly the hard way), it's that perseverance isn't always the right path to tread – know when enough is enough, you'll be thankful in the end. Safe to say, I was broken inside, I had persevered for far too long. That day cross country schooling, he ran blind across a field, and I had to bail out before I wet my knickers (or worse) – that day was the end of the road for me.

I got home that afternoon to my miserable and frequently venomous marriage and locked myself away. Dragging my knees up to my chin, I sobbed long and hard. How could I have let this happen to me? How could I be sat here broken and unrecognisable? I was barely a shadow of that fun, giggling girl that loved life so much, I felt in mourning for what I had lost. Something had to change, something huge, looking back now I can almost guarantee that I was suffering with severe depression – I spent months like this, not going out, just sad. I would never have admitted it at the time, but I was in a very bad place, one I wanted to run from and never look back. It was dark where I was and I had very few people to tell my worries to, alone again.

3 weeks later I advertised and sold my big grey lump, the very first viewer was a professional dressage rider looking for her next horse to move up the levels. I was honest about my fears and his inexperience. She was kind, didn't seem to mind me blubbering, and made me an offer. I did love Freckles, I loved him but I knew it was the right decision and I so desperately wanted to release myself from the guilt of owning a horse I was terrified of. A week later he passed the vetting* and left. I sobbed once more as the door closed on this chapter of my life. I felt nothing but a let-down, I knew what everyone at the yard must have thought; 'stupid girl, trying to be something she's not'. They were right, I wasn't that person anymore.

So, here I was, mentally drained and nothing to show for my sorry start to horse ownership other than bruises and tear stained cheeks. No rosettes* or smiling photos of me at shows, it hadn't been fun at all.

But I'm stubborn you see, I wasn't wallowing like this for long. Enough was enough, I wasn't going down without a fight, ONE LAST TRY.

I booked to go and view one of the Queens old show horses, a nine-year-old, been there and done it, gentleman type. Taking the advice of my new friends and not buying the first one I saw; I sat scrolling through a mountain of adverts only to find one right on my doorstep. Too convenient to pass up, I went to see the little bay pony first before setting off for the royal visit.

A FRESH START?

He was another young one, but 5 not rising 4, and a nice Master Imp* bred horse. His video looked promising, lots of jumping over things that I had no intention of even walking near… looked good, looked pretty safe too.

I turned up to their yard and the little scrawny nugget just stood there looking at me, shoes nearly hanging off, a little sad and poor but sweet and very polite. Freckles was almost 16.3hh when he left for his new home so this little 15.2hh seemed Shetland sized in comparison. He had come in to a very reputable breeder to be sold as a favour, not their usual line of business so he was going for little money, £3,250 to be exact. I watched a young lad ride him over jumps and I began to sweat and get a bit short of breath. I couldn't do it; I couldn't get on. Better to find out just down the road I suppose, than drive 200 miles only to shit my pants trying the other one! I was coaxed into mounting by the seller, she was so kind when I told her how scared I was and turns out the horse really was a saint. I was tense and quivering, and this little angel carried me around without any fuss. I went into trot and then canter, suddenly regaining that glimmer of what I used to know. I popped a small cross pole and I felt wonderful. I found something that minute, that split second, something that had been missing for years. I approached an oxer*, easily 90cms; he soared it, we were flying, I was flying. I cried tears of relief and ecstasy for the first time in years. I didn't want to get off. I loved him for restoring my faith that day, so I paid the lady, cancelled the royal viewing, and hacked him home. Pauldarys Master Patrick, Pat to his mates – made me VERY happy from day one.

This little horse was the most wonderful thing that could have ever happened to me back then. I had mentally detached myself from my abusive marriage and within 3 months I was confident enough to join a riding club* and do some local dressage shows. Pat would get a rosette every single time we went out, I smiled every second I was sat on this horse, he really did (and still does) make my heart sing. We made so many wonderful friends through the riding club and for two and a half blissful years, we were just perfect for each other. We competed in dressage regionally and nationally, piles of rosettes and trophies were accumulating and I was so in love, nothing else mattered in the world. You can just bloody well guarantee that when one part of your life is just plain perfect, another part falls apart around your ears.

REVERTING

Now, this was the part that was meant to say '…and they all lived happily ever after'. Not bloody likely!

My husband was posted another 65 miles west of what was already far enough and because my marketing job was becoming more of a career instead of a time filler, I decided to rent a room Monday to Friday from one of my new riding club friends and her husband. A string of violent arguments with my husband meant I was glad to see the back of him for those days too. I grew independent and loved every second of being my own person away from a suffocating marriage. It also meant that I had absolutely no money. I rode horses for other people before and after work and got a weekend mucking out job to pay my rent and keep Pat, but it wasn't enough. I was exhausted, Pat always got left until last and I felt crap again. I was forever putting fuel and food on credit cards and was slowly sinking further and further into debt. Something had to give.

I remember the day I wrote the advert, not a 'for sale' one but just as bad – Horse for Loan. I cried and cried over how I could possibly explain to another person just how much this horse meant to me. I wanted to find him a temporary home until I got enough experience to progress in my marketing career to warrant a promotion and pay increase. It might be a year, it might even be two, but it killed me all the same. Pat was my life, his shaggy Irish mane had soaked up more tears than I care to remember, how would I cope without him? Turns out, word of mouth found him a very nice lady who would let me come and see him as often as I wanted, she was local and it was the best of a bad situation. Pat and I had a glorious time at the Riding Club National Championships, and he left for his new home the following weekend. It was lonely without him, I started doing stupid things, like jogging, to fill the 'Pat-gap'. I kept on with the three jobs and squirreled away all the money I could to pay back my debt.

In December, I called time on my marriage, it had been over for at least a year, and this was closure. I had become independent; I didn't need controlling anymore and I didn't need to feel constantly depressed about what should have been wonderful. Today, I feel absolutely no negativity towards my first husband. I feel nothing but educated. I have learnt so much about myself because of that period in time and no one can ever take that from me. The worst thing, something that very nearly tipped my life over the edge once more, was not leaving behind my marriage but leaving behind my three cats. Those with animals will understand just how much they mean to you and how they can wrench you heart out of your chest when you least expected. I had three; Fatsy Kensit, Stinky Fish and Little Man who had been there for me just like Pat had for all those years. I sobbed my eyes out all the way home leaving them behind and every night after that for months. I would visit at weekends and stay in the army house with them, like a visiting order in a prison. I'm not sure it made things better or worse, but I knew it wasn't forever.

NOW WHAT?!

A blissful Christmas came, I was so happy to be free of my old life. I was a new person and I was finding myself at last. Right when I least expected it I fell in love. Yep, you heard right!! I realised right there and then that it was probably the first time too. I was totally head over heels in love and nothing, I mean nothing could bring me down.

It was 'the chap from work' who, in our house, we had nicknamed "Gary the Arrogant Arse". He was so obnoxious and rude to everyone but dig deeper and he was so wonderfully kind and thoughtful, and my Lord, did I want to take his clothes off. He wore just a little too tight trousers that I used to stare across at every time he left the room. I just wanted to kiss his hairy hand every time he gave me a document or helped me with my work, goodness, what was wrong with me?! My heart raced just getting dressed in the mornings, I felt giggly and was desperate to be left in a room alone with this poor bloke.

Now, it turns out that Gary was VERY switched on and whilst I uncontrollably threw myself at him on more than one occasion, he remained aloof, casual and ever so cool. It made me want him MORE. I was relentless in my obvious affection and made advances that couldn't have gone unnoticed. My skirts got shorter, I wore stockings instead of tights and I took every opportunity to make this combination clearly visible by retrieving things that I casually dropped near his desk. Oh, the shame! But I was smitten, I wasn't giving up and apparently all my morals had been left at home along with my tights.

It was December, I had handed in my notice (mainly because Gary the Arrogant Arse had told me that he wouldn't want to cavort with anyone from the office) and that fateful day finally arrived. The acceptance of my after-work-drinks invitation. I was shitting myself, terrified about what we would talk about when we were in a pub, alone. How would I stop myself just leaning over and licking his beard? Bugger it! We got on great actually and conversation flowed just fine, although I did laugh nervously a lot.

But then it happened, he walked me to my car and kissed me, so expertly and for such a long time, I felt my knees buckle. With his arm around my back, pulling in my trembling body, I felt like I was in the final scene of Bridget Jones' Diary, snogging the face off Colin Firth! BLOODY WOWZERS… for the drive home and the whole of that weekend, I was on the biggest high of my life!!! I didn't get off this high for weeks.

The first time I 'slept over' was a few weeks on, we attended a pub quiz with his mate and the plan was not to go home afterwards. I was so terribly nervous about being crap in bed or him having a little micro penis that I drank FAR too much wine, made a tit of myself at the quiz and didn't really remember much of the bedroom bit anyway! Once that first nude episode was out of the way, we were very quickly one of those annoying couples, sickeningly in love and totally oblivious of anyone else. Most days, even now, I still feel like that too.

In just 2 months, we rented a house together. Quick to most people, but I knew living with someone was make or break, luckily this 'made' us. It also meant that I could get my three cat babies back with me, one of the happiest days of my life. Gary was greeted by three furry hooligans who on the first meeting, Stinky Fish vomited her newly eaten biscuits all over the floor and like always, Fatsy Kensit came in and took pleasure in gobbling up the pre-chewed lumps – Gary laughed (thank goodness)!

One chilly February morning, the phone rang. A fresh clip and a bit too much nice pony food and Pat had launched his temporary mother into orbit and frightened her, I don't think it had been a one off either. It was late February when he came home, only 6 months into our yearlong agreement. I was secretly delighted – not for her injuries but because my boy was coming home. I had a better job now, a man who supported my love for this horse and I was so happy, it was all falling into place.

A BAD DAY ACTUALLY

It was a Saturday morning, I remember it like it was just last week. I watched the trailer pull up the drive, so desperately excited to introduce Gary to the other love of my life, very child-like in my emotions, I was squeaking with joy as he bumped down the track. We unloaded him and let him off the headcollar into the arena. He lifted his tail, bucked* and farted; Gary laughed. We watched him prance and snort for a few minutes before I decided I wanted to get on. I wanted to ride my wonderful boy, my comfy armchair again. I saddled him up whilst Gary fed him carrots, I led him to the mounting block and hopped on. He felt incredible, just like always. The pride was bursting out of my skin, Gary was filming from the edge of the arena. Now, I don't really know what happened next. It was all a bit hazy, but it changed my life again. That split second, the decision to ride, the day, the time; it changed EVERYTHING.

I think my stirrup knocked the fence or something startled him in the trees because in a split second, my darling horse, my rock steady boy was doing the best rendition of a rodeo bull the world had ever seen! He jinked and spun, head between his knees. I was launched into orbit before I had time to think about how to handle the explosion and landed on my head on the foot of a wooden jump stand. Massively concussed I stood up and found my very wayward bearings. I HAD to get back on, I was always taught that, even if you get on and walk two steps, it was enough. I got back on, I walked a circle and got off. All of those awful feelings came flooding back, the sweating, the tears, the tightness in my chest, it was all there just how it was before. I cried for days on and off. It's hard to put into words what this fall did to me, how it reverted me back to the days of wishing the ground would swallow me whole. I couldn't shake it off, I thought it would be temporary - it wasn't.

For 5 months I didn't ride him. I turned him away in a field hoping he would forget about that day and got him thoroughly checked over. Physiotherapist, vet, chiropractor, farrier, horse whisperer you name it, I tried it. I was absolutely terrified of riding him. I couldn't face it at all. I was lucky to have been given another horse to ride alongside him, this got my confidence back but just made the guilt of it not being Pat even worse.

away in a field again or keep him as a pet. I got on and walked up the path to the arena, it was a little bit frosty, and I could see my breath, but I wasn't cold. I was violently trembling, and sweat was running down my forehead and into my eyes. I walked a circle and struggled to get my breath. The dizziness was so bad, I couldn't breathe, I quickly got off, ran to the arena fence and vomited. I spewed bile because knowing I was going to ride; I hadn't eaten for over 12 hours. This wasn't fun anymore; it was making me ill. I sobbed into his shaggy un-pulled mane, why did I feel like this? Through the tears I explained to him that I loved him, but it was over for us, he had to have a new mummy now, but I would make sure she was nice, crikey did I sob (I am now just reliving it). At this dark stage of my tunnel there really was no other way out of my sadness and guilt than to sell him, I didn't know which of these things broke my heart the most.

In April 2016 I made a call to a professional event horse producer, talked through the costs, the process and what it involved to sell my horse. I cried twice on the phone to this poor woman. I was at my wits end, fear spiralling out of control but finding it equally as hard to let go of something I loved more than life itself. This was the darkest place I had been for years; horses consume you if you let them – a third world problem it may seem, but this was a tribulation of pure love not financial gain. I loved this horse more than life, but the guilt and fear were eating me alive. I remember sitting in my car with tears rolling down my cheeks, it was raining, I just looked through the window at his face in the barn and he whickered to me. It was probably for food, but I doubted myself for making the sale arrangements that were taking shape. I got home and I will never forget it as long as I live, that question Daddy Carrot put to me as I explained what I had done.

Very calmly, my soon to be Husband looked me in the eyes and said, "Will you regret this for the rest of your life?" – It was instant, the answer was undoubtedly "yes". He followed it with; "Imagine how you will feel watching someone out having fun with him, smiling and loving him and winning just like you should be, just like you did before." That was it. That was my motivation. Right there. In that moment, I was NOT going to let someone else love MY horse, I loved him, no-one else. I called off the sales livery and decided to deal with whatever it was after the wedding. Lord knows I needed a sunny break more than I realised!

THE I DO'S

In the run up to our wedding day it had become apparent that whilst I had been so consumed in my own equine related misery I had failed to print invitations, do table plans or lose enough weight to fit into my dress. At the end of May, 6 weeks before the wedding date, I sent out invitations, borrowed my parent's treadmill and began planning our wedding. We had budgeted £4000 for the entire thing including honeymoon and in West Sussex this was tough – but not impossible. I made almost everything myself. My dress was a £100 handmade bargain find from eBay which was actaully a size 8, I was secretly hoping that I would squeeze into it by the time the day arrived... FAT CHANCE (literally) I am and always will be an out and out size 11! With a few alterations we made it fit, and it is the most priceless piece of clothing I will ever own. It had a huge princess style skirt, fitted lace bodice and beautiful lace straps on the shoulders. I stitched a wide pink satin ribbon around the middle, and it was simply unique, a one off and I couldn't wait to wear it.

With the help of some much-loved friends and family, the day was totally magical. We had a small church ceremony followed by a village hall reception. We did a funny quiz after our fish and chip supper and our guests enjoyed a good hour of my murderous singing on the karaoke. I couldn't have been happier to have married my best friend, my Daddy Carrot; it was perfect.

The following Monday we flew to the Caribbean and by day 4, I had had just about enough of too much food, too much booze and too much sun. It appears that I am crap at holidaying, I missed the cats and Pat terribly and as a distraction I began re-inventing myself.

Day 6 of honeymoon bliss, I had a monumental psychological breakthrough. Picture this: lying on a massage table, nothing but the sound of the air-conditioning unit whirring and my new husband breathing a little too loudly on the bed next to me; I had a revelation. I began a thought process that put me in the XC start box. I was being counted down, the feelings of happiness having got through the dressage without leaving the boards and round the swim of coloured jumps without jabbing my horse in the chops too many times. I was there, just like I used to be when I was a teenager – EXCITED. I wasn't scared, not vomiting, no stains in my under garments, long story short, away from reality I was totally and utterly ready for it! Could I really feel like this in the flesh, could I go through with it?

There was only one way to find out!

We came back to the UK Saturday morning after a dog of an overnight flight and I tried to remain positive. I asked Daddy Carrot to come and get some video of me sailing over some terrifyingly big jumps, but tiredness took over. Queue the excuses... the poor pony, having had 2 weeks off getting fat would surely die of shock if suddenly, I decided to become Mrs Mary King whilst on holiday – We'll leave it for one night in the week and lunge the poor him instead. URGH... I was already losing the inner strength that I had found on that massage table.

That night, so I couldn't back out, for the first time in years I clicked that over anticipated link on the British Eventing website – FIXTURES, and chose my fate. If I planned and paid for an event that I couldn't really afford post wedding, I would feel immense guilt about bailing out! I was reluctant to say it out loud, like the date of your driving test in case you over egg it and

MORE FIZZ ANYONE?

The fateful Saturday arrived, I frequented the loo 4 times before I left the house, I had hardly eaten for 2 days out of nervousness, but it appeared my bowels hadn't got the memo! With my uneaten toast left on the kitchen side, I violently trembled lighting a cigarette as I got into the car for what could be the last drive of my life! Fully expecting to be carted off in a body bag that day, I made a note of my friend Suzi's phone number and left it on the dashboard. Suzi and I have always agreed that she would have Pat if anything happened to me, I felt like it might have been necessary for me to leave the number available that day!

I got to the yard (pretended to be brave), tacked up and hacked the 1.5 mile path to what felt like my untimely death. We arrived and to my surprise, Pat stood nicely at the meet with 70 other horses but was certainly ready to go when everyone finally trotted off. I waved my ever-supportive Daddy Carrot off and there I was, trotting off to die in a field. The first section of the ride was a long gallop up a steep hill which massively helped my nerves. I had no real control but by the top of the hill all of the horses were slowing from tired legs. Thank goodness!

I kept Pat at the front of the ride as the pace was pretty fast throughout and slippery footing meant I wanted a good run at the jumps, JUMPS! That's right, not detailed on the entry paper work I signed, but in for a penny… I clutched the neck strap over tiger-traps and logs, we soared over ditches and galloped with no brakes – It felt BLOODY FANTASTIC. For the first time in so many years I felt like I was invincible again. Tears stung my eyes through pride, for in my head I was back to that care-free 15 year old girl out hunting and absolutely loving it.

I hacked home alone after two hours of life changing riding. I screamed at the top of my lungs in the middle of an (empty) open field, the release from that shell of fear, the shell that had now cracked, I was like a chick breaking his egg…not quite flying yet but my goodness, there was some huge potential ahead!

Just playing this back in my head to write the words down has me sobbing with pride, covered in goose bumps – I never thought I would ever do anything like that ever again! I was on cloud 9 for over a week; I felt capable and as though I could do this, I could ACTUALLY be an event rider again.

#wimpyeventer

In September 2016, in a world where social media 'influencers' didn't exist, and a couple of weeks after the ride of my life, I felt that I had tormented my husband with tails of my pony woes for too long. I was desperate not to be one of those people that talked all day and night about their horses to a long suffering, non-horsey partner.

I thought I would set up a Facebook page and maybe a website to document my tales, and with that; Diary of a Wimpy Eventer was born. Originally a page to outline my fears, progress and boost my confidence, who knew that today (Oct 2023) I would have a following of over 65,000 people and have achieved so much more than the original plan.

Throughout the last 10 years of my marketing career I have grasped a good handle on how to promote other people and their businesses. It's such a different kettle of fish promoting yourself! I am so proud of how much this page helps others that are swimming against the same tide, you deserve to feel that shell breaking feeling, that dark into light that I have felt – I wanted everyone to be able to feel that.

So here we are my diary, as raw and as real as ever, documented from one Imodium fuelled experience to another.

Enjoy!

SEPTEMBER 2016

13th September 2016

Give me a hand out of this hole will you?!

So, I was massively on the up after my 'mock hunting' experience at the Champagne breakfast ride and thought this would make my day to day riding, clinics and popping a small fence in the school a doddle. With a very positive mind set, I entered a show jumping clinic at a local college equestrian centre. When the reply asked what height of fence I wanted to jump – very boldly wrote back 90 cms! I had read somewhere that you need to be jumping 10cms bigger at home and in training that you are at a competition, 90cms, what could go wrong? Well, I don't know what the actual fuck was I thinking?! I know this might not seem a huge feat to most people, but when Daddy Carrot put a 70 cm jump up in the arena to practice over for the big day – I just wanted to get off. I almost cried and, inelegantly touching cloth, almost certainly had a change of knickers looming.

Saturday morning came and I was white as a sheet walking down the field to retrieve my poor horse! I gave him a small calmer syringe, goodness knows why I didn't syringe it into my own face, and the rest of the pack of 3 I bought from the tack shop. I got all my gear on – jumping saddle (borrowed from a friend), branded jacket (that I won in a competition online) and my new riding boots, donated out of support and kindness as a wedding gift from a brand I worked for on the side of my fulltime job. The boot box arrived and the first word I read on it was "Cognac". I thought my luck was changing and they came with a free bottle. Alas, it was the colour – I have been through pairs of death boots before, and these looked not all that dissimilar. BUT…they haven't once made my feet pound with circulation loss. I feel invincible in them – I put one foot in, zipped them up and it was like someone had melted them to my legs – they are grippy, elegant and described as "the perfect choice for any top-level rider." WELL THAT'S ALL RIGHT THEN!

We certainly looked the business for our first steps to becoming an Event Rider!

On arrival to our jumping clinic, I was delighted to see the jumps were tiny and the 2 people in the group before me were hitting the deck and getting up laughing! PHEW!

We went in, perfect dressage moves across the arena, some medium trot, counter canter, I felt GREAT, but then I remembered why we had come and my heart sank. We began over a cross pole that my cats could have jumped over, clinging onto the neck strap with white knuckles – breathing a sigh of relief on landing over not dying. It wasn't the prettiest but I was doing the thing. I jumped a few single fences before being picked out of the group as the first course jumper. Well… they were around 85cms high, I didn't faint, I didn't cry, I kept a nice rhythm, put my leg on where I needed to and got each jump foot perfect. I couldn't have been happier – I jumped the course once more in the session and because of how thrilled I was to be alive, I decided to quit while I was ahead and say my thankyous and goodbyes.

I hacked home with a big grin on my face as the tension pains in my chest subsided, another happy outing doing something out of my comfort zone!

Next weekend I have pre-entered a dressage show just to get out into a competition environment where I could feel a little more confident in our capabilities. We have two competition days in a row – day one is two Novice tests and day two is a Novice and Elementary!

I have also found a chum to buddy up with at a Hunter Trial in a couple of weeks' time, result! Better get out XC Schooling so I don't embarrass myself too much!

16th September 2016

I've only gone and done it!

Well, that's.it. My feet are wet, I've jumped in with them both! – My. BE Entry. Has. Been. Accepted!

In fact, it's not my feet that are wet, it's my palms and my forehead. I'm sat at my desk looking at last year's course photos already choosing the one I might die at. With any luck I'll get balloted anyway as there are 126 in the class – that can't be right, surely?!

Anyway, not to be deterred; jumping session to look forward to Friday night before another clinic this weekend, might brave something bigger than a 1ft.6 cross pole, I've got spare pants in the car!

19th September 2016

I'm pretty pissed off that I cannot remember which knickers I was wearing on Friday night when Daddy Carrot made his largest erection to date...

We flew a jump at 110cms and I actually remained stain less. They must be the bravest brave pants in history – I must dig them out the laundry basket.

Now, as I have a following of nearly 400 people (thank you all for your support) I thought I would like to introduce to you, my lovely boy; here is his 'Pony Profile'.

Name- Pauldarys Master Patrick

Sire - Master Imp

Stable Name – Pat/Patrick/Patikins/Patsy (why do we do this?)

Colour – Bright bay.

Age – 10 (2006 foal) I've owned him since he was rising 6.

Favourite Activities - Spooking at birds, spooking at bags, spooking at leaves, stealing food.

Pony Bio – Bred and broken in Kildare, Ireland and brought to Hampshire by the lovely people at Pauldarys stud. Bought by myself in 2012 as a scrawny rising 6 year old.

Since then, we have competed for riding club teams, been to the British Riding Club National Championships, been hunting, cross country schooling, hacked to the pub, competed in dressage with wins at Prelim, Novice and Elementary, and this weekend we embark on our first ever BE event.

He is my best friend in the whole wide world.

26th September 2016

Gin and Tramadol…. A cocktail of success!

What a weekend!! Let's start from Wednesday night where the plans to run through my Novice and Elementary tests for Sunday were scheduled. I left the office, grabbed my breeches from the car and strolled over to get changed. One leg in, two legs in, yank on the too tight breeches… TWANG! My lower back left me in a crumpled, screaming heap on the toilet floor. An hour on the Tens machine and a glass of wine from nice new yard owners and I was on the horse – but only able to walk pain free.

Drat and blast… I had entered two bloody shows Show Jumping on Saturday and Dressage on Sunday, and paid upfront for them both! And with my BE event looming, I wasn't the slightest bit relieved that I might have a 'get out of jail free card'. I rested, tens machined and iced it for 2 days, the more I moved about, the better it got – enough to run through the tests on Friday night but sadly, no jump practice ready for Saturday!

The day dawned, I had my times for the 80 and 90 cm classes and I wasn't set to face my doom until 3.30 pm. Late times are good for back injuries but they also leave you with the whole day to worry about it. Bloody Marvellous. I was SICK to my stomach with nerves, by the time I had to leave. I took two Imodium caplets, a tramadol and bought a Gin and Tonic ready mixed can from the garage which I downed on the way to the yard whilst chain smoking cigarettes.

I arrived at the venue and the nerves were still leaving me utterly hopeless. I couldn't remember the course at all, I watched about 20 other horses go round and it WAS NOT HELPING! I heard the gate lady shouting my number, ARSE.

Kick, kick off we go!

As if by some wondrous miracle, I made it over the first 6 fences clear and into the timed area (which I went no quicker for) I just went for the steady clear. Mainly based on the fact that if I had gone any quicker and I would have been sick!

I had an unfortunate pole down and a very steady time but I DID IT! Totally elated, I very nearly quit whilst I was ahead and cancelled the 90cm entry but it started quick smart and I felt I ought to stay in that confident Event Rider persona all afternoon.

Well, would you believe it? I only bloody did it! Another silly pole down where I got in a bit close, but we bloody did it, I jumped the biggest course I had done in 10 years, with a dodgy back and blurred gin goggles on! WOOOHOOOOOOOOOO! I hacked home with the biggest grin and the most acidy tummy of my life!

SUNDAY FUNDAY

I was MUCH less worried about dressage on the Sunday. This was much more in our comfort zone, and dressage is pretty boring, so I will keep it brief.

OCTOBER 2016

11th October 2016

So, with reinvention going swimmingly, I am about to grace you with the first affiliated competition report that I have EVER done. I have read thousands of them written by braver riders than me, and I never imagined I would be writing my own. I will add, although I am writing this report, I am nowhere near a brave rider yet, I am an excellent actress and kidding myself into think this sport of Eventing is a good idea. I am still 95% terrified 2% determined and 3% in too deep and can't turn back!

I cannot believe what I am about to write – I'll take you back to Friday night….

Daddy Carrot and I went over to Littleton Manor Equestrian Centre to walk the vomit inducing XC course at approximately 6.37pm. We arrived, found the start, smoked a cigarette and by fence 13 – it was pitch black! Perfect! I was having a mini (internal) meltdown whilst remaining silently cool on the exterior. I was desperate to appear nonchalant to my husband over this new sport I'd taken up.

Dinner and bed (an early night, not the norm on 'Pub Friday' in our usual weekly schedule). I slept surprisingly well, woke up not too terrified but I was buggered if I could remember ANY of the jumps beyond fence 2! Oh well, I can remember my dressage test, that's a 3rd of the way down my poorly lit BE road!

Having plaited the night before, I re-tapped Pats stud holes and got him ready for the off, crikey I needed a poo. I don't think I had put studs in any horse for around 10 years so this took me a little while! We arrived in lots of time, I visited the toilet again, smoked a few more cigarettes and desperately tried to strap my spurs on through trembling hands and legs! Having mounted far too early, I bobbled about a bit getting used to riding on grass in an outline – Piss poor planning etc.... I hadn't ridden a test on grass for about 3 years. Note to self: build a grass arena in the field.

Into the test, it was *fine*, no more, no less. I did everything where I should do it but having scored nearly 75% at Novice and Elementary this year, I was annoyed that I hadn't devoted more time to improving our skills of 'field dressage' at Prelim level. We scored a mark of 33.6 – backwards to pure dressage marking, so 66.4%. Meh... neither happy nor sad over this – I know where I need to improve so I'm trying not to punish myself too much!

25 minutes later, I was 4 holes shorter in the stirrup and flying a couple of practice jumps in the warm up ring, pretty much ready to go into the show jumping – so I did! I think the more time you dwell on the prospect of jumping your round, the more likely you are to get nervous and fuck it up... do not linger about like a wet fart in the warm up – 3 practice jumps is enough to not put the willies up us, but enough to have stretched out any post dressage tension.

2023 SIDE NOTE: To this day, several events and show jumping rounds in now, and with ageing horses, I will never jump more than 5 fences in a warm-up. You are not using the warm-up to teach your horse to jump. That's what at training home is for.

Surprisingly, I remembered where I was going, didn't fluff too much with him and left him dis-united in one corner instead of tampering with the rhythm – wrong or right – it got us round CLEAR! I ACTUALLY COULDN'T BELIEVE IT!

Now onto my doom...

I was TERRIFIED, on the verge of tears. My first cross country round in forever. I had looked at the course pictures and had a pretty good idea of the route, but it wasn't helping my fragile confidence. Just re-living this now is making me need a poo! I got him ready with the help of my trusty pal and escort for the day while trying to have a bite of banana – NO CHANCE! Queue the first gag reflex!

Down at the warm-up I put my number down on a board manned by a steward and jumped my 3 practice jumps (worked for us in the show jumping, not lingering/wet fart/etc.) and walked around trying not to spew bile all over his mane. The straps of my body protector forcing the vomit into my throat; I wasn't at all ready to go. Maybe I should just stop here, go home?

"Number 123, can you make your way to the start box please?" Fucking NO, no I cannot! I want to go home please, I do not want to be here or jump any of those bloody jumps, thank you kind man, but I'm done for today.

In the box, the countdown of a minute felt like an eternity, I also explained to the counter downer that I wanted to get off and go home now please, she wished me luck – That was it... 5,4,3,2,1...crack, crack of the whip on my poor horses arse (mainly for my benefit) and we were FLYING.

Every stride down to the first fence felt AMAZING, wild and a bit erratic, but amazing nonetheless. We were galloping, flying and soared over the first fence – it was the best bloody feeling in the whole world – adrenalin just completely took over. The second jump, a row of HAYGAIN steamers, I was worried about him looking them at so one more bum smack and he flew it. I felt as though 3, 4, 5, 6 and 7 – the steps, flew by without blinking, he backs off a bit at every jump but if I'm there kicking his arse, he will go. 8 (the corner) I was worried about, no need – he was bloody flying, he felt like an absolute machine – I screamed "Good Boy!" and "YIP YIP!" at the top of my lungs before and after every fence!

Nothing was a problem for this horse today, nothing – we flew down the home straight over 15, 16 and finally 17 – I let out the biggest wail of joy you have ever heard and then through my horrendous unfit heavy breathing, cried like a baby!

I dived off and undid everything – NEVER in my life have I felt love for an animal like I did right at that moment. (Crikey, I'm now at my desk in a communal office – crying, Shit!) My horse and I; we were actually doing it – achieving what we set out to in tremendous style.

Back at the box, Pat sorted, Daddy Carrot came running over – I was currently in 3rd place! Bloody 3rd place! I didn't want him standing on the box all day so we decided to take him home and I would come back later and see the final results.

Driving back, convincing myself that the rest of the section would have overtaken me by now – I was ridiculously delighted to see ***5th*** by our names! We came 5th! Our first ever one day event, affiliated too – I was beaming – donning 2 rosettes and a great bag of prizes, I drove home. Couldn't resist stopping by at the yard to tell Pat (and my new livery pals) how amazing he was and give him an extra carrot.

We are 3 days on now and I still feel on top of the world, pride and happiness over what we achieved – what I have achieved - is just so overwhelming. I overcame some serious anxiety to even fill out the entry form, let alone give it everything we had on the day. I just want to say a remarkably HUGE thank you to everyone that has offered words of support, well-wishers and wine bringers. To my long suffering husband and team of friends for listening to my woes and mostly, thank you to my horse – he is, after all, the best thing I have ever encountered in the world EVER.

Who says the horse world is full of backstabbing, interfering arsebags?! For every wrong un' you've all proved that there is a lovely, kind-hearted and truly fabulous one'.

Thank you all.

Love, as always.

Vic and Pat

xxx

20th October 2016

Let me explain a few things now I'm older and more wisdom-ous?!

I am pretty sure that at some point in the lives of every single one of you reading this, you have felt rotten about your capabilities, downtrodden or had your chips totally pissed on by someone else. If you haven't – you are probably the one doing the urinating!

My equestrian side of life has been FULL to the bloody handle with highs and lows of the best and worst kind. Along the way, you realise the people that you surround yourself with are those that influence the success or failure the most. From my experience the pride or guilt you feel for winning and the shame or experience you get from ballsing it up, is all determined by the first 3 people you tell.

My choice of 3 include; No.1 – My husband; the realist. He almost always congratulates me on survival before any results are divulged. I am reminded that I do this for enjoyment and like we always say, the minute you stop enjoying the ride, get off the bus. No.2 – Fellow yard people; which I am delighted to say – couldn't give two shits if I succeed or fail, they are just happy peering in from the edge at someone having a bash at it! There is no hidden agenda behind their "Ooo you're alive then, how did you get on?" No.3 – My social media 'family'; I enjoy how, even the non-horsey followers give me a 'wow' like!

This hasn't always been the case though, and I won't ever dwell on that feeling of coming home from a show elated to find that Lady Big Knickers has already got her pants down ready to put your fire out. Those sorts of people, Daddy Carrot and I refer to as; Eleven-erifers. If you've been to Tenerife… guess where they've been, Elevenerife?! Always waiting in the corner to make you feel like crap about yourself.

I like to think that I have always been a good sport at dishing out credit where it's due and of course Karma is a wonderful thing but, the basics are very simple; **surround yourself with people that either couldn't give a shit, ones that would give their last shit to see you succeed, or that ones that don't know what shit you're doing!** It will almost certainly improve your life and boost your confidence.

24th October 2016

Here we are again…

It's like the morning after the night before – Sat at my paper covered desk in my lonely office, blogging rather than going through my ton of emails. Did I have a good weekend? I think so.

Friday, as you may have seen from my Facebook page, I had another 'moment'. My fragile shreds of confidence were set alight and I wobbled to my core again. Sometimes it feels as though the boat is still, the sea is calm and we can go forth into the breach… Other times, I feel like the bloody Titanic when it hit that massive iceberg. Or rather like the chap that jumped onto the propeller as it was sinking!

On reflection, Friday makes me want to cry, but so did the half dead squirrel on the road this morning and the rancid coffee I had made for me when I got to work... I think I might be coming down with something!! Bloody well get a grip Vic, for fucks sake!

Honestly, sometimes I don't know what gets into me, dwelling on negatives will get you NOWHERE!

So, let's focus on the positives - Saturday I decided to get on with it and go to my jumping clinic. I arrived a little early and got on joined by 3 others of varying levels! Sometimes I wonder whether this is the best way for us to learn but if nothing else, it gives us the chance to jump in more of a 'warm-up' environment which usually scares the living shit out of me. We jumped our round a little too enthusiastically, which always makes me smile because as the jumps get bigger he starts to back off a bit which is a welcomed relief for my twitchy bum! We ended the clinic on a high jumping around a decent 95cms course and hacked home with another smile on our faces!

Saturday night we unusually joined in with some village activities, watching the local fireworks display albeit from the pub. Someone (me) might have had a few too many drinks (totally bloody steaming) and didn't make it home until almost 1am, Daddy Carrot much more soberly in tow! Apparently, little that I remember, I was partaking in activities of the more *ahem* 'horizontal' kind until the even smaller hours! Honestly! Drinking to excess is NOT something I make a habit of and why do I not do that? SUNDAY MORNING is why! My word, it was like a diseased hamster had crawled into my ear and puked its guts out into my brain. One large fried breakfast and a sleep later and I was tying my stock ready to go jumping!

We arrived at Coombelands Equestrian Centre little time to spare and not many horses to go before us. I watched 5 or 6 go around to get the course learnt and off we went! He was flying! I was concentrating so hard on trying not to push for the magic feeling clearing a jump from a stride out - the flier! I always prefer to go off a long stride but it's not always the best thing pushing for it on my speedy steed! We had an unfortunate rail where I just got it wrong, but we were quick enough to hear our names being called out for the placings! We were 8th amongst a multitude of nippy ponies. RESULT!

The 90cm course changed somewhat, it introduced us to our first triple bar and after 10 or so riders round the course – we were in! Never mind the triple bar, I rode like a triple amputee – didn't pick him up at all – at one point, it was like time had stood still and I was coming to a big oxer thinking; 'he's doing it all by himself – I am literally straddled over the arm of sofa, still drunk!' Bless the cotton socks of my lovely boy, he did nurse us round to have another unfortunate pole – but what a horse – he was giving it everything, jumping me out of the saddle over most of them. He really did try for me, and I was bursting with pride. Where I selfishly gave him 35 percent effort, he met me with the remaining 65 and saved our bacon. I cannot tell you all how much I love this horse. He is truly the one in a million that I have dreamed of my entire life and he's mine, sod the bloody lottery!

Lastly, I want to thank everyone that wished us well on Friday and over the weekend. It means so very much to me that people give two hoots, I cannot tell you what a difference it makes. If it wasn't for everyone rooting for me through this ridiculous diary,

I would have stayed slumped in a heap on the sofa yesterday – I couldn't face a post of disappointment to all of you that had taken the time to write to me. So, with everything I have left to give…thank you very much indeed. xxx

October 22, 2016

A comment from my dear patient jump trainer today has left me feeling super - "Vic, your confidence from when I first saw you 3 years ago has gone through the roof" Mwhahaha... little does he know how I'm dying on the inside.

The reality is that Diary of a Wimpy Eventer is the best thing that could have happened to my confidence, I have a purpose now – creating a reason to carry on going – no matter what that reason is, is very important indeed. Course walking this evening at Pachesham Equestrian Centre ready for the hunter trial tomorrow - We are on at 12.42pm if anyone is interested in 'time of death'.

31st October 2016

Champagne fuelled Red Ribbons!

So, with our late entry accepted into the Pachesham Hunter Trial for the 85 cm pairs class, the usual nervous course walk Friday night was a little less toilet trip inducing than other events. I'm not overly sure why. Maybe my fragile confidence is slowly being coated in honey ready for being rolled in feathers but nonetheless, I felt quite 'alright' about most of the fences, the warm up and not dying! I had 3 small glasses of Malbec in the pub afterwards to quash any last-minute terror, I think it worked! I woke up Saturday morning feeling like I might well be able to stomach a slice of toast... VERY ODD INDEED!

I got Pat ready for a 10am pick up from my trusted sidekick for the day. Let me introduce to you my lovely friend and unofficial confidence coach, Lisa – She and her lovely little mare have been dragged to many an event in support of us over the last few months, despite having hung up her competition boots a little while ago! All ready for the off, ponies on and off we go! WAIT – 'Check the trailer lights will you?!' Sure enough 15 minutes later, we were watching the course video in a garage whilst being fixed up by some odd looking chaps - our ponies stood munching hay on the back! Off we went again...

RAIN. A lot of it. Whatever next? We toyed with turning around a few times... Any excuse! No such luck, we arrived, registered and sat about chuckling, trying to banish the nerves. It worked, a little too well, as with only 25 minutes to go we decided it might be an idea to get ready and get warmed up. What a bloody stupid thing to do – My horse needs a bit of time to get his confidence XC and I should have been ready long before getting on with only 2 riders to go before us!

Now, the nerves that weren't present in the last 24 hours double barrelled me in the guts in that short time frame. I was riding like a wet sock, totally inadequately. I relied solely on my sidekick to lead the way while Pat jinked and spooked at every bloody jump for the first 5 fences and I sat there just passenger-ing at EVERY fence! What a let-down I was to him, he deserved much more from me. I'm pretty sure the long gallop down to fences 6 and 7 woke me up a bit because I suddenly felt awake again. I stopped flopping about and started riding!!

We were flying once more, feeling confident; galloping and soaring over each obstacle – I love this horse beyond belief when we become one together going cross country – it is the most magical feeling that I cannot put into words. We are quite simply made for each other, both taking a little coaxing to come into our own.

Shit! – The bloody great Trakehner…hold on – 3, 2, 1.. Kick kick! I hear screams ahead, Lisa has managed to go flying into orbit at the last minute, hanging on by the seat of her unstained pants…. SIT UP, SIT UP! Crikey she did well to stick on. Regaining her balance, we entered the woods for fence 16 (a meaty fallen oak trunk), she was belly-aching about not being able to find her stirrup and was trying desperately to turn a circle …KICK ON! – Forget it… Pat locked onto the log and barged Lisa and little Maggie over the jump whether they were wanting to go or not! I had assumed at this point that she had regained her missing pedal and flew on to the next 3 fences and home!

WOO BLOODY HOO! Home – Fast, alive and so desperately happy that I had regained some level of riding prowess over the course – I turned to my rather red faced, panting chum and inappropriately couldn't control my laughter! Her stirrup wasn't retrievable for the last 4 fences because it had in fact flown out of the bar and was hanging miles below the saddle, dangling under the pony! What a trooper!

We walked the horses off, sponged down and had a glass of fizz before we headed off to see how we had done. Well…WOULD

YOU BLOODY BELIEVE IT? We were one of the only pairs clear and inside the time! By 23 seconds no less! FIRST PLACE! Let the squealing commence! I was elated, not just for me but for my trier of a horse, for my super-duper sidekick and for everyone that wished us luck with words of support.

We did it! I cannot tell you how amazing it feels to be doing this and doing it at an 'above par' standard to be getting placed!

Thank you, as always, to every single one of you that has us in their thoughts and wishes us luck – It keeps me going in times of (undergarment staining) crisis – This red ribbon, hopefully one of many, belongs to you.

Louise Hosking "Ive been talking about you to my friends and we can relate to you, it's great to know I'm not the only one who's not as 'ballsy' as I used to be. Keep the stories coming! X"

NOVEMBER 2016

November 2, 2016

ASTON PREP!

Twitchy bum time! The palpitations have started, the toilet trips have increased tenfold and I'm struggling to move the computer mouse due to the gallon of sweat pouring from my palms! It can only mean one thing... THE TIMES ARE OUT! My Second BE event, this time at 90cms... Am I totally ridiculous? I think probably YES!

November 3, 2016

LAST NIGHT... Pat was just utterly phenomenal! It was dark, freezing and usually the pillock will come out a bit fresh and try and have me off at least once with a monster spook! He's started on a new supplement last week - wondering if it's already working its magic on his body? Either way, I wrote a little poem to sum up my evening, enjoy!

Out of the office bang on 5,

Just down the road to the yard I drive.

Walk down the field to catch him in,

The twat trots off, and I just grin.

Finally in, I tack him up,

And quickly down a champagne cup.

Throw on my gloves, and boots and hat

And trembling, get on said twat!

Down in the school, a bulb flashed on,

He's soft and loose - surely a con?

Right from the off, back up, head low

I feel like Charlotte on Valegro!

20 minutes is all it took,

I got off and stood and shook.

The fear I feel, the nerves and strife,

All put aside for the best ride of my life.

7ᵗʰ November 2016

A tale of two halves - Our BE90 DEBUT!

So, the morning of my much-anticipated trip up to Aston Le Walls for our step up to BE 90 crept up far faster than I could have ever imagined. It left me a little flabbergasted and unprepared, but consequently less panicking time for sure! The times came out and that's when I really felt the nerves, I was seriously scared this time. And not really about the event, but about travelling the furthest I have ever been to a competition, stabling my precious boy overnight somewhere new and then remembering what the bloody hell I am meant to be doing when I get there!

Alas, we set off at 10.30am, all packed and frightened. I do remember thinking more than once; 'is it unacceptable to neck this whole bottle of port before 11am?' – Probably! It poured with rain the whole way there… assume foetal position and begin rocking at the thought of running cross country in a slurry of mud from the 3 sections of riders on the course before me! But on arrival it was bright sunshine and not a dribble of the wet stuff on the grounds of the beautiful Aston le Walls venue!

My trusty sidekick, Lisa had been a sneaky beaky and arranged for us to have a lesson with the one and only, Nigel Taylor. Unbeknown to me, this guy has done 15 Badmintons and here he was babying us round a series of twigs in comparison! My bloody horse was spooking and jinking at everything, making me look like a total amateur, Bugger it! What will be will be tomorrow!

Ponies tucked up in their overnight accommodation and us into our plush spa hotel avec Jacuzzi – we got an early night ready for a 6.30am alarm.

Alarm… Don't be daft, when you are trembling enough to wake the dead at 5am, who needs an alarm! Dressed, retching bile and pale faced, we headed to the yard to get ready for the impending and almost certain death of the day ahead. Poor Lisa – I think it's possibly catching, mildly contagious if nothing else – she was struggling to plait through the pain of her broken finger and trembling hands – team work ensued! All plaited and ready, we loaded up and off we went, both of us ready to turn for home.

My dressage was 9.49 am – I was trialling a new horse calmer today; Equine America Super So Kalm Paste – I should have taken it myself, Pat was the calmest he had ever been in a dressage warm up, especially in what felt like -5 degrees! Arse,

Crap, Bollocks! I'm being called in... I'm needing a poo just reliving it.

Well, what an anti-climax. It was FINE...again, nothing overly monumental to write home about. I'm struggling to understand what the BE judges expect from the dressage phase as this is barely a Prelim and I'm getting near on 75 percent at Novice and mid-high 60's at Elementary and still only a 33 today! Still, we live to survive another test!

Boots on, stirrups up and off to the show jumping warm up. Warmed up the same as Littleton, a couple of pingy jumps and off we went down to the arena. Well, what a bloody joke! Came up to number one, a rustic oxer with a ray of light shining on half of it, Pat wasn't looking or paying attention and spooked at the light just at the last minute, resulting in a bloody great kick from me which sent the back rail into orbit. Number 2 was a simple upright, washing lines and disorganisation meant we had that one as well. He really hates touching poles so was exceedingly upset now. Number 3 he barely breathed on the back rail this time and it fell! WTAF! Spooked like a twat at number 4 b, two very small flowery fillers and combined with the earlier upset meant another unwanted kick up the arse and another pole. We got our act together for the rest and jumped 5 through to 10 without any poles thudding to the ground! Wha a total shitter. I was very sad to add 16 jumping penalties onto our dressage score, very sad indeed. He's a great little jumping horse and I felt he was unprepared, and I didn't think about the canter, the turns, the striding, nothing really – Nerves took over and apparently the autopilot switch is far too close to the 'ride like a dickhead' switch. ARGH.

Back at the box, I had 20 minutes to change, smoke a few cigarettes and drain half a glass of Prosecco before we had to go and warm up for the death phase. I gulped as I saw the other riders in the warmup looking very professional and nowhere near as green in the face as me. Four to go before me and I was up. Being counted down is possibly my worst nightmare, it's like being walked on the plank before you're thrown over-board. And over we went! Over the first and through a gap in the hedge to number 2, he spooked, obviously! I tapped him with my whip on the shoulder to get his attention back on the job! Number 3, he spooked again, this time so violently that I lost my stirrup – Fucks sake - I felt all over the bloody place! I felt like I was going to die at any moment! 6 was the water, I got my stirrup back and started riding a bit better. 7 A and B; up and down the steps to a house as part C – BRILLIANT… Number 8, I was worried about. It looked a bit big to me! He stood right off and we embraced the beloved flier stride! Yippeeee! We were FLYING!

9, 10, 11 a double with the second bit a skinny, no dramas, 12, 13 – a skinny log to coffin – bloody flew it – didn't even look twice! GOOSEBUMPS ALL OVER ME RIGHT NOW! To the flying finish of an angled brush and we were HOME and more importantly, we were alive.

What a bloody horse! Utterly redeemed ourselves to end our very short BE season FLYING clear inside the time at 90cms!

Looking back, I am still miffed about the 4 poles that we had down, still questioning the rationality of a 33 dressage but absolutely, 100% beaming over the fact that this little horse has done a grand total of 3 cross country rounds in his life and this one was un-bloody-believable! I've said it before and I will bang the same drum until my arms fall off – I LOVE MY ABSOLUTE LEGEND OF A HORSE - now and forever more, AMEN!

8th November 2016

I've only gone and won a TROPHY!

With the eventing season drawing to a close, I turn my attention to my secret love of dressage! Over two months ago, Pat and I had a double win at Novice and Elementary which qualified us for a Championship. Ludicrously bad timing in that it fell the day after our BE90 debut at Aston Le Walls! I put him out in the field early so the poor chap could walk off any 'stiffys' he had from the previous day and dragged him back in at 11am for our hack to the championships! Arrived in lots of time and very slowly warmed up with lots of stretching to coax his tired muscles into some sort of organised outline!

Into the first test N34 and beaming the whole way round, I thoroughly enjoyed myself! I don't much like doing a Novice or an Elementary in a 20m x 40m sized arena anymore now, but if we just breathe and keep it collected we make it – just about! No dry mouth, no sweating, no near-death experiences, just breathing and enjoying it! We nailed it for a 73.8% just pipped to the Championship slot by 1.5% - Thrilled with my clever tired boy.

The second test was somewhat more of a challenge, fitting an Elementary into a 20m x 40m arena is no mean feat! Pat was quite tired now and I had to use my spurs a little more than I like to. But we got there – even the 'very nearly' wrong direction leg yield didn't put us out of kilter! A decent 65% test – our neatest Elementary to date in a short arena. We shared first place on a 65% and got a HUGE trophy for winning the Elementary league. I am so delighted and proud that he tried so hard for me after such a busy weekend. I would love to just say a MASSIVE thank you to my dear devoted husband for videoing and keeping the pony mint supplies up and once again to my absolute pleasure of a horse for just being so wonderful.

10th November 2016

So, is it just me or does anyone else feel really deflated this week? I'm really struggling, not with nerves but with motivation. AND I just looked into the mirror of my Clinique compact and goodness me! I just caught a glimpse of my haggard face in the mirror and I look like shit. This weekend is going to be spent on ME. I need a haircut, facial and no stress of competing - it will be our first weekend off in ages, so I think it's well deserved. I saved up a bit of money working 3 jobs last month, so I think I've earned it.

She says, looking at the entries for the Arena Eventing on Saturday

11th November 2016

Despite having a relaxing Saturday planned to include;

9.30 AM - Hair appointment

11.45 AM - Facial

1 PM - Snoozing with cats on the sofa appointment

3 PM - Sleeping after eating my body weight in mince pies.

I had 3 glasses of Malbec last night down the local and Daddy Carrot convinced me to enter the arena eventing at Coombelands on Saturday.

In the cold and (almost) sober light of day - the times have just been released and I am first to go at 9am and I am WELL AND TRULY SHITTING MY KNICKERS!

No time to watch anyone go first, no time to cry and look presentable afterwards - I'm trembling, had 4 cigarettes and 2 poo's in the space of half an hour!

On the plus, I've managed to get my hair appointment changed to 11.30 and my facial at 1.30, let's hope I'm not carted off in an ambulance and miss them both!

12th November 2016

I'm alive!

So, last night Daddy Carrot and I went down to the sand school with Pat to make a half-hearted attempt at gearing up for today's arena eventing... put in the terrifying 'blue barrels of doom' and he was blindingly fabulous. Pingy and calm and I was so enjoying myself after not riding since the dressage last Sunday.

One more time over the barrels and Bang! 3 strides later and my darling horse is on 3 legs. My heart stopped for what felt like an eternity. My first thought was damage to a tendon.

I dived off and he's holding up his left front leg like he's hailing a taxi! My pride and joy, how stupid could I have been to give him 4 days off and then do some jumps.

On second and less panicky inspection he's lost a bloody shoe! Pulled it clean off, no broken bits of hoof, no nails left in the foot; a clean swift pull of a shoe. I own an almost full thoroughbred and for those that don't or never have, losing a shoe for this particular type of horse is like having 46 strands of barbed wire pulled tight round his leg! Drama King! But what a relief! Farrier booked for 7.30am tomorrow morning, we headed to the pub!

Saturday – My first ever Arena Eventing Day

Woke up early but not too nervous, managed to stuff a mini mince pie in my chops AND have a cup of tea! Up at the yard, mucked out and shoe back on, it started pouring with rain! We hacked the 35 min route to the venue and as I was first to go at 9am, I walked the course and got my self together! We were soaked! And freezing. But I went in smiling as usual and jumped the first 6 show jumps CLEAR!

The next 10 were mock cross-country jumps and bloody Nora! They were spooky and all over the place! I jumped number 10, now where the bloody hell am I going?! I was very lost! I sheepishly got my bearings and completed our first ever arena eventing CLEAR, if a little steady!

Putting to bed any demons of knocking down 4 jumps last weekend and feeling utterly elated, I was slow but who gives a fat rat's ass! My horse was brilliant today, true class and truly bloody brilliant!

I don't imagine we were placed so I won't head back up in the rain.

Just thawing out before my hair appointment and girly rest of the day xx

Andi Bellini Palmadessa "I so enjoy your posts!! You're the real deal and you keep it that way!!! Win or lose, it's how you play the game!! I think you're attitude is so refreshing in what is sometimes a very shallow world. Keep it up!!Job well done... Both of you ☐"

14th November 2016

I think it's high time you knew a little more about me… I am an open book it seems!

Born Victoria Ingamells on 5th April 1986 in Boston, Lincolnshire. I grew up in a small cottage on a farming estate in Blankney, with my Mum, my Dad, 2 older brothers and an older sister.

I first sat on a pony at the age of 7 and after much begging I had fortnightly lessons at a riding school for 3 years to prove my dedication. After the addiction hit, I began helping with the hunt horses at a local private hunt yard. At 12, I started working as a cover groom for that private hunt yard, 1.5 days a week of sole charge and cubbing/hunting as often as a school sick note allowed.

I learnt from some of the most knowledgeably old-fashioned horse people in the industry of how to foal, feed, train and run (like clockwork) a busy yard filled with big athletes. For that opportunity, I will remain eternally grateful.

I trained and received the Pony Club tests and taught for a few years (signed off my BHSAI hours), ran various yards from polo to dressage and everything in between. I competed for a local family, a handful of event horses - Most of them are my dear shining stars in the sky now.

Around all of this I studied; blagged 14 GCSE's, 5 A levels and the most part of a BA (hons) degree in Marketing and PR. After a series of shitty office jobs, I landed a pretty good one, and I bought my very first horse at the age of 24.

The rest is history really! I am a funny creature of habit, I laugh often and rarely hide emotion. I love so much of the world and know which bits I don't. I have grown up under the watchful eyes of so many people that I have come to have such huge respect for, those people shaped me into something I can be proud of. I am proud of who I am. Please make sure you are too.

Diary of A Wimpy Eventer I'm so glad to be any kind of inspiration to anyone. We can all do this, it's in all of us to be brave. We just need the support of each other and a good wine xxx

21st November 2016

Mondays' Musing

I have a lot to be exceedingly grateful for. I have a super horse. I begrudge nothing about getting up an hour early to traipse out into the cold and often damp countryside before daylight. I sacrifice lovely long nails and flowing hair for a gallop across a field. Something that certainly wasn't genetic, but somehow has ingrained itself into my DNA, I live and breathe horses. Equestrian thoughts fill at least 72.4% of my daily thought process. Nearly everything I have notably achieved in life boils down to horses. They make me who I am.

People that don't think about horses or that don't have horses in their lives, will struggle to understand just HOW important scouring eBay for 'equestrian items ending soonest' truly is to us.

My long-suffering non-horsey husband understands. He understands that I am stark-raving bonkers and that if he visits the horse once a week he will get home-made baked goods, mediocre bedroom activity and a hassle-free existence!

I guess what I am trying to say is; that despite how shit it feels waking up on a Monday and dragging my unenthusiastic arse into the office, I have a lot to look forward to. Next year we are embarking on greatness, on a crusade to eventing success and non-death... I MUST try harder to spend this winter preparing as best I can and that starts with attitude.

Join me EVERYONE - Shake off the Monday blues, be positive, sit up straighter, breathe in deeper and stick a middle finger up to anyone that tiddles on your toast (your boss excluded). Have a bloody cake if you want one, smoke a cigarette if you want to - be content and feel great - because we are, in our own individual way, bloody super at something!

I feel better already.

Have a super day!

xxx

DECEMBER 2016

11th December 2016

So, a little weekend round up from us....

SATURDAY

I have been SO careful with Pat after his scary shoe pulling injury that left me counting every single lucky star in the sky. Saturday, we planned a hack with our new yard buddies Auntie Nugget and her horse, Div (Auntie Nugget – because she always has a pocket full of pony treat nuggets at the ready!). 2.30pm, swig of port and off we went. An hour passed full of chatter and giggling... this is vital to our confidence development, having people to enjoy the journey with, but wait... we were LOST! Balls! Got a mild wrist slap from a local landowner for trespassing and we back tracked home! I did manage to fly a hunt jump en-route though and Pat felt mega!

Home just as dusk set in, cuddles for Pat, dinner and back into the warm.

SUNDAY

Today was exceptionally vomit inducing for me. I had planned to jump today, the first time since the shoe pulling. I felt sick to my stomach building a double and parallel, I smoked a nervous cigarette and went down to the arena.

I did 3 cross poles before I stopped swallowing bile. Popped them up a bit and got my act together. Jumped very nicely through a 95/1m combination and I wasn't sick, result! He feels bloody fabulous, soft, and confident and I just love him so much.

I'm feeling happy, and planning to go somewhere at the weekend show wise so I'll keep you posted when I've found one

Night guys

xxx

14th December 2016

I want every single one of us to feel immensely proud of what we have achieved. Just little things, day to day that make us feel proud and great. I want everyone to post at least 1 picture to their social media today, of how far we have come. That might be dressage/jumping/ groundwork/schooling/staying on whilst attempting to do sitting trot.

After all, we are all in this together, we all smell a little bit like wee, have been trodden on and cried with frustration over our passion for horses. We are all individually achieving something every day. Why not blow your own bloody trumpet for a change without feeling like you're being judged for it!

18th December 2016

I woke up this morning with the biggest bout of crippling nerves I have had for months. I've not felt like this for ages, I think having a few weeks off from shows has made me feel somewhat inadequate as a rider and out in public; 100% worse! – I was only going to a bloody Christmas dressage show!

I arrived at the yard and got ready, plaited, tinselled and dressed up like a prize-winning turkey. We trundled off to Brinsbury for the Riding Club winter dressage series. Now, after a rare lesson yesterday I couldn't face the Medium 71 class that I had originally entered. We just aren't good enough yet. Simple.

I have taught my own horse from scratch, I don't know how to be better than we are right now, so I need help. My knowledge and skills stop at very basic lateral (sideways fancy) movements. I just didn't feel right pushing my poor horse all over the place and feeling like we didn't achieve something, so I entered the novice non-competitively and remained in the Elementary. And, as it was a festive occasion and as I am not one to blend into the background, I dressed up in full Santa costume with Pat dressed as Rudolph!

I had dulled the nerves with a 9am port swig, I felt festive and ready to rock! Thanks to my super smashing yard owners, we got a surprise Christmas lift in their lovely horsebox. I always feel like royalty sitting on the crisscross leather seats and, struggling with no transport for what has felt like forever, this was a lovely treat! Plenty of time to settle in now I wasn't hacking there so we had a jump round the clear round jumping course for a lovely clear and pretty rosette (that's now on the Christmas tree). Woohoo!

Into the Novice test, I felt smiley and as if by magic... Pat went super! We broke into canter in the medium trot but fuck it... can't be perfect all the time, can we?! As I wasn't riding competitively in the Novice class there was no placing. I finished on a shade under 74 percent which is consistent for him at this level. I was immensely thrilled with a 9 for my free walk again, something I have focussed on because of its double marks! Very happy with that indeed.

I didn't bother going back down to the warmup before the Elementary test, there were only 3 in it so not long to wait!

Apart from one small blip and rider satnav error, it wasn't a shambles. He should have been more connected and off my leg, but I wasn't displeased. I untacked and popped up for my sheet, thoroughly convinced of 3rd place (The other 2 competitors were very strong). I couldn't contain myself when the rosette I was handed was RED! I even double checked the name on the sheet it was pinned to!

Tears rolling down my face, I just couldn't believe it. My beautiful darling horse after scaring me senseless with that leg only 4 weeks ago, has come out and been utterly amazing yet again. I cannot put into words how lucky I feel to see my best friend, my lovely teammate in this sport of equestrianism, doing such a phenomenal job of bobbling me around and collecting all these red rosettes. Crying again now!

Thanks to every single one of you for your endless support, to Auntie Nugget for calling our tests so well, to Mark and Alison for your help, support and flashy taxi and to my lovely darling husband for towing the line when I smell so bad and put out so infrequently!

We've only bloody gone and done it again!

27th December 2016

Today, I feel exceptionally lucky to have found such a wonderful yard with kind and non-judgemental people on it. I just want to stress how important that is to all of us. For the last 7 years at least, I have learnt to grow an extremely thick skin and plead ignorance despite my wealth of equestrian knowledge and experience. I do this to secure my failings and not make anyone feel inferior. No one likes a 'know it all', least of all me!

I don't give two shits these days if anyone thinks I'm completely clueless, that I can't ride well or my horse isn't reaching his potential- bollocks to them!

Read it carefully - Those that mind don't matter and those that matter don't mind. Please keep that in mind when people piss on your chips!

Bloody well enjoy your horses, fall off, get scared (terrified) and overcome your fears step by step. We can all be super - just one day at a time.

Caroline Boyd "So true. We need to tell ourselves this more often."

Lois Springer "Words to live by!"

31st December 2016

A post of reflection...

At the start of 2016 I was a trembling mess. I didn't compete and I rarely rode, NEVER hacked out and feared getting my saddle out of the tack room. I enquired about sales livery for Pat because I felt sick to my stomach at the thought of getting on him.

In July, I got married to my super supportive non-horsey husband and we moved into our new house and Pat into his.

Moving livery yards transformed us, I gained enough confidence to ride every day (Sedalin fuelled to begin with until I could feel safe again). This is where our year began - with only 4 months left!!! I went on the hunt ride as a first outing and scared myself shitless jumping far more than planned but it began to fix us to an extent... every time I rode for about 6 weeks I reminded myself; if I can do that then I can do anything!

I entered a hunter trial and two days before went cross country schooling for the first time in years - I was definitely scared but more determined than ever. We successfully completed our hunter trial without death or injury.

Pat and I became best friends again, we fell in love with galloping again and he felt like he was looking after me, we were and still are, made for each other. So, we entered our first BE80 at Littleton... we nailed it for 5th place and I literally couldn't have been happier. I did lots of clinics, hacking and entered the BE90 at Aston Le Walls. Despite utter terrification we did it, pooped up our SJ but mega clear and quick cross country which made me prouder than ever of how far we had come in just a few months.

We then reverted to dressage diva and won the Elementary championships, and a few more wins at Novice and Elementary level in the few weeks that followed. To yesterday, where Pat and I went to a showing show (our first one in years) and WON the riding horse class. He was impeccably behaved and made me so super proud to own this heart throb of a horse. I was riding around the ring beaming with pride and it was the first comment we received along with our rosette. How very few people ever actually look as though they are enjoying it? – I hear this all the time, just try it next time you are out; let go of the stigma, let go of the fear and enjoy it.

Today I feel lucky, proud and extremely excited to take on 2017. I absolutely couldn't do any of it without the support of my friends, family and my dearest husband. Next year is going to be an absolute blast and I cannot wait to share it with you all.

Here's to a new year, a fresh start and a dream to pursue. If you do one thing today; decide on a dream and chase it like your pants are on fire... I'm with you every step of the way.

Love as always.

Vic and Pat

Xxxxx

Sarah Lee You don't do things by halves. From not riding to competing within a few months. Inspiring, this brought tears to my eyes :)

Annalisa Alexander Truly inspirational! Thank you so much for sharing your journey, you've given me hope that I can overcome my nervousness after years of not riding! Bring on 2017. And I can't wait to see what you and Pat get up to!

Linda Jones Thank you. I love your posts as they are so positive and inspiring that 'normal' riders can achieve a dream despite a 'normal' life.

Pamela Rutterford Inspiration at its best! All the best for 2017 xx

Maz Turvey Wow, an inspirational read as ever. Just shows what a little grit, determination and support can do. I had a tear in my eye reading this I must admit. 2017 I'm going to take a leaf out of your book, looking at lots of clinics and low-key competition to get some confidence up and to build on the relationship Ebony and I have. Looking forward to seeing what you guys get up to next year. Happy New Year xxx

JANUARY 2017

4th January 2017

Today I am suffering the effects of last night's 25 minutes without stirrups. My thighs hurt, my tummy hurts, my minky* hurts (damn gel seat saver rubadubbed my girly bits!). Now I know it was 'No Stirrup November' but we were off games then, so I am bringing you - JOYFULLY JIGGLING JANUARY.

Jiggle away my fellow followers, jiggle until you joggle! I am determined to get good at this!

.....Oh and did I mention... I've just put my name down for DRAG HUNTING on SUNDAY. Holy mother of crumbles... what have I done - I've had to take 2 poo breaks just filling out the disclaimer!!!

Gemma Conroy I can only suggest sudocreme.... before and after!

7th January 2017

Just a small musing from the bottom of my teacup this morning, how I wish I could sleep in, but every part of my human wants to get up and start the day in the hour of 5!!!

I was just checking in on Instagram and stumbled across an account which shall go unnamed! I browsed picture after picture of what appeared to be success, beauty and style. I spent 20 minutes mentally deciding that now it's 2017, maybe I should consider being more stylish, more on trend, thinner and with nicer hair?! The crux of it is - I go through this thought process about 3 times a week!!! I wish I could be more like someone else for a brief flashing moment.

Now, if there someone browsing my social media accounts wishing they were a fuzzy, ginger, marginally overweight nutbar with a seemingly average existence?! Ha, like hell!

I think what we all must celebrate in ourselves is our individual pretties. There has to be much less shame in loving something about yourself - without someone slapping an 'Arrogant Twat' sticker on your forehead!! We are all individuals, bloody fabulous for something... crikey, it might only be something small, but I bet you know what it is deep down.

I personally happen to think that I have a sparkling sense of humour, alright I'm not a stick thin, large bosomed goddess in designer clothes nor am I a wealthy or an overly intelligent business woman... but I am me and instead of spending this year wishing I was more like someone else, I am going to love being more like me every day.

Please love who you are and don't you dare feel ashamed of it!!!! Go on... celebrate and share your inner pretties, bugger what anyone else thinks!

Have a brilliant day... I'm going to hack or jump, can't decide, and then get ready for dying on the hunting field tomorrow!

Xxxx

8th January 2017

So, let's go back to this morning...

I got up and drove to the yard un-phased at this point, to skip out, give Pat some hay and not think about the day ahead. Back at home I actually ate breakfast... grilled mushrooms, tomato, avocado and a poached egg (still on the post-Christmas diet).

The Kent and Surrey Bloodhounds were meeting locally to the yard at 12.30pm (with a half hour hack and chain smoke to factor in) I needed to be plaited and ready for death by 11.45am! Bang on 10 my belly was jiggly, swallowed two Imodium and sat on the toilet for a while and I was right as rain! Constipation for a few days is a small fee to pay in comparison to soiling yourself in front of 50 people you don't know! Plus getting faeces out of my new gel seat saver would have been royally tedious!!

Off we went, swigging at the hip flask and puffing on a (almost quit) cigarette, trundled down to the meet. It was already fairly busy, and Pat seemed a bit of a frisky biscuit when I tried to accept my compulsory port snifter! Downed it and minutes later we were off!

GALLOPING was Pats pace of choice for the day, he was mega strong and likes to be up at the front, so that's where we stayed until he settled. We had a line of cantering and trotting with a blast down the gallops to warm us up before I heard the smasher of a Field Master* say that the next line might get a bit exciting!

I was crapping myself at that point if I'm brutally honest!

Covered in mud already, hip flask pretty much empty, lines 2&3 did not disappoint on the excitement stakes! We jumped 4ft hedge after 4ft hedge one after the other... big bloody bushy great hedges!!! And I tell you what, I was absolutely blinking loving it! Crikey, my tiny boy grew wings... we were flying! I cannot tell you what it felt like!!! I was crying with joy and pride soaring round those fields, until we turned and landed ourselves in front of a metal five bar gate, imagine my horror!!

Bum twitching, I kicked for a good stride and we sailed it, so big in fact, that I almost come off the back! Bugger me this was better than anything I have ever done in my entire life... we finished the 4th and last line with a huge 5ft box hedge with a 7ft drop on landing and came home with the biggest grin on the entire hunting field!!!

I cannot tell you all how today has made me feel, I seriously love the absolute bones of that tiny Trojan flying machine, he made me so blinking proud today. Looked after me good and proper.

I must also say that I have hunted a lot in my youth but absolute hats off to the Kent and Surrey Bloodhounds you have given me the best day of my life today and here I sit in my bubbly bath with a husband made cup of tea, not quite believing what we have done this afternoon.

Can you honestly believe that this time last year I couldn't even get on my horse through fear, and now bloody look at us!!!!!! Here's to a very, very wonderful horse and an exciting year ahead!!

Love, best wishes and thank you for the endless support. I await photographic evidence from the sterling Julian Portch Photography to prove my balls were almost always intact today!

Grace Reed Such an inspiration and the progress is unreal! Xx

11th January 2017

Well, its day three of post-hunting agony. I have been crippled for two days now. Stairs are a no-no, lowering my plump arse onto the loo seat - also dicey. Kneeling, crouching, or lifting my arms above my head - forget it!

I got my leg over last night though! Good old Pat stood like a rock while I jiffled myself out of an involuntary cramp... good boy Patsy! I am still on a high though, I CAN DO THIS - Look at me - I can do it after all.

The nerves cripple me: my racing heart makes me dizzy, the sweating makes it hard to grip the reins and the constant toilet visits make it near on impossible to get on sometimes, but these are the things I have no control over - I can control how I fight through all of it to feel that feeling I get when I'm home and alive and full of exhilaration.

16th January 2017

Monday Morning Musing.

Apparently, today is the most depressing day of the year - Blue Monday. Something about the weather, daylight hours, debt management, Christmas expenditure and New Year's resolution guilt....

I have to say, after the consumption of too much Rioja at our friends last night, I have felt better. My excessive consumption also resulted in me sucking a rubber fish to my forehead, meaning that I am now the proud owner of the biggest love bite in the middle of my face the world has ever seen. I've tried to cover it up... thanks Clinique, but it is still glowing through like the bloody 5th of November! When I am not having to see any more humans' bar my husband - I will be sure to post pictures for you!

Back to Blue Monday...

It all boils down to envy, we all look at other people's lives and the grass appears thick and lush and oh so green... but is it? A little insight into my life; I have 3 jobs, I leave the house at 6.30AM and come home at 7PM. I must do the washing, cleaning, cooking, food shopping and shower before sitting down to eat (usually around 8pm). We rent an average 2 bed semi in an okay(ish) suburban area, I buy pretty much everything for Pat second hand, I don't have a nice car or savings and we don't go on holiday much or have expensive clothes. I have no transport for Pat, so I work those extra jobs to be able to fund the whacking costs of dream chasing. I am tired, always crashing out straight after tea. BUT would I change it? Would I want to have everything handed to me on a plate or have none of it at all and live in a burrow in the woods?

What I am trying to say is, think of everything you do to get to where you are, the sacrifices you make for your horses, hobbies, children that make us so tremendously happy and, at times, tremendously sad. Be proud of where you are right now at this time of life, look to the future with hope, not dread. Be bold in your decisions to better that hopeful life - and try to worry less when plans take a turn off piste - My husband said, just yesterday; "The plan can change 100 times, it's the goal that must remain the same."

Be brave, enjoy it and love the life you have - don't wish you were someone else, one day you might be and you might not be happier at all.

Bollocks to you Blue Monday... I'm off to dance in the drizzle with a fag!

Have a lovely day xxx

20th January 2017

You know sometimes when things just get to you?!

Quite often I feel it, when the morning alarm goes off on my husband's side of the bed and due to earplugs, it takes him an AGE to turn it off - in the meantime I am laying there imagining the quickest, and easiest way I could wrap the cord of the alarm clock around his neck without having to move from under the covers...

Or, when your boss has categorically told you he is going to be out of the office, and you pull into the car park and see his car parked there. Never more have I wanted to ram my tiny shitmobile into the back of his car, faking an injury worthy of a sick note!

I also got to the yard to find that my bird brain of a horse had over-reached AGAIN... When will I learn to keep the bloody boots on AT ALL TIMES! Sliced into the bulb of his heel and is now the proud owner of a sick note and blue bandaged foot... Could it have got any worse?!

Well, no - it didn't, I got home, my husband had bought flowers without knowing about any of the days shit storm of events, I broke my mid-week drinking resolution - RESULT, and none of the cats had left a hair ball on the floor...

The moral of the story is - if things don't go your way, it wasn't your way to go.

Read that last line again. Don't feel sad or disappointed, just find another way to go...

Enjoy today, it's Friday after all, go make a cuppa, have a biscuit, do a star jump with one hand on your bosom (in secret... you'll laugh - trust me) - I want updates of your weekend plans - mine are writing and looking for things to sell! Pat's got his sick note in hand so might get a brush if he's lucky!

Love, as always

Vic and Pat

xxx

January 24, 2017

I'd like to talk a little seriously for a minute - Not like me, I know - but I just read something, and it got me thinking...

About something that we will all have experienced in some form or another.

Certain words, like rape or cancer, make us wince inside right to our very core. This topic does the same for many people I am sure.

BULLYING

The question on everyone's lips is 'How dare people think they can get away with making others feel so terrible?'

Now, it comes in many forms, and I won't openly share too much detail, but I have been on the end of the bullying stick and being a sensitive soul, not always been able to handle it. The crux of it is, and it took me a long time to see the light, the only thing you can really do is rise above it. There are several ways to do this but realisation of ONE very simple thing is KEY - You will NEVER stop rivalry, jealousy or bitterness that is caused by the resentment of other people's success.

SUCCESS - that word right there. You are being targeted because someone feels INFERIOR to you. Think about that - really think about it, the person being a chip pisser is actually aware that you have something they don't. Feel proud of that and lift your bloody head up. Don't fret on it when you get home - don't!

You see, bringing people down only makes a 'bully' feel better for a short time - then they are filled with self-loathing or left unfulfilled completely - After all, they are only being mean because of their own low opinion of themselves, which is the saddest part of all. The only person that a bully is bullying, is themselves. Remember that.

I've said it before and I'll say it again - surround yourself with people that either couldn't give a shit, ones that would give their last shit to see you succeed, or the ones that don't know what shit you're doing and forget what the pissers say along the way - they'll wish they were nicer when you're rich and famous!!! <3 xxxxx

27th January 2017

So, it's Friday...

What a week, my head is spinning. On the Pat front - it's been stupidly cold, and the school hasn't had a chance to defrost, so one pointless lunge this week is all we have managed. It's been over a week since my last ride and I'm beginning to feel violently sick thinking about getting back on - time off is my ultimate nemesis, good job the port supplies were replenished this Christmas! We had a visit from the lovely horse dentist, nothing to report just the usual file and buff!

I come to my Friday musing - Well there are 2 actually.

The first one is HARD WORK. Now, I have never really stuck at much in my life - probably not the best example but, being a typical Aries - I too much enjoy the thrill and challenge of change and new beginnings. That isn't to say I haven't worked hard because by gum... I didn't get this far without it!! It's time for a re-think - I have plans, major life changing plans this year that I am working hard to make sure I fulfil.

This year my philosophy of life is changing; I am focusing on working hard at the things I enjoy over things I don't just to make ends meet. I think that if you enjoy something, work as hard as you can possibly work at it, and you will be recognised for that and hopefully rewarded. Hey, I'd rather be poor than miserable any day, beans on toast are under-rated!

I guess what I am trying to say is - work hard for the things that matter, don't lose focus, and be the best that you can be at those things regardless of changes around you. Don't make excuses for not working as hard as you could, because only you will suffer in the end - the rewards will come in the form of success. Hard work will always give you something back - even if it's only self-gratification when you down your Friday night wine!

Now, moving onto the second musing (I just couldn't choose between them!) INSPIRATION. Hard work is all very well but sometimes when we cannot see the bloody wood for the trees, we need re-aligning. We need someone or something to make us realise why we are doing this, someone that is on the journey of dream fulfilment - it gives us hope and light at the end of the tunnel.

This week I must highlight an extraordinary woman that I met over a few drinks, she has put her heart and soul (and available finances) into something that isn't half as rewarding as it should be right now. She isn't far from taking a turn down the dark road of defeat and needs a light shining on her path again. I want to be that light for her, for all of you, for anyone working commendably hard and not getting what they deserve.

I feel as though I have a different purpose now, to be a torch for people when they're down a dark path - I will WORK HARD at that, harder than I have worked for anything. And YOU are my INSPIRATION, all of you reading this, so thank you.

What does the weekend hold? I plan on downing my body weight in port before hacking tomorrow. Hey, if it's not frozen, I might hack and do the clear round at Brinsbury College and then probably a lazy Sunday walk to the pub for a roast! Need to get my arse in gear on the little lorry fund and my BE season which kicks me in the guts in 6 weeks time!

Love, as always xxx

29th January 2017

Well, what a bloody joke... the nerves were back with a vengeance today, I jumped 5ft hedges and galloped for my life only 3 weeks ago and the thought of hacking to a local jumping clinic has me reaching for the Imodium!! I was so so scared today, crikey I nearly had a cry getting on yesterday too but, determined to make it big this year I need to focus, focus, focus on why I'm doing this.

I hacked, uneventfully, to Brinsbury College for my 12pm slot, shared with one other poor soul. Explained to Teachy what my issues are and why I was trembling, and we pop some poles and a cross to begin. Well... Pat clearly hasn't forgotten that hunting means you jump at 100 miles an hour, right?! Errrrr... VERY NOT FUNNY! I was clinging on like a monkey and felt utterly shit for what felt like an eternity!

It took almost 35 minutes for him to settle, he was cornering at the rate of a superbike, and it left me stirrup-less on more than one occasion. You know, I'm not shit, I know I'm not I just felt it today... a mega, mega massive sack of dog crap swinging from a stick! I think I need a re-focus from someone that knows me and Pat. He's far from a schoolmaster*, I've taught this pony everything he knows and we've cut plenty of corners I can tell you!

We finished jumping a course which felt far worse than it looked on the video. I'm ever the critic of my own poor performance! Go take a look at the videos, feel free to tell me how crap I am and how I sock his back teeth out all the time, it's the reality and things I'm working on - Operation: be less shit commenced today!

So, we are back in the game again, temporarily rusty, but back! I laughed with Pat ALL the way home, out loud like a crazy person and isn't that what it's about? I love him more than life itself, he makes it all worth the regular loose leavings I can tell you.

Peace out chirps!! And thanks again for keeping me sane, keeping me going and keeping my pants unstained!!

Love as always.

Vic and Pat Xxxx

FEBRUARY 2017

2nd February 2017

Onto our first cross country training of the year.

Well.... everyone, you will be pleased to know I am alive, my pants aren't stained and I *think* we got our mojo back!

I feel bloody frigging fantastic!

Let's roll back to 8.30am... I got to the yard and mucked out, I had to have everything ready to leave for 10.30ish. Had WAY too much time on my hands and my stomach was well and truly empty from four loose deposits before breakfast, so I had a cig and started on the hip flask. Now I'd like to add, that a good chum bought me a rather nice reserve port around Christmas time and it would surely be a crying shame not to fill the flask with it for today's special outing?! It was all too easy to drink and by 10.30am I had slurped up half of my flask, not loaded the trailer and the horse wasn't ready... but crikey, I felt mega up for it!! (Cross country that is). My dearest Auntie Nugget was driver today and had to put up with my nervous ramblings and poor directions for our 40-minute trip to the course!!

Pony unloaded, legged up by Daddy Carrot and we were off! Bobbling round warming up, not dying... this was ok, I think I was enjoying myself even at the start!!! A novelty!! First couple of jumps out of the way and I was bloody loving it!! Pat can be so mega spooky at times but today, I felt like I did galloping over the finish line at Aston last November, full of pride and confidence!

One thing I will say, I haven't had many lessons of late and I get scared at not feeling good enough, hats off to my newly dubbed 'Lord Fs A lot' he was the most incredible trainer, not for everyone I doubt but for me - simply perfect. Now, not many people could liken you to a dead pigeon in your approach to a fence but still fill you with confidence. He made clear that he despised my high hands and grinning all the 'bastard time' but this guy really has skills as a superb trainer and Pat and I were on fire because of it.

We jumped a load of different stuff, never once feeling out of our depth, even over some pretty meaty monster fences!! Steps, water, ditches, we really covered everything I needed to grow my confidence today.

I came away beaming, my horse, my bloody amazing tiddler pony has done it again, I could cry with joy and relief that I didn't come out this year a snotty, tearful wreck.

Thank you, Lord, Auntie Nugget, Daddy Carrot and most importantly, thank you Pat - you are simply the best thing I could ever, ever wish for xxxx

Over and out ☐ xx

3rd February 2017

I'm still high as a kite from yesterday, this is exactly why we do it right?! If anyone is in any doubt of whether they should stretch out over their comfortable boundaries, you should, because the euphoria lasts for days!

Like I always say, it's better than sex on a bed of money with a Lindt chocolate in my mouth! ☐

7th February 2017

TUESDAY - A lot of people's worst day of the week - you've painfully dragged your arse through the sheer agony of Monday and then Tuesday's bristly palm smacks you right across the face.

Today, Tuesday started just like that for me - I broke the Non-Midweek Drinking clause last night because of the worst Monday of 2017 to date, so I felt less than up for 8 hours of office boredom when my husband finally stopped hitting that bloody snooze button!

I felt downright unmotivated, something needed to change, like I need a darn good shake up in life, so after some excellent advice - I have set to work on a plan. If you too, are feeling like life is going nowhere and that you are stuck in a big fat rut, ask yourself...

What are the causes of your unhappiness/unfulfillment?

For me, it is full time office work - I feel trapped in the limbo of PAYE and Self-Employment. I am frustrated to the point of despair! For once, the horse side of life is playing second fiddle to this - I cannot be happy, confident and achieve my horsey dreams if this part of my life is a crumbly bumbly biscuit!

What would make you happiest, what is the main thing you would like to achieve?

This is simple for me - I LOVE to write, I love it. I laugh as I write, I cry when I read my writing back to myself, the emotion it brings out in me, the sheer joy I get from inspiring others. I cannot tell you how happy I am writing to an audience that appreciates my terrible knee jerk sense of humour and heart on sleeve honesty.

I'd also like to be dictating my hours a bit more, have more time with Pat and enjoy him more.

By outlining goals, breaking them down into achievable milestones and time-lining them, I hope I can make things happen! If you feel down, find out the cause and make a plan... baby steps remember, and soon we will all be wondering what the problem was!

I'm bursting with excitement for the future - you can be ANYTHING you want to be and you only EVER get one go at life - make it count - make a difference, and most importantly, make it happy.

Love Always

Vic xxx

10th Feb, 2017

It's Friday, My favourite time of week for a blissful musing...

Today I'd like to talk about BELIEF. Not in the religious sense, but in the 'believing in yourself' sense. Now, I am becoming an advocate of self-belief, to the point where almost every day, I have to restrain myself from physically knuckle dusting someone that doesn't have enough of it! It is VITAL and I'll tell you why...

In every aspect of our lives, in our family dynamics, in relationships, with our horses, our competitions, our work life, even fighting for the last cucumber in Tesco's, we all need some degree of self-belief. I don't think there is anything wrong with having a high opinion of yourself as long as you are gracious and polite to boot. You can only truly put others before yourself without an ulterior motive if you have enough belief in yourself to donate a slice of it to another.

I had little to none of it 3 years ago - my confidence and self-belief, in all areas of my life, were see-through... My marriage of 6 years was over, my fleeting relationship following that marriage was a royal, great big sack of rat shit, my redundancy money had run out and I was forced to take a job paying less than my first ever admin role straight out of school, so I lodged with mates in order to get by. I had NOTHING going for me, Pat was the only thing I had, I couldn't afford him, but I would have slept in his stable rather than give him up. I was not very happy and felt like there was nowhere to turn. It was Pat and my non-judgmental friends that helped me restore that once full pot of belief.

Now I have it back, I can see how important it is. If you believe you can - then you really, truly can. It sounds crap but it is true. Believing in myself meant that I could get back on Pat again, that we could enter a show again, that we could affiliate, that we could do cross country without dying, that I could meet a man that wasn't an arsehole.... I believed in myself and all these good things, amazing, wonderful things have happened.

Now, I might have been due some luck, but I know that if I didn't believe in my own abilities I would NEVER be as happy and fulfilled as I am right now. I'm genuinely fond of myself these days - I want everyone else to feel how life changing that is...

Go look in the mirror, DO IT NOW... look into your own eyeballs and find something that you like about yourself and bloody well say it out loud - be proud of who you are, don't always try to be different, you are already brilliant enough.

My weekend is going to be spent drinking from the flask of courage again as I have Arena Eventing at 11.52am tomorrow and I've just had to go for another poo just thinking about it! Have a great one (weekend, not poo) - I'll keep you posted on my hopeful non-death!

Love always

Vic and Pat xxx

14th February 2017

Happy Valentine's Day

Are you sick of hearing it yet...? I do think love should be celebrated, but not just for one day of the year. Let's talk about that feeling we call LOVE.

Now isn't it funny, when you fall in 'LOVE' you feel excited, fluttery in the belly and unable to stop smiling? Yet years in, it is likely you don't feel that it leaves you a little fooled and disappointed. It doesn't mean you care any less or feel anything less for your loved one - often you feel more, but what a shame that LOVE tricks us into thinking this is what it should feel like all the time.

I believe that you can LOVE almost anything or anyone if you let yourself. I love my husband, I love my cats, I love Pat within an inch of his tiny ears, I love my family and my friends, I love my little car, I love this blog and all of you that get something out of it. I Love Love.

HOWEVER, I am crap at love - I mean CRAP, CRAP. I love too much, I wear my fragile heart on my cardigan sleeve and it often gets bruised or damaged by the things people do or say. Love can hurt just as much as it can make you burst with happiness but that's what keeps us knowing we are alive and human right?!

Today, whether you are feeling IN love or despise the very bones of love, feeling anything at all means you have a heart. You care about yourself and that feeling called LOVE, celebrate THAT if nothing else today.

I LOVE YOU ALL so very much, for feeding my absolute love of helping people achieve greatness, have a wonderful day won't you? Remember to go and look in the mirror and choose something you LOVE about yourself today <3 xxx

15th February 2017

Today (slight sense of humour failure) I want to bare my soul a little in the hope that someone can offer some perspective and help me see the light...

So, as you all know, I use this page to address MASSIVE confidence issues that lurk under my pinky exterior. I uncontrollably and subconsciously tell myself, almost every day, that I am not good enough at one or more areas in my life. I am rarely ever a good enough wife, never a good enough friend, I'm a careless daughter, sibling and auntie to my beautiful nephews and nieces. I rarely give 100% at work and always know I could have done better and this all seeps through to Pat.

I get to the yard to ride and whilst I know I can get a tune out of pretty much any horse; I have a huge battle feeling like I'm just not good enough on my own. Line up 12 horses, unbroken, feral, and wild and I'd confidently give them all a go - madness huh! But give me my darling Patsy and I just melt into a soggy, terrified mess.

More often than not, I feel as though I don't really know what I'm doing - maybe it's because we have progressed to a level, I have no skills in yet (it hasn't stopped us before) or maybe it is the crippling fear of him shying or having the sillies and me falling off and never waking up. Either way, I have felt this way with my own horses since, well, forever.

I'm mumbling a bit, but basically - this huge lack of confidence in the areas I care most about is gradually destroying them. My marriage, my horse, my work - I simply don't know how to feel like I am brilliant, I want to - I want to feel worthy and I want to stop feeling like I'm letting people down all the time. I'm sick to the back teeth of hearing - it's got to come from inside you... I've tried - I have - I need someone to scoop me up and tell me it's all okay, that I'm not a bumbling sack of shit. I can feel another stage of re-invention coming on - Hey, I got through phase one, right?!

I'm sorry to be self-indulgent, but I know there are many of you here that will understand how I feel, I'm going back to read through some of the advice I so often dish out and take a slice of it for myself. Just a bit of a wobble, I think.

Love Always

Vic and Pat

xxxx

20th February 2017

Monday... Oh Monday how I loathe thee... Let's get one thing straight, Monday, you are NOT going to ruin my mood!

Let's talk about turning things around.

Dealing with different emotional challenges in life often leaves us feeling like we are wearing pants that are 3 sizes too small. They are uncomfortable, make us feel restricted and we know that shaking them off isn't going to be very pleasant. BUT... the feeling when you get them off is sheer delight, relief and you know never to try and get them on again.

Today I feel like those tiny bum pinchers are halfway down my thighs, still uncomfy ... but nearly off!! I'm turning things around.

Now, if something in your life is affecting everything else you do for the worse, it's time to change that thing. Can you pinpoint one negative thing that is having an influence over you that you cannot control? I personally have a few but the main one is my total and utter lack of self-worth which leads to insecurity. Today marks the very day that I am TURNING THIS SHIT AROUND!

I have been given a very clever tool by a very special person and that is to create a mentor of my mind - a facilitator to help me when I am filled with doubt. Each and every time a negative thought enters my head, there will be this constant uplifting voice telling me that I am brilliant, I am capable, and I am going to succeed.

The main thing I am trying to establish, is what will be the end goal? My goals with Pat are not overly measurable but I would like to achieve greatness. I would like to do something this year that I look back on next year and feel proud of. Ideally, I would like to overcome all odds and complete a BE100 or even a NOVICE!! Remembering that this time last year, I couldn't even face getting on let alone doing a jump, I know I have already achieved so much - why stop there! I CAN DO THIS!

Secondly, I would like to be a confident person, in control of my reactions and emotions. Just jotting these things down on here has made me feel positive, like I CAN do anything I set my mind to. We all can. WE CAN ALL ACHIEVE GREATNESS - one step at a time.

Let's go get it, start today - feel passionate and chase your dreams, we only have one chance to make our mark - take it - TAKE IT NOW!

Love you all ... Get those knickers off!

Vic and Pat xxx

21st Feb 2017

I wrote this for anyone that feels like giving up on following their dreams;

When you feel like giving in,

You feel uneasy in your skin.

Just take a minute to unwind,

Count to ten and search your mind.

Find comfort and take confidence,

And try to grasp some kind of sense.

Breathe in, breathe out and focus on

Success and just how far you've come.

Open up a brand-new door,

Find one where no-one's keeping score.

There's only you, be proud, stand tall,

I'll catch you if you start to fall.

Dream big, take steps to tread your track.

And remember – I've ALWAYS got your back.

xxx

24th February 2017

Boom boom boom... let me hear you say WAAAY-O.... (Tumbleweed for those born after 1986!)

It's only BLOODY FRIDAY! Pub night, no work for 2 days night... I am happy happy happy!! Channelling my inner positive person this week has made me feel blindingly fab. Here's something to work on this afternoon.

Stand up, get up off the bloody sofa, out of your office chair, out of the car and just for a minute (depending on who's watching - go to the toilet if you need to) - Stand on one leg, raise your fists to your arm pits and move your elbows up and down, give out a loud clucking noise and then sit back down - if you can do that without laughing at yourself, I will personally wear my pants on my head to the pub tonight!

One of the most beneficial things in life is being able to laugh at yourself. If you fall off (and you're not on the way to hospital), laugh about how your pants haven't been cut from your bare bum in public. Laugh when you forget your dressage test, only you will be able to remember the next move and stressing out isn't going to help your brain to find it! Laugh at your wrinkles, that spot on your chin, laugh at the grey hairs you keep finding and pulling out... Alright... Those are all mine, but you get my drift.

If you can master the art of laughing at yourself, it will act as a shield to nasty chip pissers that ruin your day. Enjoy being alive, only you can control your mood - people can affect it momentarily, but YOU are in control - bloody well grab it by the horns.

Weekend plans... Go on, get me the Imodium... That's right - I have a SHOW tomorrow. The leavings are loose, the palms are moist and I'm already wondering what is going in the flask! I have Combined Training at 9.36am, dressage test and show jumping round and then home for lunch to do some writing! Nothingy day on Sunday, just chilling out.

What's on the cards for you this weekend? Hope you have a lovely one.

Love Always

Vic & Pat

xxxx

February 25, 2017

Standard! Leavings are loose as a goose, sipping from the flask of courage ... here we go again.

February 26, 2017

Hurrah! We survived another outing! So, with the tail end of storm Doris licking out our heels yesterday, we trundled off to Coombelands Equestrian Centre for our first ever combined training♥ show. Up at the yard, having a mini meltdown about my missing hat silk and bridle number, trusty friends stepped in to assist! Plaited and ready to go, we hacked the 35 minutes to the scene of potential death.

Pat was unnervingly calm, warmed up without so much as a squeak- long may that reign! Number 73 "you're in" oh

Crumbs... I hate those two tiny words; she may as well have said "if you'd care to sign this 'consent to die' form". The bell sounded and four strides down the centre line and the horn sounds... what the crapper could I have possibly ballsed up this early on?! Oh, that's right, I haven't taken the pony boots off!! Buggeration! It put me right off! Good ole' Daddy Carrot to the rescue, and we set off again.

He did a sweet test, nothing flashy, just correct.

On to the jumping, boots back on, we jumped the practice cross pole twice and the spread once and went in. It's enough, I know he can jump, whatever do I need to check again and again for?! So off we go in a nice rhythm, missed the stride to the first but he jumped so well. He bashed number 10 which had a lot of people caught out but what a dear darling boy. He makes me feel like we can do anything.

So just one down, I waited for the results and I'm so glad we did. We came SECOND! If I hadn't lost 2 points for those bloody boots being left on, we'd have sneaked in at number one!! We would have also done our first sub 30% test but alas a 30.2% for us today. I'm delighted with my best boy; he was perfect today. It was great to get that run out before our first 2017 BE next week too. YEP, YOU HEARD RIGHT!

Thank you everyone for your endless support, to Gaye and the team at Coombelands and to dearest Daddy Carrot for videoing our bobblings, we got a lovely rosette and a bag of KM Elite goodies!

MARCH 2017

1st March 2017

TODAY, WE ARE CELEBRATING!

Thanks so, so much to all of you beautiful, wonderfully supportive, and fabulous people that following my mumblings. I am so desperately proud to have attracted such a kind and helpful support network of non-chip pissers. I love you all.

Today, my beloved Diary of a Wimpy Eventer has reached a massive milestone of over 8000 people in just 5 months. I am so grateful and so proud of how far I have come in confidence, not just with my riding but with my writing too. I have so many of you on here to thank for that. You have believed in me, supported me through some of my darkest, terrified times and held my virtual hand at every show. I genuinely cherish every single comment, private message and photo that gets sent. Proof that none of us are alone. I have your back, just as you have mine.

Lots of love today and always xxxx

2nd March 2017

It's twitchy bum time...

First BE event of 2017 Aston Le Walls - times are out. Holy Guacamole!

3rd March 2017

Today I would like to tell you all a little tale of courage...

Let's roll back to July 2016... Every day at 3.30pm I would begin the battle. My heart would race, my toilet visits would increase and by 4.30pm when I finished work, I could barely grip the car steering wheel through sweating palms. On arrival at the yard, I would pray for an excuse; a missing shoe, rain, the wrong colour pants on - any excuse to not have to ride - I'd take it.

I was consumed by guilt, consumed by fear unable to see light at the end of the darkest tunnel I had ever been in.

Bit by bit I began re-inventing myself.

Each day we did a little more, dropped the dope a little more and hacked a little more, after 2 weeks the day loomed of our 'hunt ride' and I was more scared than I have been of anything for a long, long time. 2 hours later I was hacking home, grinning like never before. I had done it; we were alive and I was full to the brim with pride. We were courageous for the first time in years and what a feeling!

Ever since this day, I have tried to emulate that feeling. Conquering fear is the best feeling in the world, grab it with both hands. Be brave, do something courageous, the repayments you get far outweigh the terror I promise you. After 8 months of being unable to get my saddle out of the tack room I made the decision to change the world. Just our world, the small bit of it that we take up, and look at us now.

We still battle, not hourly or daily anymore, but certainly weekly! Striving for that feeling has been the very best adventure I could have ever wished for and long may it continue.

Please, trust me and take that leap of courage - however small. If it doesn't repay you the first time, don't you dare give up - it WILL repay you in the end and if it doesn't - It is most certainly not the end.

Love as always, Vic and Pat xxxxx

Sobbing at my desk again! Cheeses!

4th March 2017

It's RAINED off! No first event of the season for us tomorrow. Three weeks to wait until the next one at Munstead and I've missed my run at 80… it's straight in at 90 for us!

For the first time ever, I wasn't scared either… I'm now lunging Pat and sulking instead!

5th March 2017

So, after Aston BE got cancelled, I had already decided to do something to get my adrenalin up, to scare myself just as I would have been going cross country today. Jumping at home is my scariest nemesis so that was that... decision made!!

We trundled down with Daddy Carrot, a camera, and my Bravery Vest* firmly clipped in, for some serious jumping action. We started off with some poles, a cross pole and then a small up right before building the oxer of doom! Gappy and large, my pony soared through the air like a podgy heron! We ballsed it a few times but what a feeling!

Was I scared? Absolutely.

Did I scream murderously, balling bad instructions at my poor husband who was out there building jumps in the pissing rain? Yes I did!

But did we die? Nope!

And do I now feel like jumping 90 cms will be a doddle? Hurrah...yes, we bloody do!

We jumped 1m15 today, our biggest jump to date, with no pant stains or death.

My lovely little horse tried so hard despite the horrid weather, what a brilliant day after the screaming disappointment of no BE party to go to!

xxxx

8th March 2017

Apologies in advance to all of those on here that are smuggling a todger in their trunks, but as it is International Women's Day, I am remarkably proud to say that on this page I have never ever encountered such support, loyalty, and kindness between equestrian loving women in my whole life.

Ladies... Let's celebrate the fact that we like a moan, whether it be the weather, the fluff and crumbs that appear from nowhere in our handbags, the remarkable difference of going into one shop and being a size ten and then a size twenty in the shop next door. We get wrinkles, eventually, we get saggy bosoms, eventually. It is inevitable that we will all at some stage, buy a coloured eyeliner or funky hair dye on impulse and change our minds about reinventing ourselves on a lonely Saturday evening (and just eat a bar of Galaxy instead).

We are a wonderful breed - Here is today's mission if you care to accept it:

Take a look at one (or more) of the wonderful women in your life and tell them why they are so special to you. A text, a PM, a call, pop over and see them. Let them know why they are brilliantly wonderful. Do they give the best hugs when you feel rotten? Do they text to make sure you're doing ok? Or do they just always have a knack of looking like a supermodel even when they are covered in hay and mud? Tell them. Make someone you care about feel wonderful, they deserve it after all.

One day, when we have nagged all the men to death or killed them off by making them build a new cross-country jump in the pouring rain - we will need each other for survival...!

And while you're at it... bloody well go and look in the mirror again, like we did before - find one thing you love about yourself and say it out loud... be proud of who you are, there is no shame in tooting on your own trumpet, toot away my wonderful friends, toot like you mean it. Don't you dare feel guilty for feeling bloody fabulous about yourself. You are all so special - enjoy that feeling.

Have a wonderful day.

11th March 2017

Pat and I are pulling out all the stops to make sure we are in fine fettle for our first event of the season!!

We trundled off for a jumping lesson at Coombelands Equestrian Centre this morning with Russell Cooper.

I was, as usual, nervous as ever! I had a poorly tummy in the night and spent a good couple of hours with my head over the toilet which made me feel so bloody wobbly when mounting my spooky beast. Lucky for me, Pat jogged and spooked nearly all the way there which helped no end (NOT), but once we had warmed up and knuckled down to popping a little warm up jump, I had forgotten about my belly bugs.

Now, I have been riding 25 years, I have ridden around 300 different horses (give or take) and I have never really been able to see a stride to a fence or ride a decent canter at one! And today I learnt why!

Within 10 minutes, clever Russell asked me when I began looking at the fence? Gave an amazing example of peripheral vision and basically spanked my ass for losing focus... I do!!! That is exactly what I do, I lose focus. Constantly! Pat spooks, focus on the fence is lost! So, with this in mind I began thinking about his feet and where they fell, miles away from the jump.

We put together a course of fences at 85/90ish and worked on the canter, I have learnt so much today. Lifting my belly button, riding with my contact on a level 2 - this is a BIG deal for me, I am usually gripping on like a monkey so if he does get strong, I have nowhere to go from already holding his mouth. The more nervous I am, the more I cling on and shut down the canter. Focus, forward, light hands, and it all just came together.

I felt capable and confident and totally loving being a brain sponge to the teachings of someone very good at their profession.

I was even brave enough to jump a few of the bigger ones at the end! Sadly, there was no Daddy Carrot with his camera today, but fear not... this is the first of many I think.

15th March 2017

Good Morning All,

Firstly, I would like to make my apologies for being a little quiet of late. I have had a bout of heart palpitations that have made me pretty lethargic.

I wanted to touch on this and why I think I have them.

Stress, panic, worry, low confidence and fear. Something I have in equal measures at different times, add all of those together and they culminate in affecting your health and general living of life.

Now, on the surface of things, I appear (and feel, most of the time) happy, at ease and full of the joys of spring but occasionally, something darker creeps in. It consumes you. It takes over your focus and makes you feel as though you can't do anything worthwhile.

I am learning ways to keep this creepy darkness from sneaking its pork-pie head into my business. Day to day, if something makes you feel less than happy or makes you feel unfulfilled - work out a way to remove it. It will eat you up inside, not immediately but eventually.

As long as you have a plan to get away from the cause, this will be enough to maintain focus. I will admit, although I have a plan - this theory is failing me! I have a plan to write a book, to sell enough of them to be able to leave my full-time marketing job. Maintaining focus is pivotal.

If there is something in your life that you have always wanted to do, don't leave life without doing it. You must grab inspiration where you can and if that's from me - well grab all you like. I am bloody well going to finish this book, I am going to make it a success and I am going to feel damn well proud of myself for taking that inspiration.

Take it, today. Make the plans, even loose Post-it note ones, and seriously - grab whatever you can and run like the wind. Worry not what people think about you or your plans - they are yours, not theirs. Be proud of yourself, do something to make yourself proud...

I'm back in the game today and I'm not going to lose focus <3

Love, as always - Vic & Pat xxxxx

17th March 2017

4.30pm on a FRIDAY.... My absolute FAVOURITE time of the week!!

WWWWWWAAAAAAAAAHHHHHHOOOOOOOOO!

Weekend plans are to prepare for Munstead BE90 next weekend (Literally soiling my skimpies over this one), learn the dressage test and jump something bigger than a twig. Going to see Beauty and the Beast tomorrow night which I need to practice the songs for (sorry fellow cinema goers)!

I am also going to start getting our stuff sorted for our 2017 eventing debut, as there won't be much time what with my frequent underpants changes in the run up to D-Day BE DAY!

Some Daddy Carrot time is long overdue on Sunday too.

Oh, and I got some beautiful things in the post today from my sponsors Foxy Equestrian, I still pinch myself that I actually have SPONSORS at all!

20th March 2017

So, all in all, we had a lovely weekend. I am totally terrified by the prospect of our first BE of 2017 THIS SATURDAY!

After the cancellation of my nice safe start in the BE80 at Aston Le Walls, I am now lumped with starting at Munstead and entered the 90. I could literally cry at how bloody nervous I am again. My palpitations are terrible, and my palms sweat whenever I think about walking the course or learning the test. I need a poo just writing this.

So, I thought I would try and outline my concerns in a hope that writing them down makes light of the situation!!

What is the main thing that I am scared of...?

EASY - The show jumping. It stands out as my most terrifying bit.

And why? Because it will be big (90 -95 is big for us) and on grass and I might lose my way or let my horse down or not kick in the right place or he might slip over, or I might die. I JUST HATE IT. I hate it, hate it hate it. I feel all over the place, I feel like I'm inexperienced and all flopity poppity all over his back! I feel like he jumps really big, and I get left behind, then get the next one wrong.

Resolution -

Jump more often, put them up to 95-1m and see that it is ok and that as long as I know we can do it, it'll be what it will be on the day.

The only way for me to stop worrying about something that may or may not happen, is to not think about it until absolutely necessary. I'm going to learn the dressage test tonight and practice that today. Then at least it takes my mind away from dying in a field.

I am secretly excited, I look forward to getting my boxes of kit ready, I love plaiting, doing my stud holes and making him look nice - years of being a groom I guess, but now I'm the jockey - it's VERY different!

So, let's see how the week progresses, how many impromptu toilet visits I make and how many times I cry!!

Love as always my darling treasures,

Vic & Pat xxx

22nd March 2017

WEDNESDAY - Oh bloody rainy horrible hungover Wednesday!

Impromptu pub visit last night! I started to get VERY excited about the next few weeks and fancied a cheeky Tuesday Tipple that turned into 3! I have a thick head; my diet has truly lost its way and I have snapped at 3 idiots in the office already!

My nerves over Munstead on Saturday are lurking somewhere behind fluffy wine head and excited 'We're off Eventing!" head... For goodness sake - What will be will be!

I'd like to share a little story with you all today.

Now, almost 13 years ago, I was riding for a lovely family in Lincolnshire that despite not being massively well off, had a couple of horses in for me to compete and hunt. I was very lucky to have a very beautiful ex-racer with manners to die for, who I adored within an inch of his tiny hooves. He wasn't bold cross country or careful show jumping, he was wooden as a board in the dressage, but we were flying in open classes at about a 1m, I think it's where I learnt to smile on a horse.

My dear boy was getting on and a second horse was bought to run alongside. Heading off to a local dealer, the owners came home with a 'throwaway' - you know those ones that no one wants, that they can't even dishonestly sell to an unsuspecting idiot. That is what arrived. He was poor, covered in scars and looked truly fed up.

6 weeks in, after a good feed and some love, I climbed aboard. Holy Moly, he was bloody awesome. He felt strong, and

powerful and gave me goose bumps as soon as we skipped into trot. I gave him another couple of months of easy work and we went to enter our first show. I looked high and low for the passport, and when I found it I almost fell over.

The thick passport had EVERY single international stamp box filled with countries you could only dream of visiting, he had travelled the world... I sat trawling the internet for the history of this beautiful animal that had been so carelessly thrown away.

His appearances included;

Sydney Olympics (2000)

Athens Olympics (2004)

BADMINTON 4* (2002) Shocker dressage and 2 poles down show jumping but fast clear XC!

24 Advanced level outings

8 x 3* runs all over Europe

And here I was show jumping 3ft at a local show!

He owed the world nothing, I did bits and bobs and pootled gaining SO much experience from the wisdom imparted by this brave and wonderful horse. He retired happy and grazing with mates in the field at home, not stood ragged in a dealer's throwaway bin.

Oh, bloody hell, I'm crying again.

The moral of this heart wrenching story is to NEVER EVER, and I mean EVER, judge anything or anyone on face value. Give them time, take a step back and look for something beyond the exterior. Try to see the good in everything and everyone and you will live a much happier life, I promise. People (and horses) can give you the most wonderful of surprises, even when you least expect it.

Love as always xxx

23rd March 2017

Holy Smokes!

Leavings are loose guys... leavings. are. loose. I have my times for MUNSTEAD! Time of expected death - 8.12 am

26th March 2017

So, here it is..... Number 1. The first one of 2017 and the last one of this book.

Back to Friday, I was nervous as hell. Having to sit in a quiet office all day, not overly busy, made my nerves worse. I had so much to do post 4.30pm and I was getting increasingly tittery about wanting to run out the door and to the cross-country course. On arrival at Munstead, I was pleasantly greeted by beautiful going, evening sun and one of my best mates to hold my hand around the course.

Now, I'm not a fan of course walking, it gives me plenty to worry about, I hated number 6 - a trappy yellow jump of mortality, number 10 - the owl hole of uncertainty and number 13 – big log with a bloody great ditch under it!! There was, however, not enough time to worry too much as it was then 6pm and I had to pick up my hire lorry at 7! By 9.30pm Pat was plaited, the lorry was packed, and we were in the pub for my last glass of wine before almost certain death!

4am... bloody 4am... the alarm was set for 5.30, why oh why are you awake this early!? Daddy Carrot was awake too!! Bugger it, we got up, made a cuppa, piled make up on (so no one can see how bloody green I am under it!!) and sat on the toilet until we needed to leave!!

Everything loaded up, at 6.15am we set off on our 45-minute trip to Munstead. We were the 5th lorry there! I was 3rd to go in my section at 8.12am so relieved to see I wasn't too early or too late. - I am still very new to this whole process, unsure how much time to leave and not really clued up on etiquette yet! Lit another ciggie, had a coffee and got him ready.

Ah crap, I was doing his studs, literally TREMBLING! I was terrified at this stage, the worst I've been for a long time but I got on, warmed up and headed off into the arena to meet my maker!! Now, I smile. You know I do. I smile like Miss Great Britain on crack, but it seems eventing judges haven't taken us too seriously in the past maybe for this reason. So, my new tactic was to ride in a much more 'prelim' frame and not smile quite so much.... looking back at the photos, there are just somethings you can't change!!! I beamed like a retard the whole way through! I felt it deserved a 31, I'd have been happy with that.

Next up - the 'shit yourself phase'. I really do dislike show jumping. It's too easy to mess up, I'm very inexperienced at it, I get tense and scared and I just want to get off now please!!! But he warmed up so bloody well. I remembered everything from my lesson two weeks ago, didn't shut the canter down, BRILLIANT! In the ring however, apparently someone ever so discreetly, gave me an epidural because by all accounts I was paralysed from the waist down! And clinging on like a monkey on his last banana, I rode appalling around what was actually a VERY nice course! I really did look like a total bloody limpet. I deserved the two poles we demolished, well and truly. But I came out smiling, mostly because it was over, but also because I got a 26 dressage, kindly announced as I sailed over fence one!

Phew.... that's the worst bit done! Not likely.... suddenly, I'm crapping it again! No time, no time... get changed, get on and wander down to the death zone waving my husband goodbye. I jumped a couple of practice fences that he backed off like a bastard at. He is not a confident cross-country horse yet, so I have to pretend to be a confident cross-country rider that shows him the way ...like hell!

Start box, oh how I loathe thee. "You've got 10 seconds" must be the single most terrifying four words I face in life. Holy Moses, off we go. Sailed the first, sticky wicket at the second. Nearly had a stop but that dear horse does go if I tell him enough and go, he did!! 3, 4, 5 went by with nothing to report - 6 I barely kicked I was so bloody scared of it... he jumped it for me. He took over for that split second, if I wasn't about to remove a lung from my mouth at this stage, I'd have sobbed with pride. 7, 8, 9, nothing to report apart from my lack of fitness. 10, I needed a rest at, but Holy McOwlhole was coming to get us, he backed off a touch but went sailing through no problems. 11, 12, all flying, 13 that bloody great ditch.... forget it,

I lifted his head, kicked like stink and we soared it, so big I almost left out of the rear exit!!! The rest of the course jumped beautifully, over the last and galloping through those final sets of red and white flags, I burst with love, pride and sheer elation. We've done it boy, we've done it!! (I can barely see to type, crikey it's emotional).

I seriously cannot put into words what this means for me to be able to be doing this. I've come from the darkest place of fear to get here; here finishing this 1st event of the season, safe, alive, and happier than ever.

I have to say, there are so many people involved that make it so truly special. Yesterday my husband made the world's best groom, best friend and best Daddy Carrot I could have ever wished for. My darling friends that surprised me with how wonderfully supportive people can be. My sponsors, I mean, I feel odd even writing that, but boy did we look and feel the bloody big balls yesterday! My yard chums, the preparation that goes in for weeks leading up to eventing season, they really have been so helpful. I can't tell you how amazing I feel right now.

Today we are giving back to the sport that I have fallen so madly in love with, Daddy Carrot and I are fence judging! But not before I go and give my horse the biggest squeeze of his life. Thank you all for everything, you are the reason we came 7th yesterday! Oh wait... yes, you heard it right... a 26 dressage and 8 show jumping with a clear inside the time cross country, meant that we attended prize giving, got a big fat rosette and a cheque for £30! Bloody elated doesn't even come close!

Love as always

Vic and Pat xx

So that's that, the first step in my year long journey to find the biggest pair of balls I can. I LOVED every second of that feeling after the event, this is what keeps me motivated to enter the next one. It doesn't mean I am any less scared or any less nervous, it just means that like all of us, I am in search of the holy grail of 'post cross-country exhilaration' (the non-death kind). Please follow your dreams, please be proud of everything you do. Remember only 10 months ago, I couldn't even get on my horse. ANYTHING is possible if you focus, stay positive and keep a handle on the fear and you CAN do this, I promise.

Turn the page - there is a list of things for you to remember, things to remind yourself of. Tear it out, fold it up and put it in your purse, on your fridge, somewhere you can see it daily. These things will keep you going when you have a moment of wobbly weakness, when you need it most. Read them – out loud if you can - keep in mind those things and I promise you will get there. If I can, then you can too.

Important things to remember

Those that mind don't matter and those that matter don't mind. Please keep that in mind when people piss on your chips!

Surround yourself with people that either couldn't give a shit, ones that would give their last shit to see you succeed, or the ones that don't know what shit you're doing.

Be brave, enjoy it and love the life you have - don't wish you were someone else, one day you might be and you might not be happier at all.

Be proud of where you are right now at this time of life, look to the future with hope, not dread. Be bold in your decisions to better that hopeful life.

The moral of the story is - if things don't go your way, it wasn't your way to go.

You will NEVER stop rivalry, jealousy or bitterness that is caused by the resentment of other people's success. – bloody well rise above it.

Work hard for the things that matter, don't lose focus, and be the best that you can be at those things. Don't make excuses for not working as hard as you could, because only you will suffer in the end.

If you feel down, find out the cause and make a plan... baby steps remember, soon you will be wondering what the problem was!

Be proud of who you are, don't always try to be different, you are already brilliant enough.

Enjoy being alive, only you can control your mood - people can effect it momentarily, but YOU are in control - bloody well grab it by the horns.

Be brave, do something courageous, the repayments you get far outweigh the terror I promise you.

If there is something in your life that you have always wanted to do, don't leave life without doing it. You must grab inspiration where you can and if that's from me - well grab all you like.

Love as always,

Vic and Pat xx

Part Two

How to stay on top

If you've made it to this second book
there will be things that have now stuck.

This book will only reaffirm
that 'chip pissers' is a valid term.

You **must** still keep an open mind
and stuff your posh and too refined.

For in this book there will be swears
and curses, tears and greying hairs!

INTRODUCTION

You cannot change what has already been, but you can make what hasn't happed yet downright bloody brilliant. You have that power, the power to change YOUR tomorrow – what is it that you're waiting for?

My adult life has taken so many turns that I hadn't seen coming, so many things I haven't stuck at, jobs I have complained about, people I have lost touch with. But let's get one thing straight, to move forward you must have dealt with things in your past and put those things to one side in order to be content in moving on.

LET'S GO RIGHT BACK

I don't really remember a time when I haven't had a mind filled with horses. Some of my earliest memories are of Skegness beach donkeys and a hand me down Sindy horse from my cousin that was a firm favourite in my pile of things. I never had ponies or parents that were remotely interested in the sport of equestrianism. But, whilst I had these loose connections with plastic horses from a young age (and hours spent riding Dobbin, my homemade wooden pony), I hadn't been lucky enough to clamber onto one until I was six years old.

I expect part of my continued love of horses beyond the first throes of passion stemmed from mild jealousy. At six years old, my closest friend began pony riding at the local riding school, she smelt of wet wax jackets and I didn't; but I wanted to. I wanted to get red faced and come home with a welly full of wood shavings. I begged my poor parents for the opportunity, over the course of a few days, probably knowing that £6.50 a week for a hobby (likely a short lived one) was a bit much for them 25 years ago. But alas, it worked, I was allowed to go! And go I did, I embraced it all. I wasn't one of the kids that came for their ride and buggered off after an hour, not me! I got royally stuck into mucking out, poo-picking fields, filling water buckets and it was then that we agreed with the yard owner that I would get a discounted rate for helping all day. I would spend all Friday evening planning the rides for all the other children that were coming along and writing "I love INSERT FAVOURITE HORSE'S NAME" in the margin.

Saturday at 8am was the best time of the week. I would pull on my new beige jodhpurs that were 3 sizes too big and handed down from the family my mother cleaned for. I didn't care, I had my own 'jogpers'. I found a riding hat at the car boot sale a few weeks later, this was when my parents realised my new hobby wasn't going to be as short lived as they would have liked. Lord knows you are probably all cringing right now – allowing your small child to get on a horse in a helmet that barely had a harness and that smelt like a nest box for ferrets. This was the early 90's, standards for helmets were looser then and the rubber chin cup protector made me sore, so we cut it off!! Oh, and the wax jacket, I had one given to me, it was too big, and the sleeve inners were hanging out the ends of the arms but I smelt of that smell… and I loved it.

One of my very first memories of riding was probably one that set me up with courage for a good few years, but equally one that could have broken me in two…

Pulling on my 'jogpurs' and gabbing my ferret smelling riding hat, I went to the stables as normal on my long-awaited Saturday. The lady waited until all the Mums and Dads had left and dragged out this little bay pony from the field, he looked nice enough – I remember he had a friendly face.

Saddled up, I was asked to get on and I was very firmly told that if I fell off, I wasn't allowed to ride her ponies ever again. I must have been shocked because I agreed to this deal and held on tighter than ever… Good job I did because she walloped the pony up the backside with a plastic shovel and sent it flying up the field! He knew the drill and stopped at the end, I walked him back to the lady and she seemed fairly impressed! I felt very good that day! I felt proud in front of all the other children that were cowering awaiting their turn. I look back now, and it became very apparent that that day could have changed EVERYTHING. I could have been a dancer or a gymnast or a chess player… but no, I held on tight, and it filled me with the biggest sense of pride I had ever felt. The danger, the speed, the desperation to not let people down… all the things that keep me going and pump adrenalin through my veins on a show day.

Funny how things seem when you look back, I always think of those days at the stables and how wet through I was! I fell in love with horses though and I didn't care about the wet or the cold. After three years of weekly pony rides, summer camps and learning the ropes on the yard, I found my one true love… He was perhaps an unusual first love for a little girl, he was stocky and opinionated and was my biggest challenge to date, but that was the best part.

A few years passed, and I had ridden all of the ponies in the riding school and had dedicated so much time to bareback riding, galloping and jumping that when the owner came home with a £200 gypsy cob, she had bartered for with the travellers in the village, I knew we were going to be a team. Django was rising 4, barely broken to ride and my first experience of getting on him was trying to get him home. I got legged up on to a Polypad strapped on with an elasticated band (we didn't have a saddle for him yet) and the owner from the car behind us swung a lunge line at him to get him going! And go he did, vertically! He reared, that's why they had sold him. I wasn't frightened though, not one bit. I loved the feeling of wrapping my skinny arms around his neck when he stood up, I growled at him and feebly smacked his bottom and with a bit of time he just got better and better. We went hacking often over the summer holidays and then the day came... I remember it so very vividly, the first time I was truly scared on a horse.

It was pivotal. I'd never felt fear, nerves or palm sweating before. We had been jumping Django for a little while now and my goodness he could fly, 1m25 at the 'Chase me Charlie' competition was nothing for him and at only 13.2hh I felt this was a good achievement. Now, one particular day we hacked across the stubble, and it was casually suggested that I jump him over a straw bale that was waiting to be collected from the field. It was easily 4ft high, the same wide and it was right there that I felt it. I mentally dared myself to jump it and as I circled my legs just froze, I had bailed out in my mind, and he refused. What was happening? I came again, and the same thing happened. I couldn't kick, I felt paralysed. The owner made me get off and put an older, braver girl on my beloved Django and he just soared it. I felt destroyed, I cried all the way home in the car and I don't think I went back for a few weeks after that. I couldn't work out why my body failed me, I wanted to give up. So young, I think maybe 10 or 11 years old, I felt fear and failure in a horrible bundle right there. I did go back though, and I did carry on, but I knew it wasn't the same as before. There was always a niggle and I felt different, just at the right moment the lady put the price up to £10 a day and my parents decided this was a bit too much money. I was secretly a little bit relieved.

It wasn't long before I missed my wax/ferret scent, and I began helping with the hunt horses at the local stables. With the experience and hard-working attitude, I had, I was allowed to sweep the whole yard in return for a ride up the long drive and back most days. These horses were MUCH bigger than what I was used to, the smallest being 15.3hh and the biggest at 17.2hh a long way up after nothing bigger than a pony! I progressed quickly though and learnt to ride the smaller of the bunch, hacking out regularly and helping as often as I could with tack cleaning and more sweeping. That hard work paid off and I remember it so vividly, the day when I was asked if I would like to go hunting. Very soon, I fell in love again. I was loaned all the clothes I had to wear for the hunt. I was very lucky because there were lots of pairs of jodhpurs and hunting coats, now outgrown and waiting to be de-mothballed and enjoyed in the big cupboard in the tack room.

I loved hunting, I loved the early mornings of getting them ready, radio on, cleaning them up and mucking out the stables just in time to devour the leftover cooked breakfast that was waiting on top of the Aga in the big house. I'll never ever forget how amazing the scrambled eggs were for as long as I live! Getting to the hunt meets, I never felt nerves, just cold! I remember being freezing and foot followers wrapping their spare coats around me when we were standing for a while. Hunting people are some of the nicest I have ever come across; they really look after each other and I loved that feeling of being part of something.

I look back now and remember crisp bright days and autumn hunting, not rain or dark days like before. I used to get changed in the toilets after school for the horsebox to pick me up from the gates to go evening cubbing. Oh! I felt so lucky. My mother was (and still is 30 years on) the housekeeper in the big house which boasted this traditional hunting stables. It's walls; black bitumen bottom halves and whitewash top halves, a Burco boiler filled with sweet smelling boiled barley and 12 fully clipped, shiny steeds- I did secretly long for a hairy pony or gypsy cob but they were wonderful, nevertheless.

The groom in this yard was so much fun, she taught me so much and I will remain grateful to her for as long as I live. Emma was and is still the most knowledgeable horsewoman I have ever met. Traditional horsemanship was paramount, knowing how to care for these athletes, the canvas New-Zealand rugs, feeding straits like oats and rolled barley, breaking horses WELL (not just shooing them with a lunge line!) and foaling at least one every year, the list of things I learnt was extensive.

We had fun on the job and one summer we had a particularly sharp 4-year-old to back which was proving a little bit tricky. Improvisation tactics took us on a trip to Ann Summers to buy ourselves a jockey that wasn't scared to get on….! We arrived back that afternoon and after inflation, dressed our jockey's ample naked body in some overalls, body protector and gloves and named him Oliver Overall. He wasn't the best at staying upright but we bound him to the saddle and added some weight in sandbags and it was only when his erratic bouncing head smacked off the corner of a wall that he slowly deflated and needed a patching up!

I spent nearly 5 years devouring this limitless knowledge like a sponge. I covered Emma's day off each week and had my first real paid job. Having the yard to myself and managing it just for one day – I'd have done it for free, Sundays were just brilliant, that was my day.

Hunting days were brilliant too, whilst the family's children were at boarding school or university, I got to ride on a beautiful palomino mare called Flossie, Highfield Gold Candy Floss. I was in love again. We even attended Pony Club rallies and camp one year too! I sometimes, rather cheekily, told the other children at Pony Club that I lived in that big house and owned all those big shiny horses, I felt great, and I look back now and still do feel great. It was magical. Flossie wasn't very confident jumping and quite often I would come over her head in front of the jump and had to run back to the box for a new pair of reins, but she taught me to stick on like glue. I remember being out hunting, just standing at a covert and her entire bridle being pulled clean off by another horse and no one noticing until we moved off!!

I laughed often in this yard and my dear teacher made this magical for me, she restored my faith in my own ability and gave me knowledge which inevitably breeds confidence. I still speak to her often for advice, guidance, and reassurance, but the difference is, I can offer it back now too, because we are the same – traditional, kind horsewomen. Oh! The stories I could tell… but that's not why we're here, I was younger, equipped with knowledge, I rode at an above average standard, and I knew fear, but I was definitely not afraid.

Knowing and dealing with fear is all you can do when you see the other side of 30 and decide to go eventing - things are VERY different now!

A LIFE LESS ORDINARY...

With the first event under my belt, and at 90cms not the rained off 80cms I had planned, I felt decidedly happy driving back to get my sheet only to find that we had been placed 7th! I can't even begin to describe what it means to get one of those top ten coveted spots that people work so hard for. It's hard to believe that we were good enough (or jammy enough) this early on to be awarded this slot in the rankings, especially as we had two poles down in the show jumping. Fluke perhaps... The hard work that goes in to even just getting to that first event, I HAD practiced hard since the 1st of January and I HAD got Pat plenty fit enough for our quest, I think that's why I burst into tears at the very thought of getting a rosette – sheer exhaustion!

The next few events were looming and one of the most awful things is having to enter weeks in advance. The only thing I can liken the feeling to is having my wisdom teeth removed (or not!) I got the date weeks in advance and bailed out twice before committing to a lifetime of paracetamol to avoid the dreaded fate of the dentist! – I still haven't had them out!

Oh! How I longed to go back to that feeling I had at 17, eventing and hunting to my heart's content. I felt no real sense of fear, just competitive spirit and the grit and determination you need to love the sport. I was so balls deep in horses back then, but everyone was talking about University, and I thought it best to have a think about my future, my career and what I planned on doing when I was a grown up! I'll tell you what, I'm 31 now and I still have no idea what I want to be when I grow up... if I grow up!

I decided I would take a course in Equine Sports Science a BSc, which after 6 weeks of being taught how to pick feet out and the most basic of biomechanics and nutrition, I soon learnt that this was definitely not for me, and BSc stood for 'Big Sack of Crap'. There were some students on the course who had never even led a horse, this was not for me and my limited patience. I had skills and experience and as an over-confident nearly 18-year-old, I thought I could teach the class a thing or too myself!

That's it then… too late to get enrolled on another course, too stiff to join the circus; I was on a GAP YEAR! I wasn't spending my money going travelling though, it would have probably only got me to Skegness pier, having never been a saver. I was skint, unemployed and in love with horses!

Lucky for me, the groom at the hunt stables got married and moved away and as with fate, I took the job full time for a year. It was perfect timing and utterly magical. I loved running the yard, writing fitness plans, drawing up feeding charts and spending every waking hour smelling of horse sweat and urine. I was in heaven. I did know that it wasn't a forever job though, as other horsey people I had often told me; "You need to marry rich or have a back-up plan…"! I didn't have much time for men so back up plan it was!

The following year I went through UCAS clearing (a system designed to aid the disorganised or disappointed!) and with my decent enough A level results, I took a space on a course called Marketing and Public Relations; a BA. I had no idea what marketing was and had absolutely no desire to relate to any kind of public, but it sounded better than bioengineering! I started the course and by week three I felt despondent, I lived at home and didn't feel I fitted in with the others living the full Uni experience (story of my life!). I wasn't the student type – I didn't like drinking cheap spirits from a mug or eating packet noodles for days on end. I like my Mum's Yorkshire puddings and I was a rural recluse deep down; I enjoyed my own company from such a young age that my late teens were no different. I remember sitting in my Biology A Level exam with my arms covered in blood and placenta from foaling in the early hours... I got off to a bad start on the fitting in stakes, I think maybe it was scent related?! I did have a large group of friends at big school though and always played the clown card, I wasn't pretty enough to be popular for that, I wasn't clever, not really. I was just different to everyone else, and I regularly used that to my advantage.

In my first couple of university terms, I wasn't attending much, I had taken a little job on a private yard which is obviously where I would rather have been, but consequently I wasn't learning much either and when assignment and exam dates loomed I ended up teaching myself using online tutorials! It wasn't all bad, my own learning techniques had me coming out with some of the best marks in the class! I figured I'd scrap seminars and go riding instead, I was still doing ok.

By February of the first year I could smell the holidays looming, I would break-up at the end of April and didn't have to be back until September other than for paper tests, the world was my oyster. I just so happened to be sat on the train that day, open on the careers section of the Horse & Hound magazine which back in 2002 was at least 2 pages worth of screaming opportunity...!! A different path to tread, one that takes me out of my comfort zone and anyway, don't they say 'change is as good as a rest'? I was about to find out.

MENTAL PREPARATION

Change is only ever as good as a rest if your change isn't going from spending 2 years only doing flat work in a confined area to then attempting to gallop and jump in an open field!

♥ Monday, April 10, 2017

Selling yourself in less than 100 words can only be done if you truly believe in these five - **I can and I will.**

Mentally preparing yourself for things that require your full concentration and for things that mean something to you, takes determination. At times I have lacked lustre and felt ever so slightly not good enough. I felt it a little bit when I look back at my first event of the season at Munstead. I remember feeling so confident in the show jumping warm up, chatting to my friend Alfie and then getting in the ring and freezing like a Mini Milk in Antarctica… I was paralysed again.

This fear paralysis makes me ride like a total turd and there is so little I can do to snap out of it at the time. It's almost like I'm not aware it's happening until I look back. I think the only way to get through this feeling of bum twitching paralysis, is to do it more. Make the muscle memory that of confident and capable riding not foetal uselessness, that was what I set out to do after Munstead. I booked 2 lessons, went unaffiliated show jumping TWICE and didn't fluff it up too much. Stage fright is awful, but stage fright on a spooky horse, knowing you could get injured is far worse. I am dealing with it, but it's not an overnight fix.

Was I really ready for a late entry into another event? It popped up on Facebook that there were spaces left in the BE90 and so with only a week to go, I entered last minute into the BE90 at Bovington. Borderline too far for me to travel with my inexperienced livestock movements but, bugger it! We were entered, after all that practicing I felt like I wanted to see if I had got any better.

At this point I will just point out that I DO NOT have pots of cash hidden away for entering shows and each event for me means; entry fee (around £90), lorry hire (£120,) fuel (£50), start fee (£15) and money to keep Daddy Carrot in chips and buy a photo at the end (£20)… that's almost £300 PER EVENT! For this one I had a ruddy good clear out of my excess stuff and had a mass eBaying session to pay for it! I also had a bit of birthday money left, so we weren't eating beans too often!

Don't ever think for a second that you get anywhere in life without sacrifice and hard work. I have worked so hard for my season this year and not just getting the horse prepared, simply affording it has left me battling palpitations and exhaustion, would I have done it differently? Unlikely! I have a point to prove, a challenge to face and a battle with fear to conquer – it makes money seem meaningless and I'd have done anything to keep going!

EVENT REPORT – Bovington BE90

So here it is, Number 2! The late entry into the BE90 at Bovington, Dorset (RAC Saddle Club Bovington) on Easter bank holiday weekend was our challenge. Now for anyone that knows me, I'm not overly keen on jumping around somewhere that I'm not overly familiar with, stupid eh?! But I like to have had a school round to feel confident enough to know the ground and at least a few of the jumps.

Bovington for us, is about 2.5hours away, I was absolutely shitting myself! Not just about the long journey but the unknown territory and the impending death. I'll quickly roll back to Wednesday, where we had a super session with my new hero, Russell Cooper. Long story short, I cracked the Pat Pony code that I've been trying to crack for 5 years! Albeit nearly getting launched out the saddle in the interim!!

Now, I thought as a reward, he could have a couple of quiet days and when I came to hack on Saturday, he was awful! I mean awful awful! Spooking at EVERYTHING! Argh! You can't get mad or upset, it just makes it worse. I spent years getting upset over his sharpness, it gets you nowhere except red faced. But it was the day before our BE day, and I was feeling violently ill with nerves. I was scared again, really bloody scared.

I got everything loaded and the pony plaited the night before, ready for our 6.30am time to leave on Sunday. All was well, and we went to the pub for a 'last glass' - much like the last supper, only I couldn't stomach food! We got home around 10pm to the bloody electric having ran out... I mean FFS, what fucking day and age do we live in! We have a key meter, yep, you heard it! A key that you take to a shop and top up with whatever spare change you have lurking! Only Daddy Carrot forgot to do this and on bank holiday it meant at least £100 worth of meat and fish in my freezer was going in the bin and I couldn't have a shower or find anything by candle light! GAH! Not ideal at all.

Our 5.30am alarm sounded and off we set! Loaded and on the road by 6.30am. The journey was swift and straight with barely any traffic. We pulled in at a Londis (lucky it had a monster car park) and bought some cigs and supplies before arriving to walk the courses and use the loo. Which I did... thrice!!

The course looked ok, apart from the biggest, scariest corner I've ever seen!! Bloody hell... I'm going to ACTUALLY die at this jump, that's it. We barely heard any of the first 20 get round without penalty which only added to my terror! Show jumping looked fine, it was in a nice big rubber arena, not on the usual grass field, with not too many dreaded fillers! I felt marginally less terrified now, I wanted to try and enjoy it as much as possible.

Tacked up and went down to the dressage, they were running ahead of time so after a short warm up of 15 minutes I thought "bugger it... just enjoy it, no pressure." And enjoy it I did. I enjoyed the feeling of being capable at this level of dressage and I rode around humming a tune, smiling away. It was great. For once I didn't care about my score or trying to squeeze every last mark out of each movement. I just felt happy.

Happiness was short lived and got replaced by nerves again as I entered the nemesis phase.... I just don't know what the bloody hell I'm doing here! But today, I felt like I almost did... it was almost a clear round too, we rolled one silly pole that's all. I felt great and functional, rather than a foetus in a sack of milk. My usual 'dead pigeon body' was lifeless no more! Hurrah! The training and practicing actually works! And I'll tell you something else for nothing... (shhhhh..) the jumps at 90 actually felt quite SMALL today!

Back at the box we learnt that my dressage was a 29 so we were heading into the cross-country phase and toward the corner of doom on a score of 33. I will always say "I wasn't bothered about the numbers; I just wanted a happy (ish) and safe day" but this was a delight to hear!

Down at the XC warm up my empty belly was churning, and I really needed another visit to my green porta-friend, but with not too many to go before me, there was no time so I warmed up and got ready for the countdown of death.

Starter: "You have one minute"

My Head: Fuck do I?! What, until I die? Yeah!

I bloody hate it, the start box, I HATE it.

I would love to be counted down from the lorry park, just amble through the start and the time ticks from the first jump (when, or if, you make it there!).

3,2,1; Out the box and a gallop to the first fence… we stormed it, he stood off the second jump a touch, so I tapped him down the shoulder! He hates a smack, so I found myself apologising to him all the way to number 3 – 'the mushroom of much doom'… he backed right off that one as expected, I kicked for my life, and we scrambled over it! 4, 5, 6, 7 fine… we were flying again, down to the corner... it had an alternative route that you could take but I wasn't going to let it get me! I lined him up, tapped his shoulder and we bloody flew it! We cleared it, but then I was heading to the next fence which I couldn't see through the tears of joy that were streaming down my face!

Round the corner to the... Oh Crap! Pat clocked the water 5 strides out and put in the best spook he's done in 5 years! I was hanging off, literally almost straight over the top with both stirrups missing, luckily my air-vest hadn't deployed! I quickly shuffled my chubby arse back into the saddle, found my stirrups and kicked like stink! He went through the water and over the jump no bother! Boy, that was a VERY close shave!

We sailed round the rest of the course, spooked a bit at the double of brushy ones but flying, we galloped through the finish line for another bloody clear!

Bursting with pride for my absolute bloody pleasure of a pony. He is by far the most rewarding horse I have ever ridden. We nailed it today but... By golly! He makes you work for it! We did it, we did it AGAIN!

Washed off, pictures purchased, and chips eaten, we set off home absolutely ecstatic. Another notch on the British Eventing bedpost and we are confidently and consistently getting mid-low 30 finishes!! Can you believe it, (banging the same old drum) that less than a year ago I couldn't even get the saddle done up out of fear? Now I'm actually out here doing it, I've never felt achievement so wonderful.

Thank you so much to everyone we met today, the Wimpy family is growing so much and for everyone's words of encouragement. You really are brilliant; without you I'd be nowhere near as brave. Huge thanks to my yard family who mucked out so I didn't have to, to my sponsors, and also to my wonderful husband.

Going out making memories with Pat and Daddy Carrot is just wonderful.

With the next event at Chilham Castle already entered, it wasn't long before the sweaty palms were back out in force!

♥ Thursday, April 20, 2017

Dreams. Today I have struggled with motivation because of dreams. It's all a balancing act isn't it. It is hugely important to have a dream. Making dreams reality is near on impossible if all you do is dream about your dream and not act on it! ... you with me?

So, today I have been dreaming about my dream. The dream is to be writing, at home, in an office that looks out onto a field with Pat munching in it. To have a holiday booked and to have the second book ready to release. It is easy to get very wrapped up in a dream. The reality is, I still have 3 jobs, a horse to keep fit for eventing (next BE Day is a week on Sunday), a husband to keep happy and a house and mountains of washing to tend to. It makes getting my shit together quite challenging and leaves no time for a confidence wobble. Dreaming makes me so happy and does motivate me a lot. But don't let dreaming take too long - chase the dream with actions, not just idle thoughts. Go

BLOODY get those dreams! I'm going after mine RIGHT NOW!

I'll remind you again of how, if you want them enough, achieving your wildest dreams is bloody well achievable. It is now October and I have fulfilled the dreams that I had in April, however, the old dreams I once had have now adapted and evolved. The dreams I had at 18 were just as far out of my comfort zone as the ones I had this year....

A CHANGE OF SCENERY

At 18 years old, those 'Job Classified' pages of the Horse & Hound were my absolute favourite, I loved reading through the descriptions knowing that I could be very capable of fulfilling several of them, even at such a young age. I had my Pony Club B test and had been teaching in my local Pony Club at rallies all year, I enjoyed teaching kids but not enough to want to do it full time. After all, you are mostly teaching the out of breath pony club mums that are running alongside little Tabitha anyway! This wasn't for me, I wasn't yet an 'everybody's person' on the inside, I found it emotionally draining to deal with too many people all at once and pretending I was fine with it! I can act up to a crowd or a camera, no problem, but it doesn't mean on the inside I feel confident and okay about it. So, teaching was a no go, I didn't fancy dressage much either (my technical riding skills were poor!), autumn hunting didn't get going until September and I was a bit too cumbersome for exercising racehorses… But there it was, the advert that changed my twenties…

'Surrey Polo Groom Required – No previous polo experience necessary.'

In essence, I had never really left my hometown much – maybe a few times as a kid, being dragged around with my brother when he played cricket for Lincolnshire. But I had no idea where Surrey was. It was February and my dad bought me my first car for Christmas just gone. A little used Ford Ka. I had failed my first driving test after a brief brush of a cyclist who totally dramatized falling off into a ditch, so I had to pass it quick smart before I could drive the 185 miles to my interview the following week!

When you have a reason to be great and failure is not an option it's amazing what you can achieve! I passed with only 4 minor faults and with my printed off AA route planner and massive road atlas (just in case) I headed off for Surrey the next day!

My word driving on the M25 even now after 13 years of driving is a challenge but doing it in a tiny car ALONE for the first time was frightening to say the least. I had to keep ejecting my tape from the cassette player because I couldn't concentrate with Alanis Morrissette bawling at me. I'm laughing out loud right now at how ridiculous this sounds but it felt ridiculous then too!

I got lost in the Surrey hills and had to pull over several times. I even remember having a little cry when someone beeped at me for the first time, it was all very overwhelming. My car also vibrated terribly at anything above 55 mph so it took an age to get there in the slow lane with all the lorries that I didn't dare overtake!

On arrival at the polo yard, I was grilled on my experiences and past jobs, and I think I had enough of what they were looking for. The lady who interviewed me was so lovely and she would be my new teacher in this unknown field. She had tons of experience, and I was very happy with the set up there. We would have 9 ponies in work at any one time, all living out, so the job was mostly riding work. The male polo player and owner of the yard would come back from his home in Thailand for 4 months and play his season in that time.

I was offered the job and accepted there and then! I was to start in April as soon as I could, ready to start fittening up wintered out ponies.

Being the youngest of four children, the rest having flown the nest, I was making the long drive back to Lincolnshire to keep it all secret until I dared break the news to my parents. In the mean time I bought the most appropriate book to teach me about my new venture – Jilly Cooper's 'Polo'. After reading that, I was fully prepared for someone with a double-barrelled surname to rough me up and burrow in my slithery cavern come the summer!

April came around very quickly indeed, I had my 19th birthday and a few days later realised that I still had to tell my parents where I would be disappearing to for the next 5 months! I told my mother and we agreed that she would tell Dad! He appeared very cross at first and I hated that feeling, good job it wasn't long until I could bugger off. I know now that he would have just been worried about how I would ever get by and probably also confused as to why I would ever want to leave Lincolnshire and my home. But I did, I knew I had big things to achieve, I knew there was more for me to explore but when the day came, I wasn't quite so confident!

I think I cried the whole way to the A1, which was about 40 miles! I had 'Big Ted' strapped in the passenger seat for company holding the AA map and a few new tapes ready for ejecting on the motorway! I was terrified. A few hours later though I arrived and settled into my little bungalow at the back of the yard, and very quickly I realised how much equipment you needed to subsidise living on your own. I had to make an emergency trip to Tesco's for a bowl, plate, cutlery, a saucepan of some kind and a few weeks food shopping so I didn't have to leave the farm for a while! I'm not sure that telling my Mum at the last minute was the best idea, she'd have sorted all this out for me! But here I was, a lone ranger, doing it all on my own!

I had by now taken up smoking too, something I wish hadn't done, because now I am a total Yo-Yo smoker. I give up and then when I think I'm not coping well, I go back to the only thing that I know will relax my brain – nicotine. I absolutely DO NOT condone it and it was something I will always wish I hadn't started, but here I was on £140 per week wages and still buying a pack of Marlborough Gold because they were the 'posh' ones. The truth of it is, they all taste awful and without a Polo mint – I would rarely have a cigarette, even now!

My first day in my new job, I turned up on the yard in smart breeches, a shirt tucked in and belted, polished long boots and my best riding hat. Very quickly I felt exceptionally overdressed. My friendly teacher and another exercise rider were in bootcut ripped jeans, Doc. Martin boots and a polo helmet with a single cloth strap holding it on! I looked a prize pr*ck and that was the first and last day I wore any kind of jodhpur all summer. I raided the local charity shops on my first Monday off and soon I blended in.

Sunday nights were party nights and the JC Polo bible I had now read twice, soon became reality. Polo is a very social sport with a lot of fun and encounters of the sexual kind that I fully embraced at age 19. It was short lived however because I began dating a fine young man who had years of aristocracy in his blood, just like the book! Hugo was a charming gent but with me using the word fuck as a comma and not being able to hold my knife and fork in the right hands, I think I soon cheesed him off! It was then that I met my, soon to be, first husband. He was a soldier in the army which meant he was away often. This was ideal as I dedicated so much time to practicing my polo swing on the wooden horse in the evenings that I didn't have time for a boyfriend anyway!

His first tour of Iraq during my first polo season was to be the first of three in as many years. This gave us no real perception of a full-time relationship. We were engaged the following year, and I was none the wiser of what a 24/7 life would be like with an almost stranger.

I did learn something this year and it was the sport of polo that taught me to love speed on a horse, it gave me skills I will use even now, of stickability and riding for your life. There is no better feeling than galloping full pelt into the side of another horse trying to win the line of the ball. I was regularly covered in bruises and had used a year's supply of vet wrap bandaging up my calves under my flared jeans because trying to look good and fit in really does make you very sore. I learnt so much about the sport and even got to play mini chukkas, which isn't very common for the groom to get a go at. My boss was a great guy too and to my surprise, never once tried to lure his way into my undergarments! Darn you for misleading me Jilly Cooper... I will never forgive you!

Returning home in September and saying goodbye to my new polo friends was very sad, but the yard kept me on a retainer to come back the following year, so it wasn't forever.

Going home wasn't all bad either, Lincolnshire in Autumn always makes me happy; cubbing turns into hunting, and with Christmas looming and local pub frivolity, I took a job in a little private yard to tie me over for money and of course this led to another year of poor attendance at university!

This little yard that started as a Wednesday morning job, just mucking out and plaiting up for the lady in the house, but this was where my love of eventing really kicked in. I had the guts and horses after earning my keep with the owners. I went out and had the time of my life under a sponsor for the first time. No costs involved, just working for the family's enjoyment of seeing their horses go well.

I wasn't brilliant, I was very average, but to them I was amazing. I made them happy and brought sunshine into their home. That was the best part for me, seeing how much difference I could make to people, just getting back after a show regardless of the results and laughing at the kitchen table over a glass of wine, how happy we all were. Those memories hold a very special place in my heart and always will.

It's a funny thing when you look back and think about how massive your balls were and how often you laughed, because right now my balls are wizened prunes, they need an injection of something but I'm not entirely sure port will do the job anymore. Back at 20 years old, the jumps were never big enough, ditches were never wide enough and galloping was never fast enough! Right now, I like the idea of having Pat stuffed and standing him in my living room to hang coats from and tinsel at Christmas.

MOVING ON TOO SOON

♥ Monday, April 24, 2017

Crikey me the nerves are back! I have my 3rd jumping lesson with Russell tonight to try and get ready for Chilham BE90 on Saturday!! I'm scared. My last one was amazing, but I was very nearly jumped off when Pat over did it at an oxer and I feel scared that it might happen again. I did feel so much more confident than this after the last session and when I jumped my round at Bovington, so maybe I'm making it up in my head again!! Either way, I have drippy palms and daren't have any lunch for fear of staining my pants later on!

So, my next D Day BE Day is Saturday, I am number 81 in section B at Chilham Castle. After that (providing I don't die) I was *thinking* I might do a BE100! Can you believe I just wrote that down?! Thing is, I have something to prove this year, to myself mainly. I want to prove that ANYTHING is possible. Anything you dare to dream, if you work hard enough to fight the fear. Borde Hill is meant to be a nice 100 so here is where it starts, that build up to the fill out the entry form without pooing on my desk chair in a shared office... ARGH! If you do anything today, make sure it is praying for me and my survival!

I did of course VERY quickly scrap this idea and thought I would do what I know is a tougher BE90 to make sure we were really ready. Tweseldown is a bigger, up to height course – that'll do... but alas, someone in the eventing fate kingdom had other ideas.

♥ Tuesday, April 25, 2017

Shit, Piss and Bugger it... I meant to enter the BE90 at Tweseldown but I appear to now be running in the bloody BE100!!! I entered and then the email confirmation came through only to reveal my fatal mistake. Holy Mackerel! I've had 2 poos since I saw my name on the list! Now, my lesson last night was GREAT, nothing to fear at all. I felt capable (for a change) and not like a limpet! I now need to book in some schooling at Tweseldown so I don't die of terror in advance of May 21st and also get to Coombelands and show jump over some bright fillers. I cannot tell you how nervous I feel right now! Focus, bloody focus I still have Chilham 90 to get my bloody boiling on Saturday. ARGGHHHHHH!

So that was it, fate decided. I knew I could have changed it and re-entered the BE90 but I thought in my head, if I did I would almost certainly die. I am a firm believer in fate, wrongly or rightly and because of that it meant that my meaty BE90 was now a meaty BE100. I will be my own failing one of these days. All the focus back to Chilham Castle now and having a super confident run out for us both.

♥ Friday, April 28, 2017

It's Friday... the times are out for tomorrow's D Day. BE Day at Chilham Castle - 11am, 12pm and 12.30pm. There are a few things I would just like to clear up before I go any further.

Number 1: I have just had to have a second poo, and do you know something...? It's DRESSAGE related! To my horror the test is bloody AWFUL. There is no free walk, the canters are around the arena not on a circle, there are so many mentions of the word diagonal... Piss flaps! Free walk is my redeemer, my point scoring movement! I just watched someone's test on YouTube, and I needed a poo. What is happening to me?

Number 2: I am getting used to sweating profusely and can thoroughly recommend Dove cream deodorant. Whilst no industrial strength product would stop my dripping pits, this at least masks the smell of level 5 terror, with the soapy scent of a 1980's launderette.

So here we are, Friday again. What a week. I want to talk about passion, it's very relevant for me right now, I have realised over the last few months that without passion, you know that fire in your belly, the burning desire to want something more than you ever have, well without it what you have is - 'Half-Arse-itus'. It's curable but you don't want it, trust me.

You might have days where you just don't want to live life anymore, you don't want to get on and ride, you feel intimidated by everything and everyone - I have been there, I have felt those things, and I promise with everything I have that it isn't forever. It doesn't have to be like that. You are so bloody wonderful and you don't even see it, every single one of you deserves to feel like you CAN do ANYTHING you dream of (Well. Maybe not flying, flying might not end well, let's leave that for birds).

What I am saying is, feel passionate about something and things will start happening whether you like it or not - magnetism, gravity, fate, who know which one, but something makes that shit happen! Get that fire in your belly...

I'm off to take my own advice and NAIL IT at Chilham Castle!!

EVENT REPORT – Chilham Castle BE90

Chilham BE90 – The One with the CLEAR ROUND

So, this morning's 6.30am alarm wasn't even needed, I was already on toilet trip number 2 by 6.00am. The balls I grew yesterday (and all week in fact) had shrivelled away to an unrecognisable size and I was SHITTING MYSELF!!!!

We loaded and left by 7.15am and arrived at Chilham at 9.30. The course walk was so bloody hilly... Crikey! I need to give up smoking! I didn't hate any part of the course in particular; I just wasn't keen on the barrels at 2 nor the jump that was far too close to the water!! But I was hyperventilating by then, so I was just glad to have made it around the course on foot without pooing myself or fainting!

Tacked up and walked to the dressage. Pat was testing my patience this morning; I was so scared. I had run through my dressage on the back of a receipt in the pub the previous night and felt terribly unprepared. Who doesn't ride the bloody test through at home?! Me apparently! I was scared, nervous, trying to hold my poo in and the twat tries to bronch me off. I wanted to go home there and then.

Now the BE97 dressage test is not my favourite. It goes down the centre line and where you would usually go all the way to C in front of the judge and turn left or right, this turn was in the center, at X! I forgot and made it to G before I remembered! Concentrate Vic, for fucks sake!

I was so cross with myself and came out thinking it deserved a 36% ish. I came back to the box unhappy with how scared I was of riding again. I could have cried.

Onto the jumping, we didn't have long. I watched a few go and decided I wanted to buy a shovel from the bright flappy tack stand lining the sides of the arena, and dig myself a hole to hide in. The arena was in fact, surrounded by banners advertising certain fatality, flapping flags of death, and there were far too many fillers to get over. I swallowed the bile down and got on board, warmed up and went in! Two lessons with the godlike creature that is Russell Cooper in the last few weeks meant we used the new skills we had been taught and we were sailing over the last fence CLEAR! Bloody clear! I sobbed into his mane wailing with joy! Fucking clear! Get in my boy!

The death phase.... no pressure, running on my dressage score. I couldn't remember the course, but in the nick of time, as I got counted down I got my act together. 5,4,3,2,1..... bloody go go go! 1 and 2 jumped lovely, he was flying... 3 on an angle that I totally screwed up, Pat chipped in, wrapped the fence hard and twisted in mid-air. I so very nearly fell off, hanging on by the skin of my bastard teeth again! 5, 6 jumped lovely, almost approached 7 from the wrong direction but we made it, legged it down the row 8, 9, 10 was a house and step down which he boldly took me into. (Now I will add that Pat isn't a brave XC horse, and I sobbed all the way down the hill to the water because for the first time HE took ME to a fence!).

Water complexes x2 rode lovely, another steep gallop up hill to the home straight, where some lovely Wimpy supporters were cheering us on! Ping and ping over the double of houses and down to the train to finish. We sailed home 13 secs inside the time!

A double clear, finishing on my poorly prepared dressage score of 32 meant we placed third! Bloody 3rd AND picked up our Badminton Regional Final ticket! I cannot tell you what this means to us, to everyone involved. I am so bloody ordinary and so is Pat. I just wanted to do my best and do it well today. I wish I had practiced my test because only one point separated us from the top spot, but who gives a shit! We are doing it, me and my beautiful boy. He truly scared me in the dressage warm up, but what a feeling on the XC, it made up for all the fear.

Daddy Carrot learnt to do studs today too... result! He's so bloody supportive, not sure what our outings would look like without him by our sides. Thank you so, so much to everyone supporting us in every context, you make this worth it, this rosette belongs to you.

I love you all.

Goodnight and God bless

Vic and Pat Xxx

So, there it was, the best possible outcome we could have hoped for, before we move up a level. It didn't make me feel any better though. 100 is such a big number. It's not just the height or technicality of the fences, it's the different calibre of people you get attending the 100 days. The 90 days are usually run on the same day as the BE80 and those people are out and out amateurs, this is what we are, and this is where we are happiest. At BE100 you are likely to be in the warmup with a professional on a younger horse, or people that really know what they're doing. This frightens me more than ever. I never really feel like I know what I'm doing, and I don't need reminding!

We had a couple of weeks before we had to face our fears, so I thought we'd better at least get round a course of 100cm show jumps first. We headed to our local venue of Coombelands for a bash at the 90 and the 100.

EVENT REPORT – Coombelands 90 & 100

So here we are, the day of doom... I arrived at the yard at 12.30pm to give Pat his 'Super so Kalm' paste that I've been trying out. It seemed to have worked, because when I came to hack my 30-minute trip to Coombelands, Pat was suitably snoozy. It didn't last long though. We arrived and scattered a few horses in the warmup with his terrifying dance moves, he knows it frightens me... why do it you knob!! I spent ten minutes learning the course and 15 minutes warming up and we were in!

Crikey, my heart was pounding out of my chest! I royally ballsed it up, by fence 5 I had 2 down because the little bugger was spooking at EVERYTHING! My nerves had crippled me, and I left him long and crap to nearly every fence. I had one more down and left the arena absolutely terrified about having to go back in when they were bigger!

The 100 course walk scared the living shit out of me. I hadn't realised that the timed section was up a peg again at 105cms and as 100 was already the biggest course we have EVER jumped I was seriously considering pulling out. Three withdrawals on the board didn't make me feel any better either. Daddy Carrot told me to get my act together and give it a go, even if I retire at number 2! Deal!

I warmed up and he didn't feel that confident over a meter oxer in the warmup and nor did I! 5 to go, I watched a few, learnt the course a bit better and then it was my turn! I went in and gave it EVERYTHING I had, and it showed! Jumps 1-6 were a meter and 6-11 were 1.05, he was flying. Upright, Oxer, Double... nothing felt too much for this little horse today. He was soaring. We had a very unlucky roll of one pole, but with only two clears in quite a big class, I was VERY happy with that (and to not have die!).

The placings were announced, and Master Patrick was read out in 3rd! The fastest four faulter! I couldn't believe my ears, I let out a little whimper of joy before collecting our rosette, prize money and Sunshine Tour qualifier! I gave it my all and truly felt deserving of that good round and frilly token. We hacked home in the sunshine and felt on top of the world - and I still do - we jumped a bloody meter course and didn't die! I didn't want to go at all today but look at us. My darling boy has done it again!

STRAIGHT TO THE POINT

Here it is, the part where no matter how rubbish you're feeling, you need to sit up and listen to this bit.

I want you all to realise that above all else, fucking things up is actually perfectly fine. I've royally fucked up a lot of things in my 31 years and I've survived and bounced back stronger than ever.

Something that is absolutely pivotal in aiding confidence for those riding, competing, tobogganing, etc. is knowing that it is ABSOLUTELY 100% FINE TO FUCK IT UP... if you don't die, you can only learn from it. Seriously, the chances of you dying are so very slim, you have almost as much chance of dying having sex or popping to Tesco to get your Imodium.

Anything less than death is just a learning curve. It's fine to have a stop XC or fall off in the dressage, it is okay to soil your pants a bit in the warmup, it really is. People might laugh, but bollocks to them, Captain Karma will soil their pants much worse one day and hopefully in public! There are times where you need to take the pressure off and stop worrying about the 'what if' moments that give you palpitations. What if you don't die? What if you take something from each experience, something you can work on and improve. Focus on making the negative 'what ifs' into positive ones.

If you take the pressure off and focus on keeping the experience as a jolly good time ... really, there is nothing to lose. Crikey... I have no dignity left so bugger it, let's be having you!

You need to get this mentality ingrained into your skull, I have it most of the time now and it makes for a much less pressurised life where you can actually start enjoying rather than fearing.

If only I had this experience earlier on in my non-horsey side of life! At 21 I wasn't massively outgoing; I didn't have the knowledge I have now or the ability to step away from a situation like that. I got married at 21. I got married knowing it was probably not the most sensible thing to do, but I didn't stop it happening. At the time I was totally swept up in planning the wedding, my fiancé was away a lot and we still hadn't lived together yet.

I buggered up my last few exams at university and whilst my dissertation received a First, I technically didn't graduate – something I don't regret now but I did for years. It frustrates me now that I didn't stick at it… but that was me all over back then!

I remember feeling worried the last few weeks before the wedding, I didn't eat much, and my dress was then too big. I dropped to 8st something and I'm not particularly small framed. I had a niggle, a seed of doubt that unbeknown to me, would grow into the biggest and most aggressive tree of crap you ever did see! It wasn't great from the outset and without a job or mates I grew lonely and massively lacked confidence.

I look back now and think about the person I was back then, I was away from my family, the people that know you best, I wasn't charismatic, or funny very often like I used to be at home larking about with my brother. I didn't really know who I was or where my place was. My husband was much older than me too and so were the people we socialised with. I remember being at an Army function and in the loo, overheard two other wives talking about me and how they didn't want to socialise with someone their daughters age, I felt sad after this. It was confirmation that I wasn't ever going to fit.

We fought a lot my husband and I, usually over how much he drank, and things escalated into a situation I wanted to get out of quicker than a fire in a kindling factory.

It wasn't all crap though, I made a very good friend in this time too, one that I will cherish for all eternity and for her home that I ran to frequently for comfort.

That brings me on to something VITAL. **Friendship**. Shut your eyes for a second and think of one or maybe two people that you really consider a lifelong friend. I have one that stands out above anyone else, and I think, always will. She and I have been there for each other in our darkest times, we have seen each other at our most stripped bare (Quite literally when she had to be cut out of her jodhpurs after a horrid fall!) and without judgement, we have picked up each other's broken pieces more than once. But just think about how much that keeps you going, even if you don't speak often or see each other every week just knowing you have someone that 'gets you' is really very important indeed.

I love being that person for people. I know there are so many people that need that helping hand and I know how much this means. Even now, when I went and did my last event of the season, she was replying to my confidence wobble text at 5.30am – we are 250 miles apart now, but it doesn't matter one jot. These are the ones, the ones we talked about before in the first book. How important it is to surround yourself with people that don't give a shit, ones that would give their last shit to see you succeed or ones that don't know what shit you're doing!

I do think though they are the first people to tell you when they think you've gone totally insane and stepping up to BE100 still being nervous as hell at 80 deserved a telling!

The week running up to my first 100 was exhausting, my body was trying to fight off the worst flu I'd had in years. I was on my knees with hardly any energy left for riding and practicing. I remember trying to have a lesson and poor Russell having to cut it short because I was struggling to get my breath. This was not boding well for the weekends challenge!

By the time the day arrived to walk the course, I felt no fear at all. I had no adrenalin left in my body that wasn't being used to fight the virus, so I slept soundly for the first time ever the night before an event.

EVENT REPORT – Tweseldown BE100

So here it is... our first BE100 report.

I would like to start by saying (for anyone that is a new follower or an old one that might not know), up until July 2016 I was unable to tack up this dear little horse without sweating profusely. I was scared of riding to the point of fibbing to cover it up. I didn't hack, I certainly didn't jump, and I would lunge for at least two days before I braved a 10 minute sweating session in the school.

Today marked our 6th BE event **ever** including the two at the end of last year. We have done 1 at 80, 4 at 90 and this one - our first 100! I'm pushing my limits; with the energy I have left after this blasted virus; I'm terrified and I'm certainly not afraid to admit it.

So here goes... Our 5.45am alarm call to leave the yard at 6.30am hit me like a train. I have been riddled with flu all week, feverish, snot ridden and unable to breathe if doing more than sitting... today was no different. I felt foul.

At the yard, a small panic soon resolved by my beloved Husband Daddy Carrot of unsticking the lorry door – I was hoping it was stuck fast for a minute and we could just go back home instead! Alas, we loaded my Patsy and trundled off on our 1hour20 trip to Tweseldown. Now for some reason, I don't like the venue. I feel it is so beautifully and professionally presented now, that I find it all a little bit intimidating. I meant to enter it to face my demons and complete my last BE90 before stepping up... well I entered the wrong bloody class and fate kept me from amending my error!

Walking the course yesterday, I felt nothing but ill! I wasn't overly nervous because I met a lovely old friend on the course that guided us around and shared her knowledge, which helped us a lot. They were however MUCH bigger than they looked in photos online! No offence to Daddy Carrot but his course walking comments usually consist of 'that looks a bit big' and 'are you sure that's in your class?!' So, a helping hand was very lovely.

Back to the day itself... We arrived at Tweseldown, gave Pat his calmer in a bit of breakfast and went to check in. I was number 467 today, I do prefer even numbers if I'm honest!

I got ready and we warmed up, he wasn't silly, he was in fact the best he's ever been in the warmup! AND this continued into the test! It went lovely, I was struggling to breathe at times, but he was soft and round and didn't gawk at anything too obviously! We pulled it out the bag for a 29.5 brilliant at this level, I really was very happy with that!

Not much time to get ready and jump because I had yet to learn the course! I put his boots on and buggered off down to the show jumping. Now, this is only the second 1m course we have ever jumped so it was still a bit of the unknown. He warmed up super and over jumped all the practice fences like a stag! I went in and had to be reminded that my bell had gone! Bloody flu makes your ears feel like you're underwater sometimes. And there it was, my ring paralysis again… The bastard spooked and jinked in front of every bloody jump! He made me work for every stride as he was clearly TERRIFIED of fillers and poles again! The reality of this is, that I was probably SO tense he thought he had something to worry about. He launched at number 3, two strides out and landed splat on the back rail and then had an unlucky rub of another, but by the end I was exhausted…my goodness, did I ride for my life?!

Hand on heart, I don't think I could have done any more. 8 faults to add and we were lying in 9th place going XC!

So, here's the thing. I left the show jumping ring and felt like a 30 stone man was sitting on my rib cage. I couldn't breathe, snot was pouring out of my face, and I just had to get my hat off, my head was thumping. I was still not nervous about the cross-country, and this worried me more than nerves. I worked it out with my very basic science, that all my energy and adrenaline was fighting infection and not making me nervous. But don't you need adrenaline to focus?! Quite right you do.

For 20 minutes I seriously toyed with withdrawing us from the cross-country. Daddy Carrot didn't really know what to say, he knows how much it means to me to not let people down or myself and so I half-heartedly said I would get ready, warm up and then decide.

Down in the warmup I felt committed... there was no turning back now, we were 4th on the board and very quickly I was in the start box (of doom) being counted down!!! 5,4,3,2...1! Let's av' it... snot drenched or otherwise- we were off!

I galloped out and got a crap jump at number 1, a very kind hanging log, but Pat wasn't paying attention and it all felt horrible. I slapped him on the shoulder as a Perky McPerk and because I knew if something didn't get better, we'd never make it round! Number 2 was a house, he stood off a little, but we had a better shot at it, up the hill to 3; a log pile, it was bigger and probably the biggest XC jump we had encountered (yet)! He sailed it, on the angle to 4 which was partially hidden by a tree. Of course he spooked, but we scraped over it! A long gallop up the hill to the WATER! The hanging log that I was shitting my knickers about yesterday jumped lovely actually, straight in the water and out at our first attempt over 6 - the dreaded Captain Quackerson (shaped to look like a duck)- WE BLOODY JUMPED IT! First time too!

Now I will add that I thought it was highly likely that we'd have been eliminated at one of these two jumps, so hadn't really planned for how I would feel about the rest!

Anyway, I found my missing stirrup, thanks to the over excitement at the Quacker and off we went! 7 was bloody massive, a big trailer but it jumped lovely, 8 a great big table on a downhill line which didn't look too friendly. He soared through the air and gave me the most wonderful jump over that, I could barely get my breath, but I yelled 'bloody good boy' at the top of my lungs! It felt awesome! 9 a log thingy, was very trappy and wide but hitting a bounding stride, Pat made nothing of it! 10 - the second water... with a jump into it! We've never jumped into water, but I thought we'd have a bash! He hopped the log and splashed in and out over the house no bother!

Down the long galloping straight to a big ask at 11, a huge table coming off the corner. Daddy Carrot didn't like that one yesterday, so I kicked and grabbed the mane extra tight and we sailed it! 12 the open Trakehner, he didn't even look at and then onto to 13 - oh 13 you bastard! 13 was a hanging log to a skinny triple brush... I flew in over the log, didn't really look, or take a pull or do anything much and Pat got confused and ran out the side. I of course just sat there like a dead fucking pigeon! We re-presented and I slapped him down the shoulder right on take-off, he shat himself and jumped through the flag! For Fucks sake! 2 refusals at one fence are costly, a 3rd is the long road home... so I trotted at it, full up 1.10m skinny brush and he popped it from a trot like it was a sodding cavaletti!

Tit! Vic you are a total tit! The poor horse didn't understand the question, he was poorly guided and I take full responsibility for those 60 penalties. We put it behind us and bounded on... 14, the angled brushes jumped very well, 15 a log pile also sailed nicely and over the scary dragon to finish! Now, I know on paper that when our 9th place and rosette turned into a 3 figure score, most people would feel a bit cruddy but it was the BEST FUCKING RIDE OF MY LIFE!

We did it, we survived, we came home smiling and full of running. My bloody beautiful boy, he sailed all those massive jumps like they were nothing, he galloped across the course just eating up the ground for breakfast. It's not about the prizes for us, it's about our trust in each other, growing that bit more with every round, the love I have for this horse is incredible.

Thank you all so, so much for the words of kindness and 'good lucks' thank you also to the commentator who by all accounts and despite having no course notes, talked about the book and about Pat and I as if we were so special. It means so much to know there are so many people that care about us. I'm dosing up and snuggling with the cats and Daddy Carrot for the evening now.

What a bloody great day!

Love as always Vic and Pat Xxxx

Just reading that back now, I am sobbing. Sadly (and you'll see why in the next chapter), they aren't tears of joy, but tears of what could have been. I'm disappointed in myself for the next series of events and how I dealt with them. I will NEVER let that happen again as long as I am sucking air into my lungs.

DON'T LET PEOPLE NEAR YOUR CHIPS

The exhilaration of the weekend's event lasted for days, I didn't feel at all beaten by our misunderstanding at fence 13. I felt empowered and I knew we could do another one. I did have to strike whilst the iron was still hot though, because I know if I leave it for the feeling of elation to retreat... I won't do it! Whilst the blood is still pumping, I always get the next one entered... I still do this even now!

I entered my second 100, somewhere that was supposed to be much more forgiving than Tweseldown and VERY local to me. It was also going to be the very last event I did in the south of the country as we had found a house up north, Gary had found a job and our move to Lincolnshire was imminent.

My heart has always belonged to Lincolnshire. It really boils my piss when people say that it's full of in-breds and flat fen land. I have no cousins that married one another, and I've seen at least two hills in the north of Lincolnshire! My first wedding was in our local church in the village I grew up in, but that was the very last day I would spend in the county before we moved 180 miles south to an Army posting. I was sad, I could tell my Mum was sad that I was going too. But 6 years later, telling my parents that my marriage had broken down and was irreparable was far, far worse than this day.

The disappointment I felt in myself for finally throwing in the towel on something you vowed would be forever, was a real blow to my pride. But I couldn't have carried on any longer, I was desperately unhappy, scared and although it feels so cliché, I had nothing left of myself. I was sad so often, I felt as though there was nothing to look forward to and dreaded my husband coming home. At 25, that is no way to live. Wrongly or rightly, I had put Pat on part livery and I had left our marital home and Monday to Friday I rented a room from a lovely couple who have turned out to also be lifelong friends.

Renting this room was the best thing I have ever done for myself. It changed EVERYTHING. The day I moved in there I was terrified; I had no idea who these people were but I had bought a numnah off her on Facebook so I knew she was probably alright! It was brilliant from the start, they made me feel so welcome and having told them about the real reasons for the move, they helped me so much to get back to laughing again.

We drank wine most evenings and Suzi taught me to cook, we laughed all the time, and I started running and doing things for myself again. I felt empowered and although I was racking up a nice bit of debt, I decided to get Pat back on DIY livery locally and then things would be perfect. They really were. I filed for divorce too, something else I had dreaded. But I did it and it wasn't so bad. I had a good job, great friends, my lovely boy back home on DIY livery and I was me. I was happy for the first time in 5 years, properly happy. It's these people, the special ones you keep in your basket along the way that make your life complete.

And here we are, 2017 leaving all these wonderful people behind to move back to Lincolnshire, I could cry at how much I miss those times, but I am so glad they happened. And new adventures are upon us now, I think I'm ready…

BACK TO IT

The fortnight before my next BE100 at Rackham, we got the horribly sad news that my much-loved Auntie had passed away, not poorly, not even old, just gone. I had made it to 31 without having anyone close to me die and I didn't take the news all that well. It's a very personal thing, grief and I wasn't sure I could carry on with my plans to do Rackham or in fact anything else, I felt emotionally drained. But during it all, I had an awful group of people that put everything in perspective for me.

In a single morning, I had banned more people from the Wimpy Facebook page than I had in its existence. By all accounts, there exists a few closed groups of people in our equestrian community that think it's utterly hilarious to make fun of others. To criticize their riding, how they look after their horses and their integrity as people. Cyber bullying, I think they call it. This hit me just at the wrong time. With the news of my Auntie and the build up to moving again, I just couldn't deal with it at all.

For the first time in a long time, I was in that dark place of depression and unable to get out, my heart was racing leaving the house, I felt like I couldn't do anything for fear of someone telling me that I was doing it wrong. I am crying now just reliving what I allowed those nasty, horrible women to do to me. I was so glad I was moving in the end so I didn't have to bump into them, no one would know where I was. I ended up on an ECG machine in A&E after 3 days of stress induced irregular heart rate. I'll point out right now, I am tough… I am not a sniffling wallflower, but this was very personal and hit me hard.

It took a few days for me to pick my sorry arse up and not allow them to get to me. My Auntie would have been cross with me for letting them ruin my fun, so I put all my efforts into enjoying my last event in Sussex but sadly it wasn't to be...

♥ <u>Saturday, June 17, 2017 at 5:18pm</u>

Just to let you all know in case anyone gets wind, Pat and I have withdrawn from the Cross country today. He is safe and well. But the heat massively got the better of him and it was 100% the right decision. We made a few little rookie errors in our dressage for a 32 which left us in 8th but then he was flat as a pancake in the show jumping, chipping in a short stride into almost everything... very unlike my big jumping boy. I knew he wasn't feeling good, and his needs absolutely always come first.

Very sad to be at home not having blasted round the course but there's years ahead of us yet. I want to thank you all for being there for us, for wishing us luck and making it all worth it.

Now despite that being the event report I submitted to the blog; it was in fact a lie. The heat was very unforgiving, but the truth is, I bottled it. I was crippled with nerves in the show jumping warm up and ended up riding next to Tina Cook of all people, which did not help! I went in the ring and left him totally wrong to nearly everything and had 4 fences down. My lovely friends had offered to drive us there, so I kept a brave face on it until I got home and then sobbed my heart out over how far back we had gone in the confidence stakes. I was right back to the beginning, I wanted to sell him. I wanted to give up and I couldn't face it anymore.

♥ Tuesday, June 20, 2017

I just want to let you all in on something that I am personally struggling with right now. I can't write this quickly and it is quite likely that it will be at least 11 by the time I have held back my tears enough to write it all down (it's now 8.15!).

For anyone that hasn't read the book yet or seen the misery, depression and times of darkness I have been through, you will all just see the exterior of what is now a braver and more confident rider. Being on the TV and blogging and shown as a smiley and seemingly capable rider will have portrayed someone that doesn't look 'wimpy' at all. The truth is, my horse has now had 3 days off after attempting my second BE 100 at Rackham on Saturday, I am dreading riding him again. I withdrew after the show jumping and I was relieved that I had the soaring temperatures as an excuse.

The truth is, I wasn't mentally capable of going around that course - there I said it. I was back to feeling frightened and whilst I had a cry over the disappointment, I was crying tears of feeling 5 steps behind where I have been the last couple of weeks.

I am crying about it again now - I had come so far and I feel like a fucking failure again. I really do take so much from the support that is offered on here and try desperately hard to ignore the occasional negativity.

It's a funny thing, confidence. Some days I feel up for jumping big jumps and then other days I can just about fill his water buckets. Your personal life plays a huge part in this, and mine is extremely up in limbo at the moment. I feel desperately low again and it isn't something that will go away overnight. I guess the point is, bear with me, that I will be back and fighting the confidence fight very soon but in the meantime I won't be entering anything like what I had planned to.

I don't want to feel like this and I need time to work it out. I'm sorry for pouring this out but I felt as though I needed to remind myself that it is okay to feel like you are failing sometimes. It's ok to not progress all the time, it's ok to sob your heart out in frustration over why you can't do it when it seems everyone else can.

I dearly love you all and I thank you once again for supporting Pat and I through this journey.

Love as always xxx

~

It's so sad to think that just one small blip like this and I'm broken, back to square one It was hard to pick myself up after this, but we had a house move to contend with and it was 200 miles, a house, the cats and the pony to move! Amazingly, we are incredibly resourceful as a couple and got it done in 3 days! We spent the week before boxing everything up and then hired a van and a horse box and did it in 4 runs up the country!

The night we loaded the furniture van was one of the oddest feelings. I had already done my goodbyes at the yard and so most of my tears were cried, but finally when we loaded up and headed off to the pub for one last drink, we realised there was NOTHING left out of the van. There was not even a pillow or duvet! We slept on a mattress under a sheet and had the worst night's sleep you could have got, ready for the long drive and unpack the other end! It was a pretty emotional day!

3 days later we were unpacked, it already felt like home and I was fully embracing a NEW START.

It's the only way sometimes when you hit rock bottom. It didn't mean that I wasn't still getting wind of the mean things people were saying about me, but I was learning to ignore them a bit more and I actually find now that I would rather not know what's being said. I am actually very nice as far as humans go and I would never, ever want to make someone feel bad about themselves. It's just a shame that not everyone feels like that. I took a piece of my own advice and decided to mentally fuck them off in my head. No one that says nasty things about me deserves my energy and worry. NO ONE.

The one thing I have gained though, is one of those nasty bastards was saying how much my hands moved and they were right… I've worked really hard to make that better, just a shame I think of their snidey comment each time I feel my arms wobble!

The bottom line is, those that mind don't matter and those that matter don't mind. The people that I love and who love me; they are supportive, they are encouraging, and they are worth one hundred of every single one of the Chip Pissers!

Bugger off my chips with your stinky piss, there's nothing for you here! And there it was, 2 weeks into moving and we were BACK IN THE GAME, albeit 80cms, but I had entered an unaffiliated one-day event.

BACK ON TRACK

So, moving back home to Lincolnshire is something I have dreamed of for over 7 years now. I am not quite sure why I stayed in the south for so long, because unless you can afford monstrous rent, you are forced to live in towns, sacrificing garden space for marginally higher salaries. You can get just as good a job up here though (as Daddy Carrot has proven) and the rent is at least 30% less in most areas!

Now, having secured work for us both and finally unpacked all of our boxes in the new house, real life commenced! Only it was different now. I wasn't getting up and rushing around every morning or dicing with daylight hours to fit in a ride. I was far more at ease and the palpitations that had landed me in hospital had finally subsided. We booked an actual holiday too! What a treat!

I was exhausted though; the last few months had really taken their toll. First and foremost, you should take care of your body and your mind, I hadn't done this, and it was letting me know!! Mental health is something I have always found a bit taboo to talk about, until now.

In the past I have been naïve enough to think that anyone one with a mental health problem needs a royal kick up the arse. People wallowing in self-pity. I now know that this is bullshit. It was my way of trying to cope with the way I felt at the time, sad, lonely, and probably suffering myself.

Chemical imbalances in the brain, grief, stress, pain, guilt, worry, fear, loneliness, anxiety; any one of those can result in depression if it consumes you enough. We shouldn't be ashamed of that.

EVER. I am taking a bloody stand right now. I have been scared, I have felt fear, I have been consumed by worry and stress to the point where I cannot think ahead of that day or even hour without feeling overwhelmed. It's more common than you think, and it is NOTHING to be ashamed of.

I'm still susceptible to it now, I just recognise what it is, and in my own way I deal with things that are getting to me and move forward. I don't just brush it off anymore or box it away and like I said in the very beginning; you must deal with things in order to move forward without them coming back to bite you in the arse.

I have now accepted that it's ok not to feel or act happy all of the time, it's absolutely okay to feel scared and vulnerable, and my word is it perfectly normal to want to curl up under a blanket and sob your eyes out on occasions. I know that's ok now, it's perfectly normal, so I just need to find things to break that sad cycle.

The most important thing for me is to be around people that understand in the same way I do, those things right there. If someone comes along and tells me to 'cheer up', OH! Expect a punch in the chin my son! That is the single, worst possible thing to say, listen up fellas... NEVER say "cheer up" if someone looks sad. It just makes you feel like you are the biggest sloppiest fun sponge, sucking the life out of everyone! All it takes is my husband to wrap his arms around me and tell me that I am wonderful to him, that's all that really matters. If you don't have a husband, that's fine too – a cuddle from your cat or dog, a drink with a good friend, a hug from your mum – they will all help because you ARE WONDERFUL TO THEM too.

Surround yourself with positive and caring people that get you. And tell them how you feel, tell yourself too, don't try and hide it and pretend to be happy, it might work for a while, but it won't long term. Fake smiles are easy to detect when you start smiling real ones that burst with joy, remember that.

I won't rest until people, particularly in our little Wimpy community know that they are safe, that it's ok to feel not ok and that you will never ever be judged unfairly. It's up there with animal cruelty for me now – and I will never, ever take for granted my mental health for as long as I am breathing.

While I'm on the topic, if you know you have said something to someone lately that might have made them feel sad or was intended to make someone feel inferior because you happen to think you're better… Come on now! Don't be a chip pisser. You really have no idea how your words might affect someone who battles with low self-esteem or depression. Yes, they might have come across a bit of a dick but you really never know what is going on underneath. It could affect them for days or years even, so be kind, be mindful of other people. Remember that everyone has a story to tell. It's much better for your own mental health to live a life never judging or keeping score. Putting other people's feelings first will make you feel fulfilled in a way no chocolate bar or glass of wine ever can.

With this in mind, and after some of the negativity I had faced of late, I was back to the frequent toilet visits and white-knuckle fear of show days, the week leading up to my next event. I had entered the 80cms and it was nice and local, so no rushing about to leave 4 hours ahead of my times. Now my saving grace was that whilst a group of people that didn't know me from Adam were being hideously cruel on the internet, I was lucky enough to have met the most wonderful people that were our new neighbours. Two of these people we share our yard with and happen to be the biggest hearted people I have ever met and ones that I hope we are friends with for a very long time to come. Auntie Smurph and Grain Pirate Dan.

These people have restored my faith in humans, they would NEVER judge me and without realising it, they have turned around my whole season this year.

EVENT REPORT – Hackthorn Hall ODE 80

Burton Hunt Pony Club ODE – HACKTHORN 80cms

So today I *might* have sneaked off and done an event without telling hardly anyone! I was having a HUGE wobble in confidence and with time off to move I was worried I wouldn't be able to get back out there and do it again! So, I entered the 80-85 Burton Hunt Pony Club - Hackthorn ODE on our first wedding anniversary no less! I've been frequenting the toilet all week trying to learn the test!! But walking the course yesterday I felt at ease with the height and decided it was a day of absolutely no pressure.

We arrived courtesy of a taxi from our lovely new yard friends Auntie Smurph and Grain Pirate Dan, and that's when it hit me. I'm actually far more terrified of getting on to even warm up than of the competition. I had no pressure to perform but I was still sure I was going to die getting on him! I need to deal with this, but today is not the day!

The three musketeers (Pat, Daddy Carrot and I) headed off to the dressage where he warmed up very nicely and actually did an ok test. I made a couple of mistakes and didn't feel that he was listening at times, but I thought it deserved a 31 or somewhere near.

A little wait until the jumping, so I walked the course (which I NEVER do, it makes me so scared actually going up to them!) and I felt surprisingly not too bad. There were less fillers than I had expected which is great for my spooky beast. The jumps were a maximum height of 85cms which I was very glad of, I could just go and have a nice time. And a nice time we had!

A sterling (if a little low flying) display from the Red Arrows overhead and we were off... very nicely over all of them just a little spook off the corner at 6 for four faults! I was VERY happy with this.

Back at the box we were melting! It was so hot. But on we got and off we went. Everyone at the event was so wonderfully friendly, even the counter downer in the start box of doom didn't scare me today!

We set off and tripped over fence one - a little log, over two and three, the house. Sailed the big table at 4 and the hanging log over the ditch at 5. We galloped over 6 and 7 a log/ditch/log combination and up the hill over a big fat log at the top. The ground was exceptionally undulating and hard work for my Patsy but he made nothing of 8,9,10 or 11 until we stumbled into the corner at 12 and he fell face first onto it! A little scratch on the neck and a check he was okay, and he popped it no bother the second time round! Over the scary blue pipes at 13 and down to a big joker fence, a 95cm palisade (that had an alternative), I grabbed the strap and kicked, and he soared through the air and galloped away like it was nothing, I felt bloody wonderful after that. Over the log, the mural painted double and down onto the water where he made nothing of a big jump in! Out and over the last, he sailed through the flags grinning just as much as me!

What a horse, what a day and what a feeling! I'm buzzing! I can't wait for the next one... my horse and me, we are on fire again! I popped back to grab my sheet and a picture (or 6!) and it actually turns out that with a dressage of 23.8! And one pole down and 20 to add for our face plant XC... he came 6th and we got a lovely rosette!

I cannot thank everyone at the Burton Pony Club enough for being so welcoming, supportive, and well organised. I love Lincolnshire and being local to home at an event was just so nice today.

I had a lovely, lovely day and now I shall enjoy a little gin and tonic with my husband on our first wedding anniversary.

Love as always

Vic and Pat xxxxxx

We had such a good day at Hackthorn and dropping back a few levels was just what we needed to get back into the swing of things. At the time of entering, I felt a bit ashamed of doing a lower class but now I've done it, I have realised there is no shame in taking the pressure off. It was the best decision for us both. It was no good going out scared at a level I can just about manage and frighten my lovely horse. Sadly, this nice feeling was a little short lived as the online bullying after this event got ten times worse. I didn't post on the blog for almost a week because yet again I had let people drag me down to that horrid sad place. But this time I wasn't going to let it break me.

♥ Monday, July 17, 2017

I want to talk about something that has been playing on my mind the last fortnight, something I haven't really felt confident to say out loud. I know I have been quiet, I haven't felt confident to write or publish anything much because of the negativity I have experienced from some serial chip pissers. That's not because I feel 'caught out' for being a fraud or that I have run out of things to 'make up' to tell people... (ROLLS EYES), I have been deep in thought, trying hard to take my own advice in times of uncertainty.

I have been doubting my ability as a rider - yes, my hands are wobbling about, yes I am unbalanced and yes I am hanging on to my poor horse for grim death at times - I do not profess to be a professional by any stretch, I have mountains to learn and take criticism well! But when the criticism is just nastiness, I struggle to make light of things. It all stems from the tiniest seed of doubt, but that seed is enough to rock the biggest boat in the stillest ocean.

I mean COME ON... don't you dare let them piss on your chips! DON'T YOU BLOODY DARE!

Our sport of equestrianism has enough challenges, we do not need other people making it harder. Why do they do it? Why does anyone feel the need to make another human being feel so desperately inferior?! I know this is usually because of their own lack of self-belief, but it's just not on! Yes, I am no longer crying at the thought of getting on my horse, I CAN jump a jump, gallop in an open field, and enter a show, does that mean I haven't overcome some huge hurdles to be able to do that? I still feel the fear, I just bloody well do it regardless.

I'm sick of feeling guilty for progressing and this is me taking a bloody stand! I know that I am never going to feel 100% confident even at 80cms, but if I can do it anyway and show the world I can, then it makes it so much more accessible for others - why is this so wrong? - I'll tell you - IT'S NOT!

For anyone that is going through any kind of negativity, don't you dare let them beat you down, focus on what you know is true, take comfort from those people that believe in you and stick two fingers up at the ones that don't.

Seriously - every single bloody one of you has something to be proud of, don't you dare feel ashamed for that. Celebrate it, make something for yourself and be bloody proud of it. I am not hiding behind my low confidence anymore!! Here's to the sun shining and to all of us feeling damn well good enough!!! <3

Love as always Vic and Pat xxxxx

I wrote this post not really knowing if I believed myself 100% but after it being the farthest-reaching post I have ever done with hundreds of stories and pictures of other people feeling proud of themselves, I knew I was right in my thoughts. This touched over 297,000 people – that one little post. Bollocks to anyone that says I'm a shit rider, I am – there, I agree but I'm a nice human and if I make life easier for just one other person I will carry on doing this, badly or otherwise!

And that was it, with my new house, my wonderful husband, my own business, good, supportive friends around me and my dear sweet Pat. I waved my sharpest middle finger at those serial chip pissing bastards and got myself back out there! I entered Frickley Park BE90, my first affiliated event up here and YES, I was still frightened!

♥ Wednesday, July 26, 2017

And so, it begins! The damp palms, the profuse sweating, the palpitations and increased toilet visits.... it can only mean ONE thing! WE'RE GOING EVENTING. Sunday is D-Day BE Day for us! Hopefully early enough times to not scare us silly! It's been a while since my fluff up at Rackham, we had a good spin at Hackthorn unaffiliated but it doesn't stop me feeling like my insides are doing the Macarena! I'm going to learn the test today and practice tonight and tomorrow in the fields on our ride, we have a jumping lesson Friday night and a good hack Saturday before the big day!! Here goes nothing!

The funny thing about fear is that for days on end it has me feeling utterly dreadful, even on the day all I want to do is pull out, but afterwards it melts away into the biggest sack of joy you have EVER experienced and makes all the bitten nails and toilet visits SO worth it.

EVENT REPORT – Frickley Park BE90

So here it is....

Pat, Daddy Carrot and I headed to Frickley Park today for the BE90. Yesterday's course walk left me feeling oddly excited to get back out and doing this sport again, I felt 75% excitement and only 25% terror after walking the somewhat boggy going of the XC course.

After walking the course we went to Auntie Smurph and Grain Pirate Dan's house for another #westfirsbycrew BBQ (did I mention, I love where we live) and played a game of rude scrabble until much later than planned! Although I did stumble upon the brilliant and newly created word 'fungina' that I now plan to include into my vocabulary. Although, this meant that silly Vic drank half a bottle of Malbec and felt like an utter 'un-fungina' when the alarm went off at 4.45AM!

Carrot drove us to get my pony and we loaded up and left! I felt SICK. Not just because of the hangover but because I just wanted to turn around and go home. Crippling nerves got to me big time today. I felt fine yesterday, well not fine but nearly fine.

I almost cried on the drive there and again when we sat in the queue of lorries waiting to be TOWED IN! Yep! I was severely close to tears now and all I could see were people skidding about in the show jumping arena out of the passenger window. It was awful, I couldn't get out and run to the porta-friend quick enough!!!

We registered, got my Patsy ready and I hopped on, as close to the box as I could so I didn't get too muddy. Walking down to the dressage warm up without my gel bum sticker-inner always makes my heart palpitations come back with a vengeance, today was no different. I have been using a gel seat saver that grips you on for over a year now and I feel lost without it! A lovely lady Wimpy follower stopped us for a chat but (I'm so sorry) I was a dreadful wreck. We went into the arena and smiled our smiles, we did everything where we were meant to and it felt bloody amazing! I wailed to pat what a good boy he was and gave him a big squeeze!

I was so proud right there, I would have happily retired after that!!!

A short 30 minute change over and we were in the show jumping. It was my worst nightmare of tonnes of spooky fillers, slippery mud and mountains of on lookers, this combination resulted in me riding like a total turd and thoroughly deserving 2 poles down!!!!

Another half an hour passed and there we were, deep breathing our way around the XC warm up. Now at this point, silly Carrot had said we had the best dressage in our section! And with 8 to add, we were 6th place and couldn't be pipped to this spot unless I failed him XC... I think after 2 stops at Tweseldown, not even making it to the XC at Rackham and the stumble at Hackthorn as my last 3 outings, it was safe to say I was rock bottom in my belief that I could still do this.

I felt weak, unfit and not sure which fence I would just plop off at... but we were there doing it, bloody doing it regardless of how green I was. I won't let my nerves get the bloody better of me! "Get in that start box of doom you great big fanny!"

"3,2,1" came quicker than expected and we were off!!! Galloping!!! Flying the brush at 1, the wall and roll top for 2 and 3, sailed over the double of bullfinches at 4 to a gappy hedge at 5, I was squealing with excitement now. It felt bloody awesome to be back there in that moment with my horse. 6, a flower dressed table caused Pat to back right off but I was there to catch him just like he does me when I'm scared, I kicked and yelled to him it was okay and he flew it and then boinged off the step down the hill!

7 a house, 8 the trakehner and 9 a shot gun cartridge all jumped lovely! 10... the first worry for me, a skinny log into the woods and a couple of strides to a second one... I don't know why I doubted that trusting little soldier today, he flew them both and out the other side like I was daft to assume otherwise! Another hedge and a wall led us to the water which he splashed through no bother, then onto my doom fence! We all have one, the one you are most likely to die at... 14 was it! A big bright CORNER! I lined him up, slowed him down, showed him the question and he answered it perfectly... bloody boing! Over we were... just like that! Down to a flower box, wagon and the home straight of a wall and sacks to finish!

Aaarghhhhhh! We did it! Bloody bloody did it! My horse is a stonking legend! We did it! Clear! The sad part is that because I was cautious of the mud and him slipping over, we went a little bit steady and did ourselves out of the frillies... but... bugger me, we bloody did it! We CAN do it.

Today I love my horse, I love my Daddy Carrot and my will to make this work. I won't let fear determine who I am... not on your life! And I won't let anyone else define who I am, me and my horse – we were brilliant today.

Thank for the endless support and encouragement, I love you all.

Love as always Vic and Pat Xxxxxx

With another round under our belts at an unknown venue and after a few weeks of emotional upset put to bed, I felt ready to fight again. I can and I will!

TWO STEPS FORWARD, TEN STEPS BACK

I started my 2017 eventing season in April and we are now 5 months in with only 3 months left... look at everything that has happened in this time, the first book flew out the door from May onwards and I am delighted to report it has been very well received – I am now writing about the reception of a book in the sequel book, not knowing how this will be received... RISKY! But, I was exceptionally worried. I am no J.K Rowling, I didn't even study English past 16 years old! (sorry about the bad grammar!) But just that small confirmation that the content was helping so many people was enough to make my heart soar, what a feeling. With each message of thanks, I still well up now, it is a very special feeling being a game changer for people and long may it continue.

♥ Wednesday, August 2, 2017

Some of the lines from my first book (especially the 'things to remember' pages at the back) are really resonating with me today. I cannot begin to tell you how much I want other people to succeed, to progress and to love who they are. Today is Wednesday, it's raining again and I woke up without my Carrot (he's in the big smoke today). I instantly felt flat. So I started the thought process that I go through when I feel like this.

Firstly, I allow myself to wallow - I think this is important, it's ok to feel sh*t, it's okay to think of all the things that are negative in your life, things that you would change if you could. THERE... RIGHT THERE... 'If you COULD' - Well you bloody well can, so step two (after wallowing in self pity) is - How do I change it?

The only way you can begin to change a bad situation or feeling is to suffocate it with positivity. Change your thought process from how crap you feel about something to 'what do I have to be grateful for?' or 'how can I make an impact on things today?' Take your mind away from things you don't have, things you can't do or things that leave you feeling like a sack of mouldy pears and start dwelling on the things you CAN do.

I started then to dwell on the reasons I am happy and the things I can improve on, that started a fire in my belly instantly!! I want to change the world, even if it is just my tiny piece of it, so that's what I am bloody well doing!! I'm not sitting there going over and over in my head, the things I can't do as well as I'd like, I'm focusing on the things I feel good about doing. They might only be small things - I make a mean poached eggs on toast, so I started there - see, small things but they came out perfectly and I felt better!! The bottom line is - divert your negative thoughts like a wasp heading for your wine glass, waft them away and sip your delicious wine... There will always be wasps - deal with it! Squash out those negatives with big fat positive thoughts! You've got this nailed, you just might not know it yet. Have a great day <3 xxxx

And so, with positive thoughts in mind and a burning fire in my belly, I entered my next event another unaffiliated one, we are doing the 90cm One Day Event at Epworth Equestrian. As we got a 3rd place at Chilham Castle earlier this year, it qualified us to enter a Regional Final. If you come in the top section of riders in this qualifying class you are on your merry way to the much coveted slot at the Mitsubishi Motors Cup held at Badminton.

This event is run over the same week as the world class Horse Trials, so we were desperately in need another confident run before our first ever Regional Final in two weeks!

EVENT REPORT – Epworth 90

Well, today was a mission of two things. Number 1 was a confidence boost before our regional final in two weeks and Number 2 was to get inside the time after being told my horse didn't make the time at Frickley because he was FAT!! I was even more determined to do it!

Now walking the course yesterday (alone!) massively put the jitters up me. I thought it looked big and beastly and there were three skinny ones that I was worrying my beans about!! The show jumping also looked big and bright! Tomorrow was going to be the first event of my whole season that Daddy Carrot would not be coming with us. It was tough to get my head around but the events keep falling on football match days and I have to be fair. Today Auntie Smurph was our taxi and friendly helper to replace my Carrot and this was the next best thing.

We had nice early times and pootled down to the dressage for our time of 8.30ish! In the warm up he was very subdued and in fact he was a little lazy. A novelty compared to the spooky monkey I usually have to deal with! In the arena, I thought it rode well, it was the same test I did at a Frickley and I definitely felt today's wasn't as good but no mistakes and no shooting off. Big pats for not spooking and back to the box.

A quick tack change and off we went to jump... only to find out it was causing cricket scores!!! Great! I am still not 100% confident that I will ever learn how to ride my horse in the show jumping. He can be a different horse from one half of the course to the other, but we will always give it our best shot! I warmed up swiftly, not too many practice jumps but no waiting about before going in either (my new tactics, thanks to Daddy Carrot observations!) I thought about what Carrot would have said "take your bloody time" don't rush to the first jump. My Carrot isn't horsey, he has just seen me bugger it up enough times now. So, with him in mind I didn't rush, I presented to every jump and kept the canter consistent...It worked....WE BLOODY WENT CLEAR! And I had heard the dressage score too... 26.3!

Now normally we are clawing at a placing by now but not this time, we had nailed it... lying in FIRST PLACE by quite a way too, we were heading cross country... I was nervous that I would let him down at those skinnies, so I rode positively from the off. Charging into practice jumps like I meant business! There was no one waiting to go so I went and asked if I could, I did and cantered straight through the start box of doom without having to endure the dreaded "3,2,1"! I kicked like stink from the off, the house at 1 jumped lovely, around the corner and a short gallop to a sneaky turn that didn't show 2 in sight until you were on top of it, Pat dropped the anchors on like a hot coal... I knew he would do this, I've had a similar thing before at the water at Bovington so I was ready for the brakes to hit and I was there with a bum smack and a "yip yip!" and he sailed it!

Out into the open for a nicely attacked number 3 and into the woods again for the first ask of the course. A barrel, over a mound and out over a skinny brush (my demon jump) well not today my friends... no sir-ee! I lined him up and locked him on and we flew it! On to a line of jumps at 5, a narrow trakehner at 6 and a roll top and coffin at 7, they all rode very nicely indeed! Number 8 he backed off, it was a big hay cart with shavings bales in front, but he flew it with a big kick from mum! 9 was my let up fence, nice and plain, 10 the water was a jump in over a boat and out over a wishing well skinny for 11. He jumped it all very confidently indeed! 12 I was crying over last night, a big brush with a ditch in front... I kicked and shut my eyes and he did stand off it quite a way, but we made it!! Phew!! Down to the castle for 13, round the corner and over the bridge, which left you down hill sailing over the flower box at 14. We didn't get the best jump at it but we made it over! 15 the Carrot box jumped great, to 16 the skinny I was fretting over... no bother, I set him up and slowed it all down and he popped over like a dream. Bobbed down the step afterwards like a pro.

Then it came, I was out of breath, long in the rein, relieved to have got over all the ones I was worried about and what happened.... the fucking cone of doom happened! It hit us, right where it hurt! A single road cone at the side of the fence and his heart fell out his mouth. He backed right off and ran as far away from the doom as he could! I swiftly turned it into a loop and growled like a goodun' and he flew it!!! 18, 19 and 20 down the home straight all galloped lovely!! And that was that! First place fell way down the swanny as the spook and loop at fence 17 hit us with 20 penalties to add!

Now there are very important things to take from today, never to get complacency when any kind of obstacle of doom lies before us, never to change the way you ride for the results you have already achieved and never under estimate the power of positive riding. I don't feel sad about losing first place, we achieved both of our objectives today and I feel on top of the world. It was a big course and we jumped clear in our nemesis phase. I feel very, very proud indeed. I'm not sure where we ended up but who gives a badger's ass... my horse was a bloody legend today! Thank you to my lovely Auntie Smurph who drove us there today and was so mega supportive. I think we both had a soggy eyeball moment when I came out the show jumping! Love him so, so much, I don't ever want this feeling to end.

Love as always

Vic and Pat xxxx

So, we survived another outing, our first one without Daddy Carrot too!! I felt a little bit deflated as it would have been our first win, if I hadn't have ridden like a total sack of crap but the fact that I had just done another 90 after weeks of worrying I couldn't carry on... I was feeling good. And this was just a warmup for what was set to be the most important event of our year; our Badminton Regional Final (only a week away!).

Now I well and truly succumbed to the pressure of this event. I had built it up SO much in my head I couldn't think about anything else. I rarely get like this, but the emotional highs and lows of the whole season were all a surprise to me. I took Pat cross-country schooling in the run up to this event, something I rarely do and I'll explain why...

The feeling that you get on the day of an event is like no other, you cannot replicate it. I have a mental block in my head about the way I ride the cross country on the day that I just cannot put into practice at home. When I get in the start box on the day of an event, I give it everything I have, I ride every fence with passion and I feel invincible in that moment. Why else have I got that ridiculous smile on my face the WHOLE way around? I'll tell you why, partial insanity but total sheer elation!!! But when I try and jump a log on a cross country course for practice... I feel like I want to cry. I feel scared, I over analyse everything, I don't ride forwards enough, and this results in a terrible confidence knock for us both. And although you might see videos of Pat and I storming around the course like our pants are on fire, Pat is NOT confident AT ALL. I have to seriously work for every jump sometimes from 10 strides out!! If I could bare it, I would love for someone else to ride him round, just to see how much you have to do to coax him over each jump. Luckily, he is more scared of doing the wrong thing than of the jumps so as long as you get the right balance of pressure to praise, he'll jump the moon for you... we've got each other sussed now, I think.

I probably should add in at this point, that I do vaguely know what I am doing. Although it might not seem like it at times! I have ridden some fantastic horses and trained with some brilliant people over the last 25 years, and I know I have 'feel' which is often something people lack and struggle to learn, so when someone comes along bashing me for not going XC schooling – I know that not going is the best thing for ME and MY horse.

I have done it a handful of times with and without a trainer and each time I have felt it has lessened our confidence. You must do what is right for YOU in this life not what society tells you is right. Crikey, there are 4* horses that can't go cross country schooling and some that even have to do fittening work in the arena because they won't hack... you tell me I'm wrong when the world's best do it their way!

If you judge your suitability for eventing on a bad cross country training session, there would probably be no need for these grass roots levels. Give it a go I say, and ride for your life on the day! As long as you are safe and not totally out of control, it's the only way you'll know for sure if you love it or not.

Right where was I…?

The day of the course walk (Saturday), Daddy Carrot and I had a HUGE falling out, because we rarely argue it always seems worse than it actually is. I was being totally selfish, stubborn, and neglectful of his feelings. I let this event take over my life and I was outraged that he wasn't being as supportive as I had demanded! It's awful really when I look back. I bet a lot of people reading this have snapped more than once at their non-horsey partners the night before a show – it's human nature but I really wasn't very becoming! In fact, I feel ridiculously sad about the whole weekend when I look back, which is a real shame. I will NEVER ever let something that is meant to be a FUN hobby affect my marriage EVER again. It is absolutely not important enough for that. I regret being hideous to him and I hate that I can't take it back. I think it was Karma, the way the day of my one and only shot at a Regional Final panned out.

EVENT REPORT – Shelford 90RF

So here it is…. my long-awaited Regional Final at Shelford.

I had been working hard all week preparing as best I can for this day. I went XC schooling for the first time all year, jumped him in the field and practiced my test. I was getting horribly nervous and putting stupid amounts of pressure on us to be the best we can be for 14 minutes of judged performance.

Carrot and I walked the course on Saturday which because of bad traffic, took way longer than planned – queue me getting increasingly ratty by the second! There wasn't anything there that

I was terribly worried about and not too many plant pots or fillers in the show jumping either! RESULT!

Now, honesty is the best policy, so here it is... I was so desperately wrapped up in this stress and pressure that I failed to be anywhere near a decent wife and quite rightly my Carrot was getting increasingly peeved over my stress and inattentive, selfish behaviour. We had a very rare argument on Saturday which wasn't helped by my transport mix up and having to drive miles to get another lorry! It was fair to say that this event took over my life. Something I will never ever let happen ever again!

I was on at 8.30 so I had to leave at 5.45am. Still stewing from our argument, I left my Carrot sleeping and thought 'Fuck it, I've got this, I'm going for it on my own!' NOTE: actually TOTALLY ALONE I didn't know anyone going either!

I arrived at the venue of Shelford, a very lovely unassuming place that is only an hour away. I got my number, notified the secretary of my lone trip, and headed for the green porta-friend to relieve my terrified bowel. I got my Patsy off the box and tacked up. Now, normally I have to get someone to feed him while I get on because I terrified of that! But I have been trying a new syringe calmer by Blue Chip Feed and it meant he just stood there at the water barrel while I scrabbled on!! I was so happy right there, it's the little things and what a long way we have come that make this journey ever so rewarding. One of my biggest fears is getting on at a show, today I put a lot of those demons to bed.

He warmed up without any tension or sillies... I couldn't believe it, I felt safe and happy and gaining confidence. Then who should arrive, my Carrot with his camera. I have to say, I was so happy just having got on by myself that I didn't give two hoots about our silly row anymore!

Into the test, and I thought it was okay, nice and accurate and everything where it should be. I have felt better tests, but I thought it was due around a 28 comparing with my other tests this season.

A quick change and into the show jumping, I have a new tactic in the jumping that I am still working out, but it is getting so much better already. He is so sensitive, spooky, and then racing about that it's hard to get a balanced and consistent canter round a course. I tend to hook him up and cripple the canter so today, just like my clear round at Epworth, I let it bum twitchingly bowl forward! It worked again! One silly duff stride at number 6 was all that wobbled us for 4 faults! I was over the moon!

I was perplexed however, to hear my dressage score was 35! What the actual fig! Bull shit did I deserve that hammering, he did a sweet test, and I rode very accurately indeed. My marks were lost because his mouth was open, that my canter transitions were abrupt and my halt 'drifted slightly' - it is the worst mark he has EVER had and it certainly didn't feel like the worst test, by a long way. I know it's all relative and everyone else in the section was marked hard too, but it left us right down the leader board and definitely not going to Badminton. At this point, I was so bloody thrilled with being able to get on by myself that I didn't actually give two shits about the score and decided we were just going out to enjoy the rest. We went to get changed and have a cuddle before the cross country.

He warmed up well and in 15 minutes we were being counted down! I screamed with joy out of the start box, YIP YIP and over the first, I gave him a little left-handed shoulder tickle with the whip as a gentle reminder that darting to the left isn't going to work today, he sailed over the palisade at 2. He flew round the corner for a giant leap at a hedge at 3, I slipped my reins and squeaked with terror as I was left shocked to the core again, he NEVER takes over, but he gave it his biggest hairy balls over that hedge!! Galloped down to a ladder at 4 and up and down a dip in the woods and out over a big log for 5!

He was FLYING, no hesitation, as soon as I kicked and shouted 'go' oh boy, he went! 6, 7 round the corner to a shavings bale filled table at 8, hit a perfect stride for that and sailed it!! Pinged the yellow pipes at 9 and back into the woods for a sticky jump over a log for 10, hopped off the step no problem and galloped down to another big log for 11. 12 was a ditch/step up with 4 strides to a hedge, he bloody nailed it. Hopped up, perfect stride and flew the hedge like a lion! Down to a huge beer barrel clad wagon, hit another booming forward stride and soared through the air, I squealed again, this time in sheer delight, this was possibly the very best he's gone, ever... galloped over a steeplechase brush with tears of pride stinging my eyeballs ....DONT GET COMPLACENT VIC, YOU TURD! Focus!

Down at the sloppy, murky water, he splashed in and out and over the roll top no bother and screamed down the home straight to the last fence... we soared it, we did it!! We bloody well did it. Ahhh, you just can't put into words, tears are beading down my face right now, I had the best round of my life yesterday. He was unreal, like never before. I couldn't have given less of a cr*p about not going to Badminton, I was and still am over the moon with the whole day.

So we did it again, me and my tiny boy. He is just my dream come true, it has taken all my effort, confidence and patience to get him here but together, we've done it again! In any other section he'd have earned a rosette to finish inside the time today.

Now I said it would be a long post today.... You may have noticed a brand-new logo attached to my saddle pad this weekend. I am absolutely delighted to announce that I have been selected to represent FALPRO as a sponsored rider! Pat has been wearing the rugs for a few weeks now and I cannot tell you how brilliant they are... I will go into more detail about which ones I love the most, but I seriously cannot thank them enough. I know we will do them proud after today.

One last thing... Yesterday was also magical for another reason. We welcomed our beautiful new boy into the family. 7 year old Bentley joined us yesterday from Cheveral House Racehorse Rehoming run by the lovely Kate, who we will continue to support for the rest of the year. She works so hard to find the very best homes for these lovely horses and I couldn't be more thrilled with our lovely boy. Watch this VERY exciting space.

So, what a day, I hope everyone takes a second to squeeze their ponies today, to reflect on how much happiness these animals can bring us, regardless of the endless heartache and fears, they are just wonderful.

Love as always

Vic and Pat xxxxx

And there it was, all the stress and heartache of trying to qualify was all over in just 4 minutes of dressage that the judge didn't like today! It's madness. No Badminton Grassroots for us, but then there's always next year. The season is very nearly over, I have a couple of runs left so I thought what better way to ensure I never get a rest this winter…. ANOTHER HORSE!

Enter Sir Bentley, or Bender as we stable named him, he was about to be called 'Feral Beryl' but luckily for him, Bender stuck! Get an ex-racehorse they said, it'll be fun they said… Well this is not the first one for me, dear sweet Sparky was the first, then India after that and a couple of the polo ponies we picked up for those two seasons I did, they were off the track too so I knew what I was getting myself in to. I had asked the lovely man that owns our yard if there was room to double my herd and he agreed. That was that. 2 days later I was off to pick him up.

I hadn't had to look far for my Bender as my beloved childhood teacher and guru had recently picked up a horse from a lovely place not too far from us; Cheveral Racehorse Rehoming. I was worried about not being suitable enough for their criteria, I know lots of people want these horses when their photos get released online so I wasn't getting my hopes up too high. As soon as I met him I knew I would love that horse very much, I think that the lady could see that and so I was therefore very suitable indeed.

Now, buying anything that is priced at £750 and described as 'unridden' in the details, isn't going to be ready for Badminton next week and I was fully prepared to play the long game. This particular horse had been turned out in a field for a year after his unsuccessful racing career ended in 2015. He was ready for a job!

The day I picked him up was the same day we missed out on our Regional Final, I was rather annoyed to be doing it alone but as Daddy Carrot was still a bit miffed about our argument, he went clay pigeon shooting with Grain Pirate Dan instead! Not ideal. I had no idea how well he travelled and yet again I was in an unfamiliar hired lorry. He loaded a little reluctantly but didn't move an inch all the way home! I was worried on a few occasions, when I took a corner a bit sharper than I should have, that he might be dead or escaped! But no, I got home and dropped the ramp and the poor love was WET THROUGH. He was clearly shell shocked about the whole thing and was sweating profusely… much like I do these days too, but he was very much alive and well!

I let him off in the field with Pat and they were friends instantly. This was wonderful to see, Pat is a proper bottom feeder in any herd so I was glad Bender seemed a nice sort. 3 days later I attempted to bring him onto the yard, oh the stress and panic that ensued! He was NOT HAPPY about being anywhere alone. That's ok, its early days. I grabbed Pat to stand with him and all was well in the world.

A few days later we started long reining him. This is a process that means you walk miles with the horse attached to long lengths of rope in front of you. You do this usually because you are too scared to mount them and feel it safer to accumulate 60 blisters walking miles instead! But 2 weeks of long reining and he was very pleasant indeed. We have had a few altercations regarding who goes first when being led (the human or the horse) and who stands on whose toes. But he is a very quick learner and didn't need telling too many times.

My advice to anyone thinking of getting an ex-racehorse is that if you don't have the patience to complete a rubix cube wearing a blindfold, forget it! You have to be kind, firm, patient and regardless of any goal, dream or milestone you might have planned for that day/month/year, you MUST be prepared to fail and move on to something else.

They are rewarding, they are clever, they have a busy brain and like a job. They also have the heart of a lion and if you win over a thoroughbred, they will give you so much joy you won't know what to do with yourself.

Some of the earliest days with Bender I sat at home in tears. I had forgotten what producing horses was like and how unforgiving it can be when 5 days of no progress other than backward steps leave you feeling empty. How no-one tells you how much you'll appreciate just a moment of calm where things go how you wanted them to.

I lunged in the p*ssing rain one Thursday afternoon trying to get him to walk nicely and just stand without spinning in on me... nearly 40 minutes of walking around a field soaked through to my knickers... and for what? A fucking halt! FFS! But that's the soggy type of endless patience it takes because now he does it on the button.

Now, in the past I have got on board long before this point because I have been royally fed up with walking everywhere! But Daddy Carrot has been very involved with Bender when the nights were still light enough and has been learning how to long rein and pointing out all the time that 'there's no rush'. He's right, the minute you rush is the minute it takes you five times as long! I had leaned over him in the yard a few times and he was very calm, he doesn't fidget when he is saddled up at all. We practiced standing at the mounting block for 10-minute stints every day for a week, being feed nuggets at the block, patted at the block, watched the human jump up and down at the block! Which meant that when the human finally put her tiny foot in the stirrup and got on, standing at the block was a piece of cake! He stood like a statue, I walked forward a few meters, gave him a big pat and got off! Secretly very relieved to not be dumped on the hardstanding!

I know it's probably ideal to be getting on in an enclosed space with a soft landing but the joys of having the horses so close to home means that we don't have the luxury of an arena. And quite honestly, you don't NEED one, it's just nice to have. For years I feared hacking and field riding and now that's the only option, I am nowhere near as scared. I'm learning to just get on with it. I used to dread tacking up and going down to the school just as much, now I just bobble about in my homemade arena in the field!

It might appear sometimes, that other people have far great chances of success than you because of what they have. Material possessions and a wonderful indoor school won't get you anywhere without hard work. They might be successful on their own merit and luck might have graced them with those things. My beautiful new saddle won't make me great overnight, and yes I am very grateful for the support of Voltaire Design, but I will work harder than ever to make sure I do them proud. That is what makes success.

♥ Friday, August 4, 2017

Here's something to think about today. Sometimes you might look at someone else's life or what they have with envy or resentment without really knowing anything about that person. Sometimes people tell you things about a person that may make your opinion or judgement of them swayed in one direction or another.

Negativity is a violent and horrible thing that, if you let it can spread like a virus and eat away at your whole life. Do you know how much happier the world would be if everyone was kind and encouraging and people eliminated negativity? I have been thinking a lot about this lately and what I can do to make a difference. I want to breed kindness, inspiration, and positivity. I want to make people feel good about themselves because it makes my life feel worthwhile. Do you know how wonderful it feels to make someone happy? To say something kind and make their eyes light up. To tell someone they ride beautifully, that their horse is a credit to them, that they look lovely today... Mean it and say it or keep quiet - IT REALLY IS THAT SIMPLE!

Words have the power to lead, to inspire, to build up and equally to break someone into a thousand pieces, choose your words with love not bitterness. We are all human and we all feel emotion, wouldn't it be brilliant if this industry was known for its support network rather than its rivalry.

Today, I want you to tell someone; your mum, your mate, your husband, your farrier, your post man - ANYONE, tell them they are great, that they are doing a good job, give them a reason to feel happy. Be kind and spread that kindness as far as you can.

And do me a favour.... Before you do that - Go look in the mirror again (one hand on the boob, if you will) and tell yourself first - because YOU ARE BLOODY BRILLIANT, you are great and you ARE DOING A GOOD JOB. You are! Believe it and spread it, do it now. Xxx

One of the nicest things about putting yourself out there in full view for all to see is that you get to help make a difference to the lives of so many people. In the last year I have lost count of how many people this Wimpy Wonderland has helped be a little bit braver or a little bit happier. It is all down to spreading kindness. I know the things I think in my brain will help other people because I know that they would help me if I read them. I have bad days and just writing down advice that I would give myself actually helps those days get better. Kindness is a wonderful thing that we all have at our disposal, why not use it more often? There's no charge and the rewards are wonderful.

So, we are coming dangerously close to the end of the eventing calendar and if I am brutally honest, I shall be glad of a rest. The stress, the worry, the battle with nerves is really getting hard now that I am tired from 9 months keeping my fear demons at bay. I was actually not dreading this next event as much as some of the others. I think because I had been to the venue before, I knew where everything was. It really makes a difference if you are worrying about getting on. We were going back to Frickley Park for another bash round the BE90.

EVENT REPORT – Frickley Park 2 BE90

So here it is... Another soggy day in Yorkshire.

All week I had felt very at ease about this one, I think after the pressure of my Regional Final at Shelford, I had made a conscious decision to not allow this Eventing lark to ruin my mood or my marriage!!! I have a new regime the week running up to an event now, which appears to be working. I must do 3 things in order to not die/enjoy the event day as much as possible:

1. Take him out somewhere, anywhere! This week we went to a dressage clinic for our new riding club. Getting him out with others means he isn't such a dork when I'm frightened getting on at a show.

2. Give him enough work and don't be lazy! I usually find an excuse to prevent riding everyday but as long as he's done something the day before with maybe a couple of rest days early in the week, it makes for a much calmer boy!

3. Jump! I don't like show jumping, I doubt I ever will, but I have put a jump up in the field and I just make sure that the day before I have jumped it a couple of times (Jeez Louise it's barely a 2ft cross pole!) - but, I think it makes it less of a shock when we get to the event and have to jump 30+ jumps.

So, with my routine nailed, I went off to walk the course Friday afternoon ...ALONE! I'm getting good at this alone time... I'm definitely not as scared to do things by myself anymore which is progress in itself. I was done in half an hour and had decided that I wasn't getting beyond fence 13 so I may as well just go and enjoy and expensive combined training!

Fence 13 was a big double of very skinny logs on a curve, I wasn't ever getting him over them in my head and had admitted defeat there and then, some things will never change, eh?!

Home, ridden, plaited and packed up for our 5am start, we headed to the pub for one! One turned into two glasses of Shiraz on an empty stomach followed by a take away curry and a later bedtime than ideal! Why do I do it, what a bloody idiot! I woke up nervous at 4.45am and feeling like a cardamom seed was implanted in my throat, I couldn't eat and despite brushing my teeth, all I could taste was Indian food! NEVER EVER AGAN! I felt dreadful, sat on the toilet for 10 minutes, toying with pulling out altogether but instead, I hauled my stupid arse out the door and we arrived at Frickley at 7am!

My dressage was at 8.12am so we had time to get registered and spend a bit of time in my green poo-box of salvation! Yet again poor Frickley wasn't blessed with sunshine, it was bloody teaming down with rain too!

Now, here's something else to note. I have had some bad experiences getting on at shows and I HATE it, I mean, I fear it more than waking up with a beard of bees... I think I might have mentioned this before. On and settled – thank goodness.

He was a total angel in the warm up AGAIN! I can't believe it, I was actually having to kick him, such a nice feeling when usually he runs from my leg and frightens the pants off me. He did a lovely test but as I feared, we got the hard marking judge we had at Shelford! Compared to our other tests this year I'd have said it deserved around a 26-28% but alas, we were on a 31.8 but in the top ten of the section on dressage score so I wasn't displeased.

A quick boot up and we headed for the phase of disaster, the make or break for us. Our show jumping scores have ranged from one down to four down and with only two clear rounds all season, I am starting to think show jumping hates me! But Pat warmed up beautifully with a small break in proceedings when a poor lady had a nasty fall coming into the oxer. Poor love, I hope she's not too sore this morning. It wasn't long before our turn, and in we go...

He barely spooked today. It was a miracle! I've started leaving it to him a bit more and it's working! Normally I hook him up or push too much or just generally get in the way, but he's usually spooking and then racing in equal measures. Not today! Just a brush over the planks at number 8 and he came out with just 4 faults! I feel like it's getting so much better when you have rounds like that, I'm so looking forward to getting my new jumping saddle now, I might take back my words of hatred!

So, having decided that I wasn't getting past fence 13 on the course walk, we re-named cross country; the 'fuck it phase'! A quick change and we were in the warmup swallowing bile and deep breathing. Pat was reluctant to stand in the start box today, he was jazzy and, ordinarily, had I not have been pooing my pants over the course that lay ahead of us, I'd have probably been scared of his jazziness, but I think he's just starting to love this part a lot!

"5...4...3...2...1"! Boom, he flew out the box like a whippet! A short sprint to the first and he was FLYING! He felt so up for it today, none of his usual spook related reluctance! Up the slope to number 2, a palisade, he soared on a big long stride and I was beaming! YIP YIP.. down to number 3, a roll top, he backed off it! What the actual fudge! It was nothing, but by Jove it made me buck my ideas up!

Now that I was actually in the driver's seat rather than the boot of the car in a duffle bag... I rode for my life. Short reins, determined grit, number 4 the hedge oxer sailed by, 5 the box jump and drop step left us feeling confident for a long down hill gallop to a spooky White House at the bottom. I kicked and YIPPED and he soared! Wowzeroonies... what a feeling! 7 the trakehner, was a 'shut your eyes and kick' job and it worked a treat! 8 was a big feeder type jump and one of my let-up fences, he took the bit and flew! 9a&b, two skinny logs with mushrooms in the woods, he didn't even look! Just locked on and with a bum squeeze, he pinged over both and galloped down to 10, the hedge! Flew that and the same over 11 the dressed dry-stone wall! Oh bumders! 13 was creeping up...

Into the next field that I was sure to be eliminated in, I had to really work hard to get him over the army tank at 12 (great start to the field of doom). Here it was, 13... I found a good line, I held it, I kept a short rein and a firm holding leg and he locked on and jumped it! Shit the actual bed! Now what... turn, turn, turn, you moron! I did the same at part B and it bloody worked! Arrrrrrgghhhhhh! Bloody YEEEEEEEAAASS!

Yeehaaaaaa.....

Oh buggeration... I hadn't thought much about the rest of the course! We splashed through the water and over the boat house but wait, the doom wasn't over because 15 was that awful white and green corner I hated the last time I was here! But I took the same tactic, short reins and firm leg... he went! He bloody flew it. Then to 16 the flower box, he thought about darting out to the side but mother had turned into Mary King today and he had no chance! Boing!

A long gallop down to the ornamental wall and he stretched for a big one, full of running we galloped down to the last fence and with a kick, he soared it. We flew through the finish 6 seconds INSIDE THE TIME!

Bloody Nora what a feeling! Bursting at the seams with elation and adrenalin, I sobbed. He listened to me, I rode him, I rode him well today. Probably the best I have ever ridden in my whole life, and he was just unbelievably brilliant. I am utterly delighted with him, what a way we have come from that fearful little lamb I nursed around at the start of this season!! He is an absolute wonder, taking any small shred of confidence I can give him and storing it away to make the next run even better. That is why I love horses.

We finished 11th out of 43, with 0.1% holding us back from a rosette! But who gives a finger of fudge! NOT US! What a horse. He is my heartbeat, my very best friend and I just adore the absolute bones of that tiny boy.

Thank you all so much for the support, as always, you are the reason I keep going, I keep pushing my limits and facing my fears. Really. Thank you. I truly wouldn't be able to do this sport without your help and encouragement, thank you so much for believing in someone so desperately average.

What a bloody run that was, I am looking forward to feeling like that more often. That is progression for me. The placings and rosettes mean nothing if it was all a fluke on the day. I was riding better, feeling more in tune with my horse and actually enjoying it more – that's all the progress I need.

Back at home, educating Bender was getting interesting too.

♥ Tuesday, September 12, 2017

So, we are entering Benders third week with us. There has been a minor setback in his settling and Thursday evening I had to put him back in the field after I slapped a wet fish around his chops for ploughing through me more than once!

He had clung to Pat and apparently as Pat left his eye line he took Benders manners with him! We have since parted them in the field and I gave him a couple of days to let that sink in. Last night I tacked up and lunged on a huge loop in the field. He trotted over some poles too! He truly redeemed himself and made my heart sing. He is getting quite a character now his slippers are on and his chair is warm. I sharn't be letting him forget his manners and become rude but I do want to earn the trust and respect of my new love.

There is a VERY small margin for error here and you need to be able to re-adjust the plan in the blink of an eye without feeling disheartened. Firm and fair is my tact and always has been. The balance of trust vs respect - he needs to trust that I'm a good, safe leader but I also need the respect of an animal 10 times my size! It's about pressure and release, be a dick = pressure on... less of a dick = pressure off! I love how super his attitude is to work though and I will be keeping these initial sessions to 20 minutes of fun and praise as long as possible!

With my patience tested for the millionth time and Pat being such a golden boy, I wondered often if I had done the right thing doubling my herd. I think you only really know for sure when you get on them, when you feel that initial reaction to what you're asking, that connection of being on their back. Are they going to listen and respond or are they going to destroy your last hope of ever falling in love…? Well it wasn't until week five that I braved wriggling on, it's funny because I have this uncanny ability to detach myself from horses that aren't mine and I don't feel scared. Apprehensive, maybe, but not terrified like I have been getting on Pat some days. Bender although he belongs to me, doesn't quite feel 'mine' yet. He is a gentle soul but I have a feeling there is a little stubbornness in there too.

♥ Friday, October 6, 2017

Educating Bender week 5! What a happy Friday, after wriggling on him for a sit after a ride and lead the other day I knew it was only a matter of time before I was properly astride my new love. He had Weds/Thurs off whilst I was at HOYS so today, I tacked him up, lunged for 10 minutes over his usual 3 poles on a curve arrangement in the field. He was keener today, usually he is a slug and takes a lot of vocal encouragement on the lunge but having brought the mounting block down, it was now or never. He stood stock still whilst I wriggled on, I sat up and worked out the best way to make him move without me needing a parachute!

Ordinarily you would have someone on the ground leading at this stage but I don't have that luxury in the daylight- I am usually alone. I clicked, nothing! I tried turning, nothing! I wiggled and joyfully repeated "walk on", nothing! I had to use my leg, lord knows this horse is likely to only have been ridden with a racing saddle on and won't have felt 11st of porky wimp nudging his ribs, but he responded as though he had been in a riding school for years! Obedient and calm. We did 4/5 circles on each rein, tons of praise for him softening into the bend and I then asked for trot... He trotted, it was a wonderful feeling. Unbalanced but he's so solid it's not unnerving.

3/4 circles of trot on each rein and over the poles! Massive cuddles and lots of treats for Bendy Wendy today! I'm so, so happy with him. I also took Pat out for a hack to test our fitness ready for autumn hunting TOMORROW! And having given Bender some fibre nuggets in the field, he barely whinnied! Such a huge improvement on his field pacing and screaming! So Pat is going hunting tomorrow and another little ride for Bendy.

There it was, the start of ridden work for my 'unridden' ex-racehorse. He is such a gent and not at all the sharp prickle that Pat can be. But you heard it correctly, I was hunting tomorrow… HUNTING. The last time I did that was with the Kent and Surrey Bloodhounds last Christmas and I jumped a 5ft hedge! This time it was set to be much more sedate, so I wasn't sweating too profusely.

HUNTING REPORT

So here it is... day one of my autumn/winter regime, Autumn hunting with the Burton Hunt. With the meet being at 3.30pm and only 500yrds from home, I had all morning to fret. I woke up early and went back to bed with a book, a cat and a bucket of tea! At 12pm I was prematurely dressed and ready to go so I delivered pink parcels to the post office and stopped in for a cheeky swifty at the pub next door. I rather annoyingly bought and smoked a ciggie, but by Jove it calmed my jiggly belly!

I got up to the yard and went to ride my Bender before getting Pat ready for the off. Totally took my mind off hunting and I really enjoyed our first little canter. All the ponies brought in, I brushed Pat and tacked him up. Our chaperone for the day was our trusty Grain Pirate Dan (husband to Aunty Smurph) and he too was ready to rock and/or roll!

We mounted and rode the 10 minutes to the meet in which time I had guzzled half my flask and smoked another cigarette! I turned around and Grain Pirate was swigging whisky from an Evian bottle... I haven't laughed so much in ages! This is how we roll! I had one glass of port at the meet and we were ready for the off!! Pat was terribly excited and wouldn't trot anywhere, canter was all he could muster even on the road, silly bum!

We had a good blast and jumped a few jumps that all were nice and familiar so didn't scare us too much, then standing at the covert Pat was not for stationary momentum. He was READY FOR ACTION! At this point my bum twitched slightly, he was silly and I was a bit scared and it was like telepathy... Daddy

Carrot came round the corner (foot following) with an apple and all was well again.

We jumped a couple more fences and a small hedge and flew down the side of a field of maize with very little control but guess what...? I wasn't frightened, not a jot! I had the time of my life! We stayed out until dusk, finished my flask and met some really lovely people. What a wonderful warm welcome we had, thank you so, so much to The Burton Hunt and to their Supporters Club who made the most delicious burgers and sausages for supper afterwards. I cannot wait to be out again.

Love as always

Vic and Pat xxxxx

Sobbing tears of joy this morning writing this book, my very first BE event was a year ago this weekend and I cried tears of fear for a week before that day, we've come so far and I'm so proud of what I've achieved in my brain area. You really can do anything to set your mind to and I know it! You really can, not only could I not face getting on my horse; I was often shy, introvert and even avoided food shopping at busy times. I didn't like making a fuss or feeling like an inconvenience and I expect being able to achieve so much in one area of my life has led to the confidence growth in another. I am now one of the most assured people I know, I will make conversation with anyone and I can finally be myself without feeling guilty for it. I know my own mind now and what makes me happy and what doesn't. I'm not afraid to have a different opinion to someone else either.

My life has changed a lot in the last year, I now work from home, I have my own business (something I should have done years ago but never had the balls) and I am very content. There are still days where I feel very alone in my thoughts but that is 100% normal and I have learnt to be content with that.

On a business front, I know there will be many people reading this that wish their career was more exciting, you wish you had done something different or didn't have to do a job you're not passionate about. Well, I'll tell you what.... WHAT THE FUCK ARE YOU WAITING FOR?! 40+ hours a week is a long time to spend wishing you were somewhere else.

And don't think for a second, I had a net to catch me if it all went up the badger's backside… I had no windfall, rich parents or savings account. Nothing changed for me financially in order for me to do this, the only thing that changed was having the confidence to do it. I had about £600 in the bank as a buffer for the next month's bills, I saved this up over 2 months by selling anything not nailed down and knowing that I only had a month to build the business up I got to work straight away! I haven't ever wished I could go back, not once. It was the absolute, best decision I have ever made. I worked 10 years for other people, 10 years of being instructed by directors that didn't ever understand 'my' vision, just theirs.

The only thing I do regret is not doing it much sooner. I was probably good enough to go freelance in marketing 5 years ago, but I didn't believe in myself. I had controlling bosses that were very demanding and I always felt downtrodden even though sometimes I was more skilled than them. Now that I have that confidence, I use It wisely and as long as you are prepared to work harder than you have ever worked and for just enough to get by… you might just be a lot happier? Give me beans on toast eaten with a smile any day of the week… Leave unhappy steak eating for politicians!

The basics; Life is too short to spend it worrying about a job you hate. You don't get another go at life, why not make something monumental of it?

Look at the bigger picture, what have you *actually* got to lose? Your dignity? Well mine buggered off when I told the public about my frequent toilet habits… Dignity is over-rated, happiness is what really matters.

Make it happen don't wait for it to fall in your lap, YOU CAN DO THIS, I BELIEVE YOU CAN because I did and I know what it takes. Don't give up. You owe it to yourself.

♥ Friday, September 29, 2017

It's FRIDAAAAY! I've just woken up in my third hotel room in 4 days but today it is for VERY EXCITING reasons! I enjoyed a lovely late dinner and drinks with an old friend last night and we reminisced about pony times gone by. It was wonderful, I love taking myself back 5 years and looking at how much different things are now. I woke up this morning so determined to make the next 5 years just as monumental. Starting RIGHT now. It is so important to grab life by the big hairy bollocks as soon as you can. It's refreshing, gives you a buzz like no other and can truly make you feel alive. I'm grabbing today, and tomorrow and the day after... I feel different, I feel totally in control of my own fate and you can too.

I have just spent a few minutes (WAY longer!) browsing photos, I have chosen 3. The first is where I've come from. The innocence, the filthy face, the loving family and grounded hard-working roots that have always been in me somewhere and always will be. The second; a photo of me doing something I never thought possible JUMPING A BLOODY GREAT JUMP- the present. I am NOT brave, I couldn't do it every day but I know I CAN do it. And finally, the future, happiness- the end goal, what it all boils down to, smiling at my husband in front of our little house.

Look at where you've come from, what motivates you and what you want from life. WHAT DO YOU ACTUALLY WANT???? Be honest with yourself. Feel the buzz, the passion, the love and work for it. I believe in doing as much as you can for as little in return (I'm no Lord Sugar!!) because on this basis you will be wealthy in far more areas than money. You will be repaid in gratitude, loyalty and love, and isn't that what really makes us rich?

Go, make a start today, feel inspired, be fearless and remember don't give two shits what people think if they're pissing on your chips... they'll wish they were nicer when you fly off on a magic carpet of success without the smell of urine! Fly free my loves, YOU (and only you) are in control of today.

THE END IS NIGH

With only one event left, I started feeling a little bit sad and despondent that I hadn't managed to bring myself to enter another BE100 before the end, it's likely that we were capable, I just didn't feel ready mentally to put that kind of pressure on myself. Our confidence is so fragile that if I broke it, it might be that I never signed up for eventing EVER again! And who's keeping tabs anyway, I like 90, I feel safe there and that is where I plan to remain for next season too. Maybe even an 80 to get us going. It's about me and my horse, who gives a shit what other people think.

I had heard my last event at Norton Disney was set to be one of the kindest on the circuit, so I looked forward with excitement this time not full of dread to the week's countdown.

We went to our regular outing in the week leading up to the D Day BE Day, this time it was evening dressage where we celebrated a super win in the Elementary class and a second place in the Novice. What a confidence boost. I even got on from the side of the trailer without any help too!!! SHOCK HORROR – I wouldn't have done that 8 months ago! That brim full confidence was short lived though, why does it have to be so bloody hard?

♥ Wednesday, October 18, 2017

So here's the thing... I went to dressage Friday and what with one thing and another (avoidance), I didn't ride Saturday, Sunday, Monday or Tuesday - not once, not either of the horses! Yep, that's right! I have my last BE event this Sunday and I can't even get on and go for a mooch round the block FFS! One step forward blah blah blah!

I woke up this morning and felt lethargic, I felt stale, I felt like I just want to keep pet ponies not riding ones! But something hit me, it was around 10am... something spurred my soulless arse into gear. I got dressed in actual jodhpurs and seized the moment! It was like something inside me took over. I arrived at the yard expecting a royal fuss when taking Pat away from Bender but NOTHING! A whinny and then head down eating. I think I may have been looking for excuses...

I tacked him up, I got ready and off we went, off the yard in the wrong direction! (I usually go the same way because superstition tells me I will survive going right and not left!) but in for a penny! I trotted for 15 minutes, cantered for 5 and then had a walk break, back into trot I dared myself to jump a set of rails outside Auntie Smurph's house and we did it! Another stretch of canter and another set of rails and wall (which was my goal jump when I first arrived here!) WE JUMPED IT... perfect stride, galloped away down the field together, so merrily skipping along I could have cried!

Back into canter up another field and lined him up at a hedge... he backed off it a bit and I almost wished I hadn't done it, but I was there 'Yip Yipping' and we bloody flew that one too! We walked home grinning from ear to ear after the best ride I've had in forever.

Now, I know it's not hugely safe to jump alone like that but there were farm workers around and I had my phone, Daddy

Carrot got my compulsory "I'm hacking" photo and would be awaiting my safe return text! But what a frigging ride! After all week of building it up, of dodging the most wonderful bullet... I bit it and it was GREAT!

If like me, you are dreading it today, grab this nugget of courage and run like the wind for your saddle...you can do it. I know you can! I hope you have a just as wonderful ride and fill your heart back up with happiness, I'm full to the brim and very happy to share it xxx

~

I do this a lot, avoid riding because the thought of it can fill me with dread even now. But I get there and get on and even if it isn't a good ride, I have never ever regretted a single second in the saddle, ever. That's the point isn't it – the pressure we put on ourselves, if we couldn't ever ride again… how much would you wish you had just one more go at it.

I've been writing this book that you are reading for weeks now, and I have told myself that this crucial week to get it completed, that I am not allowed to ride until it's finished. Well, I've cleaned my tack ready, picked out my new boots for Pat and Bender and I'm just slogging through the last few chapters because I WANT TO RIDE. I actually want to. – You're probably best not to read any further because I'll be rushing it and it'll likely be full of typos!

So, here it is; the very last one, the grand finale, the home straight.

BUT WAIT…

♥ Saturday, October 21 2017

What is our weak point...? Skinnies... Just walked the course and guess WHAT! 5 out of 18 jumps for tomorrow are slippery little skinnies. I'm loose in the leavings but CHALLENGE ACCEPTED!

EVENT REPORT – Norton Disney BE90

So, here goes... (tissues advisory, wine compulsory) I'm struggling to know where to start so as usual, I'll take you back to Friday night....

This week had been a write-off, I lacked enthusiasm at the start and finally pulled my finger out of my arse on Thursday with an excellent ride, jump and grin! Friday night I took Grain Pirate Dan for a confidence boosting ride of his life and we sailed the hedge again and a set of rails and had a few good canters.

With two good confidence boosting hacks and I was feeling much better about Sunday morning eventing!

Saturday, I got up and went early to walk the course, rather unusually minus a hangover! I came back white as a sheet. Now, I don't know about anyone else but fear triggers Adrenalin in me and it either spurs me up or knocks me out. Well, I slept for 2 hours when I got home! By which time Storm Brian Big Blows had come to town, just in time for me to run through my dressage test! Fucking salt in the wound my friend, salt in the wound!

I trundled down the field and bizarrely Pat couldn't give two shits about storm Brian and he went the best he's gone in ages! I do love him dearly! Everything packed up, pony plaited and ready for our 6am departure, I went home for fish and chips and a glass of wine!

At this point I felt okay about not being able to get round the XC, we've got plenty of time to practice over winter and if I enjoy the dressage and don't cry getting on it'll have been a good day!

I woke up this morning and my mate Windy Brian was still pounding twigs at my front door; I was so close to bailing out. Auntie Smurph was taxi today and she said it was my call... Urgh! Mine, my decision. After much deliberation on the loo, and a message to my beloved best friend at 5am, I decided to pull my knickers up (literally) and get a grip.

It was still pretty dark on arrival and after a twitchy bum loose horse moment in the car park where a chestnut figure was careering past us, the mount of death almost brought on a little cry. I was leading him round fretting about it for ages, I'm very lucky with Auntie Smurph; she does not judge me for being scared or irrational or asking strangers for cigarettes!

Finally, I got on and he settled really quickly in the warm up! Into the test and he was so obedient, I had a lovely ride. We happily plopped round for what I thought deserved a 28ish. Lucky for us we got a 29.3, with a slightly samey sheet of 7s, nothing more, nothing less. He's never got less than an 8 for his free walk but today lucky 8 was what gave us that sub 30 yet again. We were in the top ten marks in the section again so I was very happy with that.

Now to the phase that permanently lets us down. I was so terribly nervous again, I ran to the green loo box and stayed for a minute hoping it would lock fast and I'd just have to stay there for the day! I had a cigarette, yep that's right, and I got on... We warmed up and I have to say, I felt 100% more confident than I ever have in this phase. I'm putting that down to the French Knights in Turquoise Capes who came to visit a couple of weeks ago... they brought with them my new Voltaire Design saddle that was now holding my leg in place, keeping me in balance and to be honest I worried so much less.

I went in the ring, I didn't panic, I didn't rush, the fences came one by one and I addressed them all as they happened. And it really was that basic because look...WE WENT FUCKING CLEAR! Clear! We went clear! Our second ever affiliated clear round EVER! I was so frigging delighted; I can't even put it into words right now.

Oh Crikey! Now it meant something, the course I had resigned myself to getting eliminated at, now meant a placing. URGH!

The pit of my empty stomach still managed to churn as I got changed for the death phase. On board and into the warm up, I jumped a jump and went to put my number down on the board of people ready to face their doom. However, if I had been wearing my number, I might have been able to! A quick spin back to the trailer to put my forgotten bib on and I was back warming up trying to pretend not to be flustered. It wasn't that long until I was called over to face my doom.

In the start box I have learnt not to cry or whinge or turn for home and instead just be still, enjoy these last few moments of aliveness and breathe without burping bile.

"5...4...3...2...1"! Bang, like a rocket we soared out the box like our pants were on fire! Number 1 always jumps crap, I never get a good shot and this was no different, it was a green palisade type jump that looked nothing, but by Jove did it make me buck my ideas up! Number 2, a wooden box fence jumped very well indeed, a gallop around the corner to a dip and up a bank to 3, a roll top; I got a lovely jump over that and 'yeehaaared' my way to the croquet set at 4, he backed off that and I howled at him and smacked his shoulder with my whip, he sailed it enormously in reply! The first skinny was 5, off a turn where I knew there was an alternative route, I didn't take it! I held my line and kicked like stink and over we got! YES bloody yes! One down! A gallop up to a log for 6 and a skinny log on the mound for 7a, down the bank to 7b, a skinny brush, well who ever said; look straight ahead and mind your knees... I frigging well looked ahead, locked him on and kicked... we flew it! It felt amazing! I could have stopped there and been ecstatic!

But alas... Down to 8 and 9 a set of double rails and palisade that both flew by without trouble, up to 10, the steps (2 of) ping ping! Up we climbed! Down to 11 another downhill into a box house skinny! We were on bloody fire! He soared over it, and we were away. I'm pretty sure his neck was sore from all the patting by now! 12 was the coffin and trellis and he popped through no bother on to 13, one I toyed with the alternative again... bugger it, he was jumping for his life today and so was I, we went for the direct route and it paid off! Only one skinny left Yip yip!

There it was the water barrels! He flew and splashed his way through the water and down to the house at 15! We were going for it now... 16a&b and 17 were all in a line and jumped very nicely with a howl and huge pat we galloped to the last, sailed the shot gun cartridge and burst through the finish!

Yyeeeeeeeeeeaaaaaaaaaaaasssssss!! The absolute best ride of my life. I cannot explain that feeling, once you've felt it there's nothing that compares to sailing through the finish line having ridden your heart out to end on your dressage score!!

A double clear! I've only ever had one other and that was at Chilham back at the start... it all came together again today! What a feeling, what a day, what a horse!! 29.3 double clear! We finish 6th in our section!

I am so immensely grateful for the support and confidence I have been given by every single one of you on this page. This was for you today. You made me this brave, you got me through this BE season and you earned this feeling too. I thank you with everything I have.

Another huge thank you to my wonderful sponsors and everyone else who has supported us this year, I really wouldn't have been able to do it without you. It's humbling that you have taken a gamble with an average rider and her average horse who thanks to you, appear to have become anything but average.

I am sobbing with pride over what we have achieved, anything is possible. Never ever give up on a dream. Ever.

Love, as always

Vic and Pat Xxx

So, that's it my friends, not a dry eye in the house. I get quite emotional these days, every time I think back to the days of hiding my saddle and pretending that I forgot it so I didn't have to ride. The times when every reply to 'did you have a good ride?' was a lie because I didn't even get out of the car. I cry, not with sadness, but with pride, pride for what I have overcome, or how I still feel a lot of the time and regardless of that fear I bloody well get on with it. I have never done anything this well or worked this hard in my whole life. That's the point isn't it? Hard work really does pay off. Be passionate, set goals, change goals, make a life to be proud of.

– What are you waiting for?

♥ Wednesday, October 25, 2017

I have a question for you... I was sat pondering my 2017 eventing season and how far I have come in my confidence. Not just confidence as a rider but as a person. I'm more independent, I'm stronger and more able to love and give help to people because of this strength.

I'd like to know, what is bravery to you? What defines success and failure? For me, bravery is feeling scared out of your skin and still going through the motions, it's giving it all you can despite your crippling fear and learning to enjoy it.

I've learnt to enjoy always being a little bit out of control. We ride horses, you will NEVER be 100% in control. Fact. Learn to have fun, train yourself to smile through a spook or sigh at a stop, the other options are cross stitch or chess... Success is in the tiniest step, less palm sweating, an open field canter, 3 days riding in a row... it's looking back and realising how little you thought you could achieve at the beginning.

18 months ago I thought I'd never ever enjoy getting on my horse ever again, I never imagined smiling over a jump or screaming with joy through the XC finish line! I know that I've taken hundreds of tiny steps this year and some massive ones right back to where we started but the success is in the trying.

My biggest success to date is getting on Pat by myself at Shelford BE... my proudest moment to date (normally I get Daddy Carrot to feed and hold so I don't feel so scared). Something so trivial to so many people but such a huge step for me.

Try to let go, give less of a sh*t what it looks like, what people think, drop the stigma, don't be afraid to look like a d*ckhead... it WILL change your life, I know it will.

Failure is not an option, as far as I'm concerned it doesn't exist. The only time I will ever fail is if I don't try in the first place... failing off isn't failure, nor is coming last, learn from it and you will never fail again.

The opportunities that have opened up to us because of this public display of fear conquering have been amazing. I was very kindly offered and accepted a column in a national equestrian magazine and by the time you read this you will likely know which one (the best one!!). I have been invited to some amazing places to do some brilliant things; taking the course walk at Blenheim Palace Horse Trials for Falpro was a highlight with memories I will treasure forever. We have lots to look forward to as well. I have signed some wonderful contracts for next year with some impressive companies that will help me to grow this mission I am on. I won't stop until I know I can't help people anymore. As long as what I write gets people out of bed, keeps them smiling and helps them worry less – what more can I ask for?

So, what does the future hold for us?

Well, Pat will have a rest, he likes to be doing a job so it won't be too long but I will let his fitness down for November and December ready to start getting him back to work in January for next season (Yep! That's right, there's a 'next season'!). I have loved being part of the eventing community for the most part and next year we will be campaigning hard to make sure the equestrian community is kind and welcoming for everyone that wants to have a go. Our Wimpy world is growing and it provides a safe place full of encouraging people to help each other and that's what it's all about.

Bender will be developing his gentlemanly nature and hopefully his confidence in being alone so that we can enter into the world of SHOWING. This is new for me, I haven't done a lot of showing but I have the rather ambitious goal of riding at The Horse of the Year Show so I better work as hard at this as I have at eventing this year! And if he doesn't want to do that, we'll just go hacking instead!

Daddy Carrot is going to ride a little more if he can find some suitable underpants. I think he is much happier being chief in charge of studs and photography though!

And I will be practicing my show jumping, writing more, learning to make decent Yorkshire puddings and making every day the best that it can be. From now on, I will be living life for us, for my boys and not in fear of other people's judging eyes.

Look back often at your life and how far you have come but don't linger. If there is something in life that you want to achieve you must first make a plan (do it TODAY), you need to work hard for it like you've never worked before and adapt your plans along the way. You must also remember to tread your own path because although a trodden path may be easier to walk down, there is likely nothing left for you at the end.

You cannot change what has already been, but you can make what hasn't happed yet downright bloody brilliant. You have that power, the power to change YOUR tomorrow – what is it that you're waiting for?

Over the page there is a list of things for you to remember, things to remind yourself of. These things will keep you going when you face a rocky road or difficult chapter, for when you need it most. Read them – out loud if you can, keep in mind those things and take those bold steps forward, you won't ever regret anything you can learn from.

Important things to remember Part II

You know the drill, tear it out and keep it on your person...

Something that is absolutely pivotal in aiding confidence for those riding, competing, tobogganing, etc. is knowing that it is ABSOLUTELY 100% FINE TO F*CK IT UP... if you don't die, you can only learn from it.

The bottom line is, those that mind don't matter and those that matter don't mind. The people that I love and who love me; they are supportive, they are encouraging, and they are worth one hundred of every single one of the Chip P*ssers!

I have been scared, I have felt fear, I have been consumed by worry and stress to the point where I cannot think ahead of that day or even hour without feeling overwhelmed. It's more common than you think and it is NOTHING to be ashamed of.

Fake smiles are easy to detect when you start smiling real ones that burst with joy, remember that.

It's much better for your own mental health to live a life never judging or keeping score. Putting other people's feelings first will make you feel fulfilled in a way no chocolate bar or glass of wine ever can.

My advice to anyone thinking of getting an ex-racehorse (or any horse for that matter) is that if you don't have the patience to complete a rubix cube wearing a blindfold, forget it!

It might appear sometimes, that other people have far great chances of success than you because of what they have. Material possessions and a wonderful indoor school won't get you anywhere without hard work.

Look at the bigger picture, what have you actually got to lose? Your dignity? Well mine b*ggered off when I told the public about my frequent toilet habits… Dignity is over-rated, happiness is what really matters.

Make it happen don't wait for it to fall in your lap, YOU CAN DO THIS, I BELIEVE YOU CAN because I did and I know what it takes. Don't give up. You owe it to yourself.

Don't ever think for a second that you get anywhere in life without sacrifice and hard work.

Be passionate, set goals, change goals, make a life to be proud of – what if there wasn't going to be a tomorrow, then what would your today look like?

A CARROT'S EYE VIEW:

AN INTERVIEW WITH DADDY CARROT

Sum up eventing in ten words or less

It isn't as bad as watching dressage on its own.

Describe a day out eventing with your wife and her horse.

It starts way before the actual day with a gradual build-up of apprehension. The night before usually means her drinking more than I would if I had to get up at 5am, travel three hours and then ride all day. First thing in the morning my wife tends to sneak out of bed and disappear into the toilet for a while. Sometimes more than once.

Even though we get up at the crack of sparrow's fart, there is never any time to eat anything or have a cup of tea. We go straight down to the yard where hopefully she's loaded all of her cr*p in the horsebox the night before so we don't have to linger about too long. She won't let me drive her precious cargo so we have to drive at around 10mph and it takes far too long to get there.

On arrival she will always scurry off to some tent next to the bacon roll tent, but there's no time for bacon – I know not to ask this anymore. Next, we go back to the lorry and she dresses him up in diamonds. She is NOT chatty at this point. I am usually left in the rain holding the horse while she visits the toilet again.

The first part of the day is down in a grass field about a mile and a half from the horse box. There are loads of people trotting and walking and trotting and walking and trotting and walking. It's like watching paint dry. At this point I take photos of her warming up, which apart from the other riders in the background, look exactly like the photos of the test.

When she gets near the white planks they beep a car horn, which is good because then I know the actual test has started. I know it's finished when she's smiling and heading towards me.

We go back to the horsebox (back past the food vendors from earlier – I mentally note what's on offer and bide my time) then she changes clothes and the boring bit is officially over. Hopefully we haven't parked too far away from each bit, because walking ten miles isn't much fun when you haven't got a horse to help you.

In the show jumping warm up (which is always near the food vendors) my job is to stand at the most dangerous spot in the middle and put the poles back on the jumps after she knocks them down. Invariably this means I become the official show jumping warm-up helper, picking up the poles for EVERYONE. Tedious. Around this stage she will appear slightly less nervous, but may still snap at me if I get in the way.

Show jumping is probably the easiest bit to spectate. I have no idea what's happening in the dressage and I only see the first and last jump of the cross country. Pole down = bad. Pole still up = good. This appeals to my logic.

Experience has taught me that immediately after the show jumping is the opportune moment to sneak off to get myself some food. She is likely to be far too nervous about the cross country to care where I've gone.

Back at the horse box for the final wardrobe change of the day. This time into something far more protective than a piece of tweed cloth. By now she has usually lost a bit of the nervous tension and has subsided into a kind of morbid acceptance of certain death.

I watch her over the first couple of jumps on the course which seem to be a bit smaller and easier than the middle ones and then wait for her to come back to the finish. I like to find out the optimum time for the course and keep track on my watch. She usually goes too fast but it doesn't matter because at the finish she becomes what I like to call, "High on Horse". She's finally enjoying herself now it's over!

Back at the horsebox I am almost ready for another bacon roll, but we have to wash him, put him in pyjamas, wrap stuff on his legs. Sometimes I get given a "manly" job like taking out the studs, thus warranting my presence for the last six hours.

Then we check the scores and see where she has finished, which can sometimes be a long wait for absolutely nothing. However, without fail she will always purchase several photographs to take home, despite me having well over 100 (free) pictures on the camera I brought with me.

What have you learnt most?

It is usually best not to say too much until the cross country is over. Just remain silent and close to hand like a dust pan and brush.

I have learnt not to arrange anything else on an event day. Despite what time she says you'll be done and home, it takes ALL day.

I've learnt that flip flops are frowned upon as event day attire. Turning up on a motorbike is also frowned upon.

The catering vans usually do the rounds of all the local events. Establish your favourite and stick with it. With a bit of luck, the vendor may come to recognise your loyalty and reward you with extra bacon.

Most of all, I admire my wife for her passion and dedication and what she has achieved. I actually quite enjoy going and watching her ride and it isn't anywhere near as unbearable as I have just made out.

P.S. Always have a carrot in your pocket.

Love as always

Vic and Pat xxx

(And Bender and Daddy Carrot)

Part Three
How to get yourself off

"You always look so happy when you're riding...."

With thanks to…

My horses.

Every single one that has graced my life and that has touched my heart. Without them, none of this would exist. Without them, I would be a very different human (probably a wealthier one).

We owe so much to our horses; the tears that fall into their manes, the squeals of joy we share galloping down a stubble field, yet they remain so unassuming.

Horses do not know that we've had a bad day, yet they are always there.

For all of them.

So, here's the deal... my first ever event season ended on an absolute high. My placing at Norton Disney was the absolute icing on the 2017 cake. I came from the depths of confidence hell to conquer a BE100, complete several events and be a whisker away from Badminton Grassroots.

I had two amazing horses, ending the season buying my darling Bender (Sir Bentley) who came from a racehorse rehoming charity, and he fast became the apple of my eye alongside Pat. I was certain he would be destined for Horse of The Year show, as Pat was for Badminton, and I felt full to the brim with love and excitement.

But as with anything involving horses, basking in momentary bliss is exactly that. Momentary. You soon wake up to a cold, dark December and wonder what the hell you were thinking taking up this hobby. Instead you could have been cross stitching patterns of Salisbury Cathedral onto a piece of cloth in the warm, dry comfort of your front room. There would be no hay to buy, no mountains of sh*t to pick up in the field, no mud to scrape off before getting freezing cold and wet out on a very average ride. But there is something that keeps us going, there is something I struggle to put into words that keeps me from buying several thread colours and a donut bum cushion. It is that musky horse smell, the feeling of exhaustion, but still the remarkable ability to take on the world of full wheelbarrow pushing through a hail storm. It's the days you sob so hard into your horses' neck because only HE can understand. That is why we are all here, why you have picked up this book. You and me. We are those people and you get it, just like I do.

I hope you learn as much from this journey as I have, and I hope you can now see that if everything went according to plan, I'd have won the lottery years ago and they'd be no need for this nonsense at all!

MOMENTARY BLISS

Now, with the event season over, what I should probably have done is turn my horse away for a little rest. This appears to be common practice in the eventing world and I do get it, but Pat is a total knob after time off. Instead I thought I'd tackle some good positive dressage outings, while we were in the right frame of mind and leave his holidays until the New Year.

With Bender going SO well and after a little quiet time and time to settle in, I had really begun to up his workload and retraining. He had such an AMAZING attitude to life, that even after a week off I could tack him up and he was just like an old man with his slippers on and getting him going had me sweating. He would stand like a rock for me to get on and wouldn't ever dream of moving unless he has to. From the outset I decided to treat him like the old arm chair ride that I wanted him to become, and he really was 80% there already - some race horse eh?!

I hadn't really asked too much of him in the contact yet either, mainly because we had been concentrating on leg aids (forwards) and my seat aids for stopping! But we did have stop and go installed and so it was time to learn the frames that are required for his muscular comfort.

I am a very firm believer in 'building the bridge' - developing the muscles over the spine that my fat arse bounces on (especially with a TB having been inverted for most of their ridden lives), how can you get the head and neck lower if the bridge has collapsed under you...? A strong bridge is vital for them to drop the head and neck comfortably and be able to work in 'the outline' we ask… Or that's the way the theory of biomechanics works in my head!

Up until this point the contact and head/neck position had been a mixture of giraffe (for his balance) and peacock (because it avoids dealing with the contact). In a nutshell, I would keep a low, wide but consistent contact and do a lot of kicking!

To help him understand a bit more, I would make the giraffe moments not so pleasant for him and give a firmer feel for him to know it's not ideal. And then lifting and vibrating the rein on the peacock moments to 'oi oi' him out of that dipping. Consequently, I would have a lovely soft contact after about 15 minutes, and he was a very quick to learn when I spelt it out clearly. Of course, there would be inconsistencies but as soon as we had done a whole 20m circle with that shape and softness, he got to have a rest.

This is how I have trained all of my horses, and it has worked for me. I'm no expert but clear, definitive instructions and very obvious rewards are always a good starting point in my book.

I then spend his second 15 minutes (I would only do half an hour with him at this stage) encouraging a longer, lower frame. So that would mean more kicking to get his belly up and feeding the rein out with little squeezes of pressure and release, giving away as much as he will take. By the 5-minute point the penny usually drops, and he just exhales and plops into a lovely long frame. I always like to do this training in trot because you have that natural swing to work with. He would work like this consistently and very happily for 5 minutes through bends and changes of rein and gets lots of mega pats.

I just love this big boy so much. He's so loving and has firmly got his feet under the table.

Bender would do 3 days a week of work like this and 2-3 days on the long reins out around the little lanes near our yard. He wasn't massively settled for me to hack unescorted yet and this was something that started eating away at me a lot over the next couple of weeks.

2nd November 2017

Right... I'm on here because I need to offload. I don't often feel like this but today I do.

Do you ever just get days where you just want to cry.

I can't pin point a reason in particular either, I've asked the question; 'what's making you sad?' and I have no idea what the answer is.

People can look in from the outside and judge me wrongly sometimes, I hate that. I'm not rich in anything other than love, nor am I spoilt. Far from it. I work so hard that sometimes when you get criticized, it really feels very personal. Now, even though I work for myself, I still work a full time job - Crikey probably more hours than before! I still have a book to tie up in a fortnight and I have so much going on I just can't handle it.

I have a list as long as my arm to get done, 2 horses to ride (or Bender at the very least) and a mountain of washing to do. I need to go food shopping too because I have nothing to cook my Carrot for his tea, and all I want to do is curl up under a blanket and cry.

Yesterday I went out in my lunch break and followed the hunt on opening meet for a bit. Someone, a lovely, kind man who I have known for many, many years had a nasty fall and was air lifted to hospital. Things aren't looking good at the moment. This has made me worry a lot for him and his lovely family too. My mind is all over the place.

I want to be a cheery ray of sunshine but today I feel like an oozing sack of rabbit droppings. I need a cuddle and a kick up the arse I think. It's not often I have days like this but I feel so self-pitying and I bloody HATE it!

SNAP. OUT. OF. IT.!!

Seriously, I read this back now and I just want to slap myself! People have crappy days, people are allowed to wallow in their sads a bit, but please just think of how lucky you are, just for a second. Think about your current situation. Are you homeless? Are you in poverty to the point where you cannot eat unless you steal? Do you have the ability to breathe in and out and move around and feel something other than emptiness? How dare I not see that, and that's the thing… On days like this, I need to realise, not just how pathetic it is complaining about trivial shit, but how lucky I actually am.

I have friends, a job, my horses, my husband, my health, a family… it's endless and yet I allow myself to complain like this.

Well LESSON NUMBER ONE: Realise how lucky you are. Yes, things might not always feel perfect or go how you'd like them to. But you are so lucky to be alive. And for anyone feeling the same, go do what I just did... put on some mascara and go look in the mirror, tell yourself how wonderfully brilliant you are and flash yourself a boob... you'll laugh and then you'll realise things aren't so bad, just focus on that for five minutes whenever you feel those sads creeping in.

~

And when you do wake up not feeling your best, this is for you…

Imagine if today was all you had left to prove your worth, today is all you have left to make it count, to tell people how you feel and how much they mean to you. Imagine if today is your last ride, the last time you will ever get to feel the wind on your face and the cold in your toes as your horse gallops you across the grass.

What if it really was? How differently would today pan out for you?

Grab life by the big hairy testi-baubles today, don't wait for tomorrow because what if it doesn't come?

Love like it's now or never, ride like it's your last time and laugh like no one's watching you! You can be as wonderful as you like, you've got it in there… let it out. You won't regret it. Stop worrying about what you look like, how you come across and how life may or may not work out for you.

Live for today and I promise you, it will be the best bloody day you've ever had!

Go… bloody well do it now!!

Go on!!!

~

Anyhow... I digress! Back to my blissful November!

Now, two weeks in and I was happily hacking the boys out on ride and lead hacks and I was also climbing up the field gate to clamber onto my arm chair of a horse ... BENDER! He was SO relaxed out hacking with Pat, and as Daddy carrot is determined to ride more, I thought I had better prepare the horse for a novice jockey!

With Carrot wanting to set sail on his maiden Bender voyage that coming Sunday, I did everything I thought Daddy Carrot might do...I clambered onto him kicking him on the rump as I swung my leg over, took an age to do the girth up... fed him a whole packet of mints and guess what…? He did not move an inch!

Off we went striding out in front the whole way, hardly a spook or shy, and he is just the comfiest ride. We had a good trot and a little bit of canter (all in a pretty decent outline too) I was absolutely ecstatic with him! Like he had just got me round Badminton happy! It's the little things with horses that keep me going and this might have seemed such a small feat to most people but to me, it was the best day EVER!

Minding your Manners

When Bender arrived I think it is fair to say that he had been a bit of a Feral Beryl and just turned away in a field for a few years. I stand by the importance of good ground manners in all aspects of horsemanship, and sometimes these pony ground manners need keeping in check. It's also a great exercise to do when you don't feel like riding. It's good to see them working on the ground so you know areas you need to work on and see how they're improving.

Pat is VERY polite almost a little too shy to handle at times, so it just involves a lunge for him, lunging over a single pole on a big loop. Lots of forward and collecting in the trot, timing the pole on the ask for forward. It gets him pushing and round and working his muscles.

Bender next, back on the long reins... he has been getting a bit upset and excitable coming home from a walk/ride and it isn't very nice when you're on top, so today we went up and down the drive in both directions 5 or 6 times before I took him in a field away from everybody and did a ten minute lunge.

He settled down to work after 5 minutes of stressing, but as soon as he settled and did a few loops in a nice walk and trot, I put him away. He will do this every day now until we break his anxiety patterns. As soon as he is calm and does a little bit, back to the field as a reward.

There might be other ways of dealing with this, but I can't just ride him in the field next to his mates forever!! I'm toying with the idea of taking him on holiday down the road for a few weeks where they have arenas and coloured poles to break the attachment to home, but I'll do another week of today's routine and see where we are first.

Winter is hard to maintain momentum at the best of times, but it'll be so worth it in the end.

~

I was certainly finding this new horse and his stressy personality a challenge and the thought of taking him on a hack filled me with the fear of death. I was really struggling to bond with him because of that. We had a lot of issues with him in field too. Our yard is really small, just my two boys and Auntie Smurph with her two. It does mean that none of them would ever be alone in the field, but Bender wasn't happy unless Pat was there. This also meant my rides on Pat were being increasingly fraught too. Every time I took Pat away, Bender would run the fence line until he was white with sweat and be constantly calling to his buddy. I tried separating the field in half, I tried a calmer, I tried having him next to the sheep and next to other horses, but he wasn't interested. He just pined for Pat.

My heart was breaking and I was very aware that all of the confidence that I had spent all season building was coming crashing down around my ears. Something had to change. I made a few calls to people that I thought might be able to take him on training livery but the costs were so high, I didn't really have the money to put him on full livery. So after a call with my friend Piers who owns a local equestrian centre, I packed Bender's suitcase and he got collected the next day. He was going on part livery at Willow Banks, where I could go and ride him myself to bring the costs down but where they would help me out with one end of the day.

I found myself struggling to muster the enthusiasm to go over there, my heart and my confidence were bruised, and although I loved the updates from Piers on how well he was going, I felt really sad about the whole situation and in honesty, full of regret.

25th November 2017

Here it is; honesty.

I haven't ridden for two weeks. 13 days to be precise, and I feel like total and utter shite about it.

There is a lot going on, it's too windy, the book, bla bla bla... EXCUSES!! My Mum has been in hospital since Wednesday and I've spent at least 4 hours a day with her the last two days, but again another excuse!

I'll tell you what, I feel selfish. I have two lovely horses - a luxury not everyone has but here I am, an ungrateful cow, not riding them.

I'm having a day of refocus. The book has gone to print today, the calendars are done, and I have all Pink Thursday orders placed at the embroidery company.

I just feel all over the place, I want to relax and get excited about Christmas but I'm feeling constantly on edge about something.

It's not even 8.30 and I'm stressing, worrying, and trying to be better. What I'm actually going to do is get dressed and go take Pat for a ride. Just us, just like it used to be.

These problems, worries and things I'm stressing about are so trivial. I know this, writing it all down helps me to see it. I haven't laughed in ages, so that's my aim today (look out). My hair is bushy, I have a spot, my eyebrows haven't been pencilled in and I've got eye bogeys, but HERE I AM. I've also got Ringworm, a wart on my foot and bunions (I'm dealing with it, alright!!).

If you are like me and have things on your plate that seem overwhelming, spew them out... I'm all ears. It's made me feel better already.

~

I did in fact go for a ride that day and I got a glimpse of what life used to be like when I wasn't stressing about Bender or money or something else! Why do we do this to ourselves? Put ourselves under this extreme pressure and get wound up about it? I was on a roll it seemed and the weekend had arrived, with no plans in place I had the bright idea of getting some photos together for the blog;

27th November 2017

Yesterday I managed to find a small slice of MOJO hidden in the depths of my moth ball infested spirit. I grabbed my Carrot and we headed off down to the yard.

I tacked up Pat and hopped on. I try not to plan what I'm going to do with him at the moment and just let the mood take us, so I don't feel disheartened not having fulfilled the plan.

After 10 minutes of trotting about the field, I jumped my one and only jump (yes, we have more coming soon I hope) it was a 2ft ish cross pole and he felt GREAT and I felt SAFE. I had my new jumping saddle on, not the dressage saddle, so I thought 'bugger it, in for a penny'. I laid out a couple of placing poles and popped the cross to an upright. Now, anyone that knows me will know that I have a certain stigma with jumping uprights, I fear them falling more than any other jump. But without any more wings, I was forced into it.

We started it at about 85cms and jumped it in both directions, then popped it up to 105 and came around and jumped it a few more times without terrifying myself!!

I felt so happy to be doing a jump, it might sound pathetic, but I felt capable and confident, and it really showed. The difference in my lower leg from just a couple of months ago is VERY noticeable and I have the saddle to thank for that.

I also went over to see Bender that weekend too, he was going SO well and really wasn't that stressed at all over at Willow Banks, not like he was a home. He was often left until last in the stable without a fuss, and his educational work was coming on really well too. I was getting regular updates from Piers about his progress and videos of his ridden work which looked great, sympathetic but no nonsense. I had so much hope that we could work this out and get him home in a few weeks, it was back to momentary bliss….

DECEMBER 2017

TIMES OF UNCERTAINTY

With a fairly noneventful week been and gone, my Mum given the all clear to come home in the next few days, I realised my anxiety was sky high again. I had been seriously nervous about something for a while. I couldn't put my finger on it, but I was about to find out. On Saturday 2nd December I had agreed to speak in public.

Most of you will by now, see through the façade of laughter and frivolity and know that I am a very insecure person underneath all the bravado. I've probably always been that way, and actually, I am usually quite comfortable in my own skin. But the thought of talking in front of people and on my own was one of the scariest things I could think of doing. But it was for the most wonderful charity and I couldn't possibly let them down with an excuse of FEAR... I was supposed to be the one conquering bloody fear, not running from it!

Anyway, we packed up the car with an over-night bag and made our way to the Wobbleberries Awards Night somewhere in the depths of the Midlands. I didn't prepare a speech or anything else for that matter, I wanted to be real and that doesn't come from reading off a sheet, or so I thought. So, with a rough introduction planned, I hoped other things would spring into my mind after that bit was over!

On arrival, I was greeted by the lovely founders of the Wobbleberries charity, and then by the other speaker for the evening, Andrew Hoy. Yeah that's right! The gold medallist, the international superhero. And media trained, comfortable speaking in public, Andrew was my partner in entertaining crime for the evening!

Anyway, I was up first so I was very relieved! I started by asking everyone in the room to shut their eyes… like always. I have found after doing a couple of these that people usually do as they're told when you've got a microphone in your hand and have the power to single them out at any moment! I then ask anyone who has felt fear around horses and riding, to raise their hand. Seriously, I feel something so magical when I'm standing in front of a room full of people all with their hands in the air. Even Andrew Hoy had his hand up. Covered head to toe in goose bumps, I welled up good and proper. Right there, in that moment… that was it, where I knew I felt at home; making a difference to these people. I talked about my experience with fear and I felt very emotional at one point, I dare say those there felt it too. I read a chapter from the book and that always gets me right in the feels. It's real you see, and although these books and social media, and all the crap that goes with it might look like a load of fun and be entertaining for everyone. My fear and journey is so real it physically hurts inside sometimes. I still battle with confidence and fear every single day, and I probably will for the whole of my life, but I won't ever let it beat me.

I have felt scared, I have felt desperation, I have felt like giving up on life, but I tell you what the most wonderful bit is, I have also found something from somewhere each time and fought through it all. You don't need to be the best, the bravest or create a Freddie Mercury legacy, you just need to find that strength to drag your arse out of the dark days. The rest you can worry about later. **LESSON NUMBER TWO: SURVIVAL.**

Survive, and worry about all the other shit later. Get through today, get through that week, get through that hour if that's as far as you can see. Just get through. Happiness, fulfilment, pride, comfort; that will all come in time, I promise. -But you need to survive first. Chances are, as soon as you strip it down that far, you'll find yourself recovering much quicker and laughing at how a chocolate Santa, under the foil, looks awfully like a giant erect willy!

Whilst we are on a 'getting to know you' mission, I thought it might be fun to list 30 things you might not have known about me. Here goes...

1. Favourite smell? Hot horse, you know the sweaty smell after a jumping session or the smell of the steam in the air when you gather at a covert post gallop out hunting - that smell. Or cat paws, they smell a bit like popcorn.

2. Biggest fear? Losing the people I love. Hands down. I am shit scared when Pat bronchs with me but nothing comes close to loss.

3. Favourite pizza? Black olive and Palma ham... I LOVE a thin crust too, none of that doughy stuff!

4. Favourite Flower? Roses, Honeysuckle or hydrangea, or Wisteria if I could get the bloody thing to grow!

5. Favourite breed of dog? Not a huge doggy person but I like the non-stinky kind!

6. Favourite place to visit? Christmas markets or my Mum and Dads for Sunday dinner!

7. Roller Coasters? Definitely not, maybe a steady log flume.

8. Favourite Ice Cream? Homemade (with far too much condensed milk), strawberry.

9. Pet peeve? Eating with your mouth open or hearing people being nasty about others.

10. Shorts or jeans? I dislike both in equal measures, I'm a chino/legging or skirt person! Jeans make me feel FAT, they're restrictive and scratchy and I haven't found a pair that don't make me feel monstrously fat yet!

11. What are you listening to right now? My typing?! I'm writing a book if you hadn't noticed!

12. Colour of your vehicle? Pearlescent white!! Not just white… oh no, Alfa Romeo kindly named the dingey, off white of my cheap hatchback something far more fancy! – It's not fancy, it's dented and full of horse items that smell worse than Pat's show day excrement!

13. Colour of eyes? Green/hazel – Oh and while we're at it, I'm not naturally ginger. Mousey brown with notes of auburn but it's what suits me best I think and now I've got a fuck ton of grey hairs, I will always colour it!

14. Favourite Foods? Blue cheese, prosciutto, creme brûlée

15. Favourite Holiday? Seriously, anywhere with my Carrot that doesn't bankrupt us that is hot without too many flying insects. Ha ha ha… pretty much leaves us with Skegness for that one hot day of the British Summer then!

16. Night Owl or Day Person? Day, I can't stay up late… I'm nodding off on the sofa usually around 9pm.

17. Favourite day of the week? Saturday, oooo or maybe Friday afternoon. It's like, what do you prefer; Christmas Eve or Christmas Day… is the anticipation better than the actual?!

18. Do you have a nickname? Well, I'm almost certainly not a Vicky, it's just not my name! But Vic is fine :)

19. Favourite Music? Dolly Parton

20. Tattoos? None! I don't like paying for pain.

21. Do you like to cook? Yes, very much.

22. Beer or Wine? Wine, but only good wine... a Chablis, Gavi, Rioja, Tempranillo, Marlborough, Malbec... I love good wine, but there isn't much I dislike more than bad wine!

23. How's your driving? I'd say pretty good. I used to drive a lot and I was very good, but now I'm motoring less, it's got a bit wayward!

24. Do you wear perfume? Yes, most days

25. If so, what kind? Lancôme

26. Favourite colour? PINK! If you hadn't guessed.

27. Do you like vegetables? Yes, all of them I think!

28. Do you work out? Never, apart from riding, the only exercise I do is walking to and opening the fridge!

29. Do you wear glasses? No but I definitely should.

30. Favourite season? Autumn or winter. I like wrapping up warm and I LOVE mulled wine, open fires, dark nights, big jumpers, fluffy socks... I'd sacrifice dry fields and clean horses for that any day!

3 Fascinating Facts:

I was runner up Miss Lincolnshire 2008

I have been a contestant on the X-Factor, didn't get on the telly though.

I am absolutely terrified of the dentist.

Back to it.

So, it's mid-December and Bender has been in the new yard for nearly a week. He's doing SO well and I might just be getting a little carried away, but…

I have just got all the dates in the diary for HOYS qualifiers! I mean, call me optimistic but, I don't see why this isn't something we should be aiming for. Everyone needs a goal, right? The Horse of the Year Show is something I have dreamed of for many years, and having always bought cheap ex-racers that haven't always been that well behaved or that well put together, I've never made it.

The HOYS qualifiers are all over the country and on writing them down I soon realised that I might need to take out a bank loan or seriously reconsider bringing my planned Lottery win forward by a few years! They start in April and run through to August, around one a month, but none of them very bloody local!

Just to add, we will be entering the SEIB Search For A Star Racehorse to Riding horse class, which is for anyone that owns a horse that has raced under rules in the UK and Ireland.

At this point, I didn't know what he would be like at a show, I didn't have any of the gear I needed, and I also hadn't managed to canter a 20 meter circle or trot in a straight line yet but they were all forgotten when I visualised Bender and I in that big sparkly arena. Drummers playing us in and the music singing us into our final gallop down the long side. My Carrot on the side lines holding a fancy show rug embroidered with 'Team Bender' and me; smiling like an asylum escapee as the judge pulls us in in first place! I could see it now; Vic and Bender ROR champions, nothing else seemed to matter much.

December 10th 2017

Today has already been one of the happiest days ever. I've been feeling a bit groggy this week and with so much to do it was really not good timing.

I got up early and went for a frosty mooch on Pat around our favourite ride, losing almost 2 hours catching up on chit chat with Auntie Smurph, which always makes me happy. Then back for sausages and Christmas snuggles with my Carrot.

At 2pm we drove up to have my first ride on Bender in his new residence. He has been with Piers and his team at Willow Banks since last week and I am just utterly astounded at the difference in his manners in general.

Piers has been lunging him in the Pessoa, and really getting him working forward and round. I thought it was time to be the pilot in his new environment, and I can report that Bender went the best he has ever gone.

We just did a few circles in walk, trot AND canter, and my word... the softness, the ease of the canter which I haven't really worked on at all since I've had him. I could have cried with delight.

He felt so balanced and so relaxed, far more than Pat sometimes. He was lazy though and this was really hard to adjust for me. Pat is SO sharp of my leg, and I found this very exhausting indeed.

I can't tell you how happy I am though. I was truly in despair over his separation anxiety and I thought I had reached the end of the line, but all my worries have disappeared.

He isn't calling, napping, getting anxious in the stable even though he can't directly see another horse.

For anyone dealing with this awful issue with your horses, there is hope, there is happiness to be found, and today I am happier than I've been for ages knowing my horse is content and rideable.

Now for Lincoln Christmas market and a few mulled wines to celebrate.

Love always,

Vic, Pat and Bender

Xxx

~

The rest of December was a total mine field. I had to go away with work, and at this point I was still working pretty much full time, albeit from home, as a marketing manager for a group of construction companies. I also had 4 days working at Olympia horse show and I was seriously struggling to get all the book parcels out in time for the big (Santa) day. Being away and living out of a suitcase for over a week was beginning to take its toll on my emotions.

To add to this heart ache, whilst at Olympia my lovely, and last remaining Granny died at her home back in Lincolnshire. I was taken aback. First the shock hits and then I was just beside myself with worry for my Mum. I cannot imagine how she must have felt only months after losing her younger sister, to have now lost her Mum too. I'll never forget either of those phone calls from my sister for as long as I live. We just sat, hundreds of miles apart and cried together for a while. It makes me realise how isolated I have made things for myself. I still feel so young and so little when things like that happen. I am the youngest of four; two boys and two girls, and they are all so strong and people I can really look up to. I'm the only one without children of my own too, and I think that changes things for you. I've always been the childish one, the 'not quite grown up' and I needed a cuddle from any of them right then. I wanted to be there for them too and be strong, but instead I sat in a corner of the Olympia stadium and cried into a bottle of bramble whisky.

I missed home, I missed my Carrot and my family, I missed my boys and my cats. Working for a living is exceptionally over rated. But it was just one more hotel, one more day, one more speech delivery, 3 more trains and I'd be home for Christmas.

This is the thing isn't it when you feel like this? You must work hard to have horses, you need to earn more money than if you didn't have them, and this was the sacrifice. Just keep smiling, keep upbeat and keep focusing on why we work hard. Dry the tears, have a glass of wine and remember that you get bugger all in this life unless you make sacrifices.

LESSON 3: YOU DON'T GET ANYWHERE WITHOUT SACRIFICES.

Sometimes it might not seem fair. Often, I see people who don't go to work, that have so much money that they buy saddlecloths they will never use or have 2 lorries and one just sits there all year doing nothing. But really what do we know about each person's individual's sacrifices? The answer is; nothing. From the outside looking in, I have these two lovely horses and loads of daylight hours in which to ride them, but I work hard for that. It's easy to look and judge, but the answer is that we are all on our own journeys, every one of us is different and have different things we must do to get the enjoyment from our lives. But I'll tell you something else, the wine you consume on a Friday night tastes SO much better if you've worked hard for it.

Chances are, if you are feeling restless about something in your life or somethings don't feel like they are going well, you just need to push a little bit harder. It will pay off, maybe not straight away, but it will in time.

23rd December 2017

I'm feeling nervous, apprehensive maybe... I haven't ridden for a little while now because of work and someone (my friend, Piers Warmoth) thinks he's a funny Christmas Cilla Black and is matchmaking Bender and I with the demon that is SHOW JUMPING…. tomorrow!

Ho ho ho-ly shit! Pass me the Imodium!

The support from Piers and his team at Willow Banks is just so overwhelming that I'm actually going to trust him and jump a whole course in fancy dress with my Bender! A course of poles on the ground is still a course, right?!

~

Now, the hard work I had put in to enable me to afford having this horse trained by Piers was making such a remarkable difference to his progress. There is no way in the world I would have got to this point alone, in my muddy field so soon. I mean, we would have got there, but not after 3 weeks! Now I know all those long hours away were worth it, even if I was totally staining my undies of the thought of it.

The Christmas Show

So, it's Christmas Eve and what better way to spend it than sitting on the toilet waiting to complete a round of show jumps on your ex-racehorse that has never jumped a course before.

I awoke early and went to visit the golden balls pony (Pat), who I wished was my trusted steed for this morning's events... alas it was Benders' turn to shine.

Having been coaxed into doing this only yesterday by Piers, I took his word that death was far from imminent, and off we went.

I nervously tacked up my unflappable thoroughbred only three months into his retraining and mounted him for the first time in 10 days! I felt instantly at ease with my Carrot by my side and bobbled about the warm up avoiding the jumps.

Now, I have jumped Bender once in the field and he had a little pop on Thursday this week, but this is as far as his training has gone. So I entered the 30cms class.

He went in and jumped every single one in his half-arsed style, but we got our first ever first place rosette! And I have to say, 30cms or not, I felt like I'd just gone around Badminton, my beautiful bold boy jumped all those jumps for me.

I did eventually manage to jump something more than a leaf in the warmup and decided to enter the next class at 65cms.

We went in and did a very stylish clear and mostly in canter too! I was bursting with pride hearing our names read out in FIRST place AGAIN! Seriously, I've never had such a lovely time with a monstrously green horse on Christmas Eve! He tried so hard, coped so well in the warm up and gave me a lovely feeling over a jump too, I cannot ask for more.

Huge thank you to Piers and his team at Willow Banks and to all of you for your endless support. I'm also ever so lucky that my Voltaire Design saddle fits Pat and Bender because I stuck to it like glue today.

What a day. What a horse. What a happy girl and her beautiful boys.

~

Whether Bender was in fact ready for this show or not, the reality is, I just got on with it. He went into the ring alone, didn't fuss about leaving the other horses behind in the warm up and he gave me the best Christmas gift ever. I don't think I have felt such joy for a long time and my hopes of HOYS were edging ever so slightly closer even if it was all costing me a lot of money.

New Years Eve 2017

I can't help but feel a little bit sad about this brilliant, brilliant year being over tonight.

Pat and I started the year determined to be the best we could be, and today we will end on some fun 80cm show jumping and pairs relay with Auntie Smurph.

Sadly, today was a day for survival, and I can't help but feel a little bit sad at how desperately scared I was again.

Pat was monstrously fresh when I got into the warm up, and all those demons came back to get me. I couldn't put my leg on, he bronched with me, and I almost went flying twice before I anchored myself down with my neck strap. He hasn't done that for months, and it's purely down to excitement that boils over. I can honestly say that it totally fucking terrifies me. He is so short coupled that when he balls up like that you are literally sat on NOTHING!! I wanted to cry. But that was the first time he's been out to a jumping show since Norton Disney at the end of October, so I should have seen it coming.

We eventually got warmed up and settled and jumped a lovely round over the 80cms for 4 faults, due to a momentary blip where he just didn't appear to take off, and I ended up almost on the floor! He was the quickest 4 faulter in a big class though, and we got 6th place!

Auntie Smurph and I then went back in for the pairs relay and came 3rd with 2 super-duper clears. This was SO much fun!

I feel like both Pat and I have gone back a few steps in confidence so lots of outings in the new year planned before we get back out on BE adventures again!

I feel also feel a bit sad that I close the doors on this truly amazing year, one that has been the absolute making of me and my horse.

- We went from be80 to be100 and cleared jumps over 1.10m! I never imagined that this time last year I'd have done anything like I've done 2017. I couldn't even visualise getting on him without breaking into a sweat.
- I have self-published TWO books, and we have posted out over 19000 orders from our sitting room floor!
- We relocated 200 miles north and I now have my own business!
- I have now got my own column in a national magazine, Horse and Rider UK.
- Most importantly of all, I have grown as a person, I had goals and dreams, and I fought some huge battles to achieve them.

If you have a goal even just a tiny one, write it down NOW. You can do ANYTHING you set your heart and mind to. Trust me, you can.

I'd like to take this opportunity to thank you all for your endless support, for your motivation to keep going when I'm at rock bottom. YOU are the reason I have succeeded, and I will be eternally grateful.

Here's to making a life to be proud of in 2018

JANUARY 2018

GOAL SETTING

January! You get me so full of hope and motivation to make myself thinner, richer, more successful and actually stop drinking my body weight in wine every week. This January was no different. I had decided to take on DRY JANUARY, where stupid people like to cease all alcohol consumption in order to act the smug baastard to all of their mates. I was fully intending to break my challenge by week 2 but my Mum always told me; "It's the taking part that counts." And there I was, sober as a judge for over two weeks! I get it, you might think I'm a little dependent on booze by now, and I might well be, but Friday night when you've worked your arse off all week, you just want 3 glasses of wine as a reward… is that so bad?! It's not like I'm drinking Tesco's own brand whisky from a brown paper bag on a Tuesday morning. – Now there's a New Year's Resolution if ever I saw one!

So, the new year started just as I had planned. I set out with a plan for this year, to get Bender to HOYS and Pat qualified for the Badminton Grassroots 2019 or, at the very least, a couple of Regional Final tickets. I had mapped out my season and realised I was going to have to work my fingers to the bone for it to happen.

And that's right about where the wheels fell off!

15th January 2018

Today is Friday. I have been away since Wednesday morning, not ridden Bender since Tuesday or Pat since Sunday... the motivated start to my new year is NOT going well!

I have today and tomorrow morning and we're off again back down to London this weekend. These are things I cannot get out of and it's making me feel that sense of guilt creeping in.

Motivation is a funny thing, I can feel totally powered up and ready to go when there's no chance of me being able to knuckle down! But chances are, when I can... I won't want it half as much enthusiasm!

Today is actioning day!

I am desperate to raise the remaining money for my lorry now. Visualising having him sat on the drive or being able to get in him and have my own freedom to pop to the beach on an afternoon would just make me so happy. Never mind save me £160 on my event cost every time!

So what needs to change? Bender will be coming out of full livery. This has served a brilliant purpose of weaning them off each other and getting him going in the arena but I have to think about the long term goals. The lorry will progress him more than another 3 months in livery will, I'm sure.

Budgeting; I'm going to write down ALL of my income and outgoings and strip everything back. I need to know where every penny is going so that I can go to shows as well as save for my lorry.

So, I've written it all down. I feel more motivated already, grabbing life by the horns today and getting stuff done.

And just remember; you are on your own journey, no one else's. Live a life of being true to who you really are inside, be kind and you will always have people who love you.

Have the most wonderful weekend, make sure you laugh often, enjoy the moments that matter and squeeze a pony or two. Fill your heart with love and it will radiate from your face like the toasty glow of a log fire! Enjoy it.

Love as always Vic xxxxx

Having ridden Bender a few more times at Willow Banks and made the decision that we might be ready to cope on our own, I decided to move him off full livery. I also chose not to move him back home straight away because it was royally muddy, and I really needed an arena to ride him in, so we could keep things consistent.

I found a lovely little DIY yard with an arena around 11 miles away. This seemed doable, and I moved him there the following week. He settled so well and despite them having limited turnout, he was amazingly calm and just as good to ride as he was at the other place.

On that subject; I want to talk about retraining.

I'll add right now, I am NO expert, but I do have experience and I'm not afraid to use it!

So, you have a horse that has inevitably learnt to go a certain way, who favours right over left, head in the air instead of round and soft. He wants to run through the bridle when you put your leg on or spooks constantly and has zero trust in you... any of this sounding familiar?

Now I don't know if I have just got unlucky but all 4 horses that I have owned have all had bad habits, learned from a previous way of going.

Horse 1 – India 4yo thoroughbred mare: Bought out of NH training and had a flighty nature. She was a feisty, hard mouthed 4 year old that took my very last nerve to re-educate. Her problems were purely inexperience and age related but nonetheless, I had a tough gig for my first horse.

Horse 2 – Freckles 4yo warmblood gelding: Bought as a very green baby and he had dreadful issues almost resembling agoraphobia. The further we got away from home the higher and further over he reared, this was again down to inexperience and age but not great learned behaviour that I had a job fixing.

Horse 3 – Pat 5yo thoroughbred x Irish draught gelding: Pat had fear seeping out of his skin, he was scared of everything and wouldn't take any kind of contact in the reins without dipping behind the bridle. Team this with the sensitivity and sharp nature, and I had a ticking bomb under me many times!

Horse 4 – Bender 7yo thoroughbred gelding: Bender is probably the easiest of the bunch, but his separation anxiety is probably the worst I have come across in all of the 500+ horses I have looked after in the last 20 years.

Now, each one had something to work on and all of them had the potential to get better and be wonderful. I was trained from 7 years old (that's 25 years now) by some of the country's most practical horsemen and women, using traditional methods that I know work. And I know they work because with each of these horses, the same theory has improved each one.

Good Groundwork – is ESSENTIAL.

Lunging, long reining, leading, tying up, rugging, grooming, loading. MANNERS are vital. Don't let him bite you, head butt you, pull you over, etc. I can't think of anything that I find more frustrating than seeing someone get dragged around by their horse, it's not fun and it's certainly not safe.

Gain respect without fear and you've got trust.

That comes from good rules on the floor. Teach him to back up, to stand and lead nicely. It might take months, but you'll have years of enjoyment in return. Repetition is key, do things over and over until they are so boring you want to stick pins in your eyes.

Know when it's time to get on; there is a pivotal point in the groundwork training where the trust is established enough to have a good, safe first ride. I won't mount until that point – it could be a week, it could be 3 months. But don't rush it. What's the rush anyway?! You'll have gained respect and trust on the ground that will make mounting your horse safe and isn't that what you want?

Ridden work – basic, solid footings.

Don't over complicate things, if it's not working do something else. Have eyes on the ground at least once a month from someone you trust to set you straight (no one is right all the time!).

Think about 3 things;

1. STOP: vocally during groundwork you will have used a command that will aid the stopping when things are getting a bit onward. It's that simple- make sure stop and rest commands work before you kick on.

2. GO: don't just kick! You might be launched into next week, you've earned the trust - use it. Be vocal. Daddy Carrot is learning voice commands with Bender and does a very good woman's voice for 'walk on'!

3. Steering: well, more flexion and getting the horse to use his abdominal muscles. It's key to getting control of their whole body and having them use themselves correctly. Once they learn to bend around your leg and lift up their big barrel bellies, you'll find the neck drops, the frame relaxes, and you don't fight for an 'outline'. Having control of their body means you also have a fall back if things don't go as you planned, move the body to break the naughtiness, simple right?

And that's just it, keep it simple one thing at a time. Repeat things often and don't lost patience. It might take your brain a second to process something, but a horse is 8 times your size with a walnut for a brain…. remember that when things aren't going how you thought they would.

You'll also find, if you're focussing hard enough on correct training, every ounce of fear you ever had just evaporates. Yes, I still get flutters of racing heart but, believe what you are doing is correct, don't be afraid to ask for the right kind of help and stick two fingers up to people who look at you like you've got 'Tw*t' marker penned across your forehead. You'll show them.

Enjoy your horses, first and foremost. Cross stitch feels very under rated when you're getting hauled through a hedge by a bolshy beast!

~

10th January 2018

7 weeks on Saturday ladies and gentlemen... 7 little tiny, tiny weeks.

The countdown is on and I need to tick off the following before then;

XC training

Set up my field arena

Jump at least once a week

Hack three times a week

Sort out my calmer doses so I don't die

Save money for entry fees

Find my balls

Clip off remaining fur!

Lose a stone or buy new breeches!

I could go on but it's just terrifying! Gearing up and getting in the zone is hard enough but it doesn't feel five minutes since the 2017 season finished.

First event will be Epworth BE90 (or 80, I haven't decided quite yet!).

It's hard to keep a focus when there are SO many things to focus on! I read something somewhere that it's Blue Monday coming up too, this is meant to be the most depressing day of the year. Everyone's skint, the daylight hours are giving everyone SAD and you can't see light at the end of the dark January tunnel. – I'll be looking forward to that!

I don't think I dislike January as such, it's not poor January's fault you can't get your arse in gear! But I do want to say a big, fat, hairy 'Bollocks' to Blue Monday!

Let's roll back 18 months; It was a balmy late August evening when I finally located enough of my own hairy balls to get on and go for a ride outside of a confined area for the first time in a while. I slugged hard on my hip flask and led my half-doped horse out of the stable.

Trembling at the knees and sweating in the palms, I lugged my fat backside onto the sticky gel seat-saver and off we went. I think I had reached the 1/2 mile point before I dared to release the death grip, I had on the neck strap in order to light my cigarette.

I exhaled a huge cloud of smoke and port fumes and finally relaxed to about 65% of what was my natural state. I trotted for a while and edged into a small canter on the verge. It felt amazing, all those feelings of failure and guilt of 'not doing' melted away, and there I was, 'doing' for the first time in ages.

I came home a short while later and untacked my horse, I slumped into the corner of the stable and cried. Not tears of sadness, but tears of relief, utter relief that I wasn't a failure, that I could do something despite the fear.

There it was; the realisation that fear doesn't have to win.

Fear causes mental blockages that I now know can be unblocked. The paralysis, the sweating, the 'not doing', these are all things YOU CAN control.

So, big hairy goat bollocks to you Blue Monday, because I'm better than feeling sorry for myself these days, I'm better than dwelling on the negatives, I'm a fear fighter and I'm doing alright!

~

I was doing alright, looking back can often make you see how far it is you've come. Don't be afraid to look back. Pat and I have a lot of history. Some of it isn't stuff I want to remember, but doing so, I feel like we are getting somewhere and not just spiralling into more darkness. I think it is much harder to gauge when you are head over heels in love with your horse too. He was like the leather jacket wearing, motorbike riding, spunky boyfriend that I probably should have steered away from… but that's my Carrot in a nutshell too! I am my own undoing!

And on that front, since moving back to Lincolnshire in July, having a lovely Christmas in our new home and feeling much more content, our marriage was as strong as an ox. It's very important to have an ally to tell everything to, one that doesn't judge you despite the (often) bad decisions you make, and one that will help you pick up your last scraps of dignity without belittling you. It took me until I was 27 to find him, I married the wrong one first time around and had a fair few wrong ones in the middle, but I got there. I do think there is someone out there for everyone and it might be that they're right in front of you and you just haven't noticed yet?

~

Now, as the January days slip away, I am driving 44 miles a day just do go and do Bender on DIY, and it's becoming increasingly difficult to keep both horses going. My confidence is in tatters after one bad ride.

I stupidly got on Bender In. A. Bad. Mood. This is always a BIG mistake but what made it worse was that Bender, for the first time, properly got the hump with me. After 10 minutes I ended up getting off before I lost my temper. I was angry that he felt wooden, I was frustrated that he couldn't pick up left canter after how hard I'd been working on it. I was raging that I couldn't get a tune out of him and NONE of this was HIS fault. It was all mine. The cracks were staring to show.

Days like that, you should NEVER get on a horse, never mind one that needs hand holding or training. But I did, I'm not perfect!

I then spent the next few days resenting him and the time I spent over there trying to form a bond, whilst Pat was playing the lead part in 'Feral Beryl the Musical' at home. Since I moved him to the DIY yard, I had spent over 2 hours every day fussing with him and grooming him, in some kind of hope that I would find the connection like I had with Pat. I didn't feel happy around him very often and this was making things very hard all round.

FEBRUARY 2018

STRIPPED BACK

I was finding things all a bit too much, and I was massively running short of money having entered early (so I didn't back out); Pat's first two events at Epworth and Oasby, in March. What with the livery and fuel and time away from working to spend with Bender at the other yard, I was running myself ragged and skint!

In need of some kind of solace, I went to Pilates for the first time. Now, I'm not one for communal exercising of any kind, but this was so relieving of my anxiety. I found it really cleansing and I felt very emotionally balanced every time I came out of that musty smelling village hall. It was during one particular Pilates session that I laid on my borrowed mat and had a moment of total clarity.

In my head someone asked me; Are you enjoying these horses? – My reply was, No. They asked if I have ever enjoyed Bender at all and again, apart from the two rides at Willow Banks over Christmas, I hadn't enjoyed him at all. He was breaking my heart. I wanted to love him, and I wanted him to fit in, but he didn't. So, on 9th February 2018 I wrote this;

Do you solemnly declare to tell the truth? The whole truth? And nothing but the truth?

I do.

I'm not coping.

Not at all.

Here it is; the saddest and most heartfelt post I think I have ever written down.

My nerves are trashed, totally frayed. And not just riding, which is the saddest part of all. I'm lost. I've been getting very upset almost every day for the last 2 weeks and the pressure I have felt has been incredible.

I am exhausted, I'm working very hard at work to keep money rolling in, but having the two horses and in particular Bender who is totally breaking my heart, is the cause of most of this sadness.

He is the sweetest, most affectionate horse, and I've been trying everything to form a bond with him, but it's not working. Every day I have spent hours with him, we don't work together, and I don't know why. He was lovely for Piers at Willow Banks and never put a little hoof out of line, but he senses my insecurities, and I can't fix them. Left alone, I am causing him to feel insecure too, and it's breaking my heart every day.

I know if someone came to me with this message, I would say that life is too short to be so unhappy. Horses are my hobby and when they make other areas of your life sad, you should look at resolving it before you spiral down that dark road again.

Pat and I just get each other, he looks to me for leadership and I can give him it, I look to him for comfort, and he gives me that in return. We are best friends. And I'm destroyed that I can't find even a glimmer of hope with Bender.

This isn't a decision I have made lightly, and I am thoroughly expecting a whole world of disappointment from people that wanted to see us do well. I'm sorry. I do feel a let-down, I've let him down too.

I need to find him someone that will love him, continue his training and give him what he needs. He is a beautiful horse and will make someone so very happy.

I really am sorry.

I know that this is the best thing for the horse and that is, and always will be, my main priority.

Reality hurts more than ever now that I've opened the wound for everyone to see.

For anyone else, in any 'normal' situation, I don't expect they would feel as though they have to justify themselves all the bloody time like I do. When I make a decision like this, I don't just feel as though it's me I am letting down.

There were so many people that wished us well, that were rooting for us to go to HOYS, that sent messages and wrote comments of support. I just felt like a total fucking let down. And of course, no-one voiced that. I was already broken enough, but I tortured myself about it for days afterwards. I knew that I wouldn't want to go up there at all now I had made the decision. But it was a new day, the plaster was torn off and now I had to find my boy the very best home possible.

His advert was also quite hard to write because I didn't want much money for him, only the best home. This can sometimes bring with it; joy riders, inexperienced people or ones that won't have the money to look after him properly. I'd had him for 6 months, during that time we had established that he is a much happier horse in a bigger yard not just in a pair where he can get quite clingy. That type of living arrangement probably wasn't going to be free, the buyer needed to be the right one.

He had had a year off before coming to me, so I'd spent 2-3 months long-reining and in hand manners training before getting on. He had a very lazy disposition but was NOT confident hacking alone with me. This is where we hit a brick wall I think. He would long rein on his own, so it was likely to be my nerves making this an issue.

He absolutely loved jumping though, and didn't spook at any fillers, he wasn't silly in the warm up at the show and was an angel in the ring. But his new Mum or Dad would need to be able to kick as he wasn't a speedy Gonzales!

What I was looking for was someone that had a good knowledge and empathy, that was looking for a partner to love and cuddle. – This might be harder than I thought.

~

Over the next two weeks I kept him ticking over as the first buyers were set to visit. They came and rode him, and he went so beautifully that I felt like retracting everything I said and keeping him after all. I hadn't ever seen anyone on him and he looked amazing for the lady that day. I drove home so seriously confused and unhappy about my decisions and just hoped they would come and take him before I changed my mind.

They arranged a 5 stage vetting using a vet they chose all the way from Cheshire. It was such a windy day and I totally bottled out riding him for the vet. It became very obvious how much my confidence had been dented just lately. I was full of fear yet again, something else that was making me feel like utter crap, never mind the guilt of selling him.

I recognised that anxiety creeping in again.

I felt it badly when I left the house one day that vetting week. I was meant to be driving down to West Sussex for work and I had already cried that morning when Gary left for work, not at all like me. I got in the car and went to do Pat, then to Bender. Getting on the road about 11am and just 20 minutes into the journey I had pulled onto the hard shoulder. I sat and cried so hard into my scarf I thought my head was going to explode.

I couldn't cope; with the drive, with the vetting, with work, with anything. I felt truly desolate for the first time in years. I thought I had a handle on this now, I thought I was okay. I was meant to be fine now we moved to Lincolnshire. I was not fine.

I felt sick, I felt empty inside. I would never say that I felt suicidal, but I felt nothing for life. I called the doctor right there on the side of the road. I needed to talk to someone, someone who didn't know me.

I explained to the lady on reception that I needed to speak to a doctor who called me back within 10 minutes. I told her how I was feeling and where I was and what I was meant to be doing. I didn't even feel stupid, I didn't feel a burden either, because I knew I needed them to help me. I took the advice I was given and drove home.

I attended an appointment the following day and talked through all of it again. I cried a lot, but I felt so much better for letting it all out. That's the thing with mental health you see; the more you ignore it the worse it gets. Never ignore a niggle. Recognise when something isn't right. I wish I had done something sooner, I hadn't been feeling right for a little while.

I went down the homeopathic route (due to us trying to conceive) and started taking a high dosage of St. John's Wort. I do get that this might not be the most effective way, but I was happy with the decision and within 2 weeks I was like a totally different person. I don't know whether it was the remedy or the fact that I had got it all off my chest, but I felt like me again, full of life and ready to get going.

And yes, you read it right; Conceive! I might not have mentioned this to date because, you know... some things are private. But we've come this far together, I have nothing to hide from you.

In September/October time we made the decision not to renew my next contraceptive injection, and do, what we like to call; 'not, not try'. Keeping things very nonchalant, and if it happened then GREAT and if not, we wouldn't be too worried about it.

In hindsight, I should have put two and two together because that imbalance of hormones hit me harder than I ever thought possible. I felt like a totally different person, and the withdrawal from this drug I had been injecting into myself for 3 years, was probably the culprit of my breakdown in mental stability at that time.

9th February 2018

Anxiety and hormones, go on... Fuck off!

(Sorry gents!)

So here it is, another brazenly honest word vomit...

I'm struggling. Still.

In November I released my body from any kind of chemical contraception. Prior to that I was injected 4 times a year so that we could carry out exercise of the horizontal kind without fear of producing a sizeable litter. (Sorry mum, **I have sex**, there I said it!)

December I felt fine, but two weeks into January, and I was not at all fine. I have felt sad often, cried often, felt worthless, lifeless and unmotivated. It totally spiralled out of control.

Now, I'm never hormonal or a sobber so I knew this wasn't me. I literally wanted to go fucking crazy at people for no reason what so ever. Scream at people for doing things that pissed me off, where normally I'd let them wash over me! I cried for three days in a row over absolutely nothing, I couldn't tell you what I was sad about. I was just heart wrenchingly unhappy.

I made everything into a problem to the point where, for almost a week, I hibernated with the curtains shut so I didn't have to face life. It's reality and it hurts to even talk about it.

I have turned a corner in the last 10 days, I have picked myself up with the help of St. John's Wort on recommendation of the doctor. But here's the thing;

Don't ever feel alone.

Ever.

Promise me right now. Because it's just horrible. If ANYONE reading this ever feels sad and alone, you come to me. I've felt very alone these last few weeks and although I'm bettering these feelings every day, I want people to know that this is real f*cking life, and you WILL feel better soon.

I love you all very much

Vic

xxx

Please don't ever suffer alone. Promise me.

~

Now, where was I? Ahh yes…

Bender was so lovely that week and I even had a jump on him in the school which was very bittersweet! And I was about to realise that fate has a very funny way of telling you something wasn't meant to be.

He didn't pass the vetting.

He had a few weakness related issues that may or may not be a problem later on in his life. Bla…bla… bla…!

Seriously, my blood boils for this subject.

I have NEVER had a horse vetted in my life, granted I have never spent that much money on horses, and they have always been bought more as pets than investments, but;

NUMBER 1: the horse has no concept of its value. It could just as likely injure itself in the lorry picking it up than have some long-standing degenerative disease. You shouldn't gamble all your money on a horse. Ask yourself; "can I afford to write off the purchase price?" if not, seriously reconsider the purchase until you can. They are animals with feelings, nerves, muscles, bones and tendons. They also have a 500kg body and a walnut sized brain... you do the maths!

NUMBER 2: If you cannot tell a horse is sound when you try it, you should be taking someone who can tell, or reconsidering your animal purchase. Lame hamsters are much less heartache.

NUMBER 3: If you need to get anything done, get bloods and x-rays. Cold hard facts. Failing flexion tests do not mean the horse won't come to anything. There are several top Olympic horses that have failed a flexion test on an off day in their careers.

I feel quite strongly about this topic because a very good friend of mine had a horse vetted by a qualified and practicing horse vet, who turned out was embroiled in the most revolting scam with a couple of horse dealers. There were horses with feet glued together, hidden ailments, fake passports, broken and fused bones; most were injected up to their eyeballs with enough cortisone and steroid to numb a rhino, just to mask the pain for prospective buyers. It was DISGUSTING and from that day I have never taken any notice. You must be knowledgeable enough to know that something isn't right and as I said, if you're not, just find someone you trust that is.

Anyway, the prospective buyer pulled out, there and then. And I do understand. Sometimes you might not have the money if it did go wrong, but I felt sad for him too, it would have been a lovely home.

So, February was turning into a bit of cruddy old month! I felt like burying my head in the sand and calling time on this whole horse thing! I had some nasty comments on social media again too, something that I thought I was dealing with quite well, but I just took something to heart about my riding and my intentions, meaning things weren't improving on the mood front either.

Yet again, I let fear and insecurity take a hold of my life.

16th February 2018

What a week, not at all the one I expected to have

So here it is, I've withdrawn from Epworth and Oasby. I know what you're all thinking, and you're probably half right. But the truth is, I'm not ready to do it yet, and I'm not going out there half-hearted and ruining my horse's confidence because mine isn't intact.

My first BE event will be the BE80 at Norton Disney in April (my birthday weekend). So, with that in mind, and not one to dwell for too long…

Tonight, I am heading to Hartpury for the Mary King demo and doing a takeover on Instagram for Horse&Rider Magazine! I'm hoping to leave feeling mightily inspired and ready to take this season on!

Funny thing about this Wimpy world I have created, I don't always want to live in it and sometimes I forget how judgemental others can be.

I just want to make sure no one ever has to feel like they are worthless because of what people say on the internet, or anywhere else. If ever you feel like shit because of a comment on the internet, just stop and think how sad they must be for doing it in the first place. I will support you, without judging or demoralising you.

The love and kindness shown by people in the Wimpy community must be celebrated. We must build each other up to help us reach those dreams. Make equestrianism a sport of support and friendship for a common love of our horses.

Fucksake, I'm not asking for world peace or the end to global suffering. I'm just asking that people refrain from tearing strips off one another for wearing the wrong shade of turquoise numnah!

Think before you speak, think about how you might feel. Give people the benefit of the doubt, perhaps they just need help or advice instead of berating. Keep that in mind when you hear gossip too, correct people, be a voice of reason and don't just join in a crowd of bullies.

Isn't it a nice feeling to be nice, to say something kind? To help someone when they feel sad? It's a much nicer one than the sour taste of putting them down.

~

I had the most amazing time at Hartpury. I went with my friend Dave and, despite us getting a little bit lost on the way, he bought me KFC for tea and weren't late after all.

In the break, I took the brazen, but opportune moment to accost poor Mrs King. I grabbed my baby pink and blue hat silk from the car, and, like an over e-numbered toddler, I ran and knocked on her lorry door.

What the fuck I thought I was doing, I don't know. But, with my Sharpie in hand, she welcomed me in, finished necking her Peroni and signed my hat silk. RESULT!

I literally couldn't believe I was standing there in her lorry whilst she drank a beer. I'd loved to have shared one with her, but alas, I was merely some marker pen wielding groupie encroaching on her bevvy.

I left graciously, and to this day, I will never forget meeting the person that I had spent years gazing at on my bedroom wall posters, in a wet carpark in Gloucestershire (at the age of 31 and 3 quarters!).

~

Back home and hitting reality with a bump, I had a few messages about Bender and followed a couple of them up. One was from a lovely local lady who had a yard not that far away, and who I knew was VERY experienced. We spoke on the phone and she really liked him from the videos. I also explained that my confidence wasn't great, and that I didn't want to look like a bumbling buffoon showing him off for her, which she was very kind about indeed. That weekend, she picked him up. Only on a trial basis, but I knew she would love him and do her best for him. I wrote the money off there and then if I'm honest. I wanted him to have a good home, and if that meant that she didn't feel like she could gamble on him financially, I was okay with that. His happiness was worth more to me than money.

I received regular Bender updates for the next few weeks. Videos of him hacking out on his own down the road made me smile the most. Sometimes, some horses just aren't for you. That was us. He was settled and took everything in his stride and I don't think his new mum would be bringing him back in a hurry!

Not forgetting, in the middle of all of this was little Pat. Who had a season's eventing ahead of him, and who hadn't been ridden for nearly two whole weeks, it was far from ideal! The DIY yard I had kept Bender on was paid up until the first week of March, so I decided to use this as a kick start for Pat. I shipped him into the space and began knuckling down to business.

18th February 2018

I'm on cloud nine...

Yesterday I moved Pat with the help of lovely Auntie Smurph and we now have an enclosed space in which to get my confidence back.

Part of my Horse&Rider Magazine contract is a monthly video of us tackling some of the magazine exercises and today, we had filming to do.

I FLOATED OFF TO HEAVEN!

After almost two weeks off, I thought he would come out a little stiffy plank but, boy was I wrong. He went the absolute best he's gone in the whole 6.5 years I've had him!

I didn't do much, and some people will probably roll their eyes about the sheer delight without rosettes or jumps involved, but he was unbelievable today.

It's the best feeling in the world being on a happy, stretchy, swinging horse that's glistening underneath you. I'm struggling to put it into words how happy I felt. Just did 30 minutes of flatwork but I didn't actually want to get down. I rarely feel like that, hardly ever these days and I am moist in the eye area feeling it once more.

Anything is possible.

~

Turns out, having daily access to an arena for the first time in months was actually doing us the world of good. I still maintain that I am better off without one, so that I'm forced to hack (which I am distinctly more scared of) and not just ride in the comfort of an enclosed space. But there are some things that you cannot do in a field in winter when you work for a living and don't have flood lights! I was buzzing to get up there and ride him every day, just because it was a novelty and I wasn't used to it, I guess – something I definitely used to take for granted.

Having this safe arena space and jumps, also meant I was getting my confidence back in bucketful's, and the change in Pat was very noticeable too.

MARCH 2018

IT'S ALL COMING UP A BIT SOON!

You know sometimes, when you sit and think for too long, you talk yourself in and out of decisions? You feel confused and need guidance on which way to turn?

The decision to leave that job you hate, to get married, to start a family, to try something that has an end result that is out of your control.

It leaves a seed (or boulder) of doubt or uncertainty lurking around. That is inevitable and anyone that tells you otherwise is bolder than the boulder itself.

My battle with fear has taken on many forms this year, and it was only March. My main concern used to be a fear of fucking up, of disappointing people and not doing as well as I know I can. Now I couldn't give two shits about ballsing it up. I'm now scared of hurting myself, more than I ever have been. I'm scared I might fall off, that I might hurt myself or that Pat might run off and get hit by a car.

But, here's the reality.

The bottom line is; with horses, **YOU WILL NEVER BE 100% IN CONTROL**. Unless they're dead or heavily sedated! You must learn a way of embracing that feeling of being a little bit out of control and I had mastered that last year. I loved galloping in a big field I LOVED it, so that's what I need to do. Learn to love being a little bit out of control again.

Fear takes many forms, and it changes faces often too, rationalise what it is you are actually afraid of and deal with it, don't let it rule your life.

Don't let fear be the reason you didn't take that opportunity, enter that show, marry that person... who knows, sticking a finger up to fear might just be the best thing you've ever done!

You see, I am scared. But I'm doing it anyway. And regardless of that fear, I will continue to do it until I don't feel so scared anymore. I think that's the only way if you're too stubborn to give up, like me!

Once, I actually said it out loud. Addressing my spooky, fresh horse; "Please don't do that, you're frightening me!!" He didn't reply, obviously! But I didn't feel in control and that's what I was most scared of. I felt like, at any minute, I could have fallen off.

And that's when it hit me; Do you know how many times in the last 7 years of having Pat, that I have actually fallen off....?

TWICE. Two times. Just 2 falls in 7 years. And before that, I think I fell off maybe 3 or 4 times in total since I was 22 and owned my own horses. Crikey, growing up I fell off a lot, but that's how you learn to stay on, and how you teach yourself to be balanced and ready for anything. I do feel ready and I do feel balanced, I just need reminding that I'm good enough sometimes. I'm realising that this is definitely a battle of confidence and not skill that I'm fighting.

Remember: Knowledge is Power.

Back to March, and the early spring SNOW had arrived! Yep, it came just in time to fuck up my pre-season training and leave my horse standing in his stable for days. Pat is not great being cooped up, and starts getting restless, very sharp to ride and not great to deal with in general. Queue March disaster number 1:

8th March 2018

The little shit escaped! Yep, that's right ... he was tied up outside his stable being skipped out when I wasn't there, and he pulled back and buggered off!

This snow has an awful lot to answer for I can tell you!

~

Over the next few days, I was able to give him a lunge in the small indoor school at the DIY yard, and when I eventually got to ride him again, I had ended up getting off far sooner than planned and not because of pant stains!

Pat was very tight, more spooky, crabby, a bit bucky and guarded in his movement and just not himself. I hadn't pushed him because it had been desperately out of character, and I felt as though he was trying to tell me something.

I decided to bring him back home to the field ASAP and back on 24/7 turnout which I was convinced would help him feel better. Lord knows the event season is starting for most people and mine should be too, in just 3 weeks! It wasn't looking hopeful!

~

By the time I got him home, he was back to his jolly self, and I was so relieved. He hadn't had a significant amount of down time either which meant that he wasn't exactly lacking in fitness to wobble us around a BE80. It was competition practice I was lacking and so instead of going straight out to do an affiliated event in April, this happened:

22nd March 2017

The balance of fear and doing...

I've just done something really, bloody stupid! I've entered a 'pre-event'!

So, I was feeling desperately unprepared for my first BE event on the 7th April, so what do I do? Enter an unaffiliated one for the 1st. April Bloody Fool! I'll be the only one looking a fool I can tell you!

I'm calling it a practice run. Most local XC schooling venues have events on at weekends now, so they aren't available for plopping round as practice. I'm using this as my practice! – Ever the prepared pilot.

I've been to the toilet twice since registering my interest, but I just don't want to feel like this anymore. I'm sick of being beaten by nerves. And the only way to banish them is DOING it!

I'm going in with no expectations, no pressure and hopefully no vomit on my shirt! I'm doing the smallest height they had available too, so I can just get over this total gut-wrenching dread I have developed over the winter.

I know that so many of us feel like this, I question often if it's all worth it. So, I leave you with this…

My first event of last season was a year ago this weekend. I was SERIOUSLY frightened, in fact, I nearly followed through waiting for Carrot to get his morning coffee! But I got on and rode the dressage, and then got back on and did the jumping and if that wasn't enough, I got on a third time and nailed the cross country. You can do things even if you're scared. That is a FACT.

There's the focus, the determination epicentre.

Let's do this!

~

Best thing really!

I'd had Pat back in the field on the farm near our house for just over a week before I started feeling much more myself! We hacked every day possible and I also did some pole work in our squidgy field. I would just walk down to him with a brush and my saddle and clamber on from the hay feeder. It might not sound much, but I felt very chuffed with my change in confidence and progress as the season was eking ever closer.

25th March 2017

Yesterday, after a shove from Auntie Smurph on the way home from her show, I booked into two dressage tests for today at Hill House Equestrian.

Two novice tests, and to be brutally honest, I didn't care which tests they were. I didn't care if I came last in each class or did a

20% test, I just wanted to feel safe at a show again. I wanted to get on him and not feel on the edge of a coronary.

I spent last night cleaning, polishing and preparing all my things, washing my favourite numnah and making sure everything was sparkling, mainly to keep myself busy and not fret!

I was surprised to have only made one nervous toilet visit whilst learning my tests and only one more this morning when reality kicked in.

First job...I gave him a calmer syringe! I'm now doubting myself if these are for his benefit or mine, but nevertheless, I'm sticking with it for now!

I got him all plaited and loaded and we arrived with plenty of time to spare in the glorious spring sunshine.

I think the last time I went to a show was New Year's Eve, so you can imagine how full of dread I was about getting on. He just lights up when we go out and I'm scared. I'm scared of his tense upright neck, his bulging eye, seeing his heart pound in his chest, I HATE it. It makes me scared to get on. Today I chatted to Auntie Smurph about this seasons' show attire and took my mind off things.

Surprisingly, Pat was super chilled. No fidgets, no eye bulging, nothing! I got on, no humpy back, no serpent head moments, not a squeak I worked him in outside, away from other horses and then took him indoors to a warm up ring with 5/6 other people riding... BLOODY NOTHING! He was AMAZING!

Into the tests and my word, he was a Dolly Daydream. In fact, it was a far cry from what we are capable of at this level because he was SO chilled! He wasn't forward enough at all, but I felt so safe I could have cried with joy. I didn't once grab my strap or feel that tightness in my chest, I did however, sweat buckets trying to get him going forwards!

So, we earned and deserved our 66% and 68% tests (that could easily be 5% more when we are on top form) for a WIN and a third place. And here we are... back in the game.

I have learnt today; that it's not so bad after all and how you really must get on and 'do' to release your fears... Oh and not to give him the calmer after all, maybe just try without it next time?!

Love as always

Vic and Pat xxxxx

~

Sometimes, just getting out there and realising things aren't as terrifying as you thought, is the only way to get over your fears. I think quite often, your fears are very ridiculous and usually stem from not being prepared enough. Most of the time, my fears are quite likely to be guilt related too, because I know I could have done more in the run up. This is what I'm learning about life and about myself and I'm learning it all through the power of equestrianism. They teach you so much about yourself these horses. And with that the call from Bender's trial mum came in…

She loved him, she saw his potential, but she wasn't in a position to offer me money for him. I was so glad that she loved him, and that he had been going so well, that I didn't care about the money by then. It's not like I'm rich but it would also cost me a lot more emotionally to argue the toss. The lady had taken him hacking, jumped him, taken him to 2 dressage shows where he scored nearly 70% in each prelim and he sounded so happy. He wasn't the straightest horse or the most level, but he was happy and doing a good job, so I know it was the right thing for him.

Sometimes, you need to know when to pull that plaster off. **LESSON 4: DON'T HOLD ON FOR TOO LONG**. It might just break you. Whether that's horses, relationships, jobs, cars, houses, packets of bulgar wheat that you've carried around through every house move for ten years… Get rid of the sh*t that isn't making you happy, the stuff that lingers on your conscience and keeps you awake at night. I mean, do your best to fix it if you think there's hope but when you know deep down that all hope is lost. **GIVE UP and MOVE ON.**

You have not failed in giving up, you are in fact stronger and more powerful than ever. Making decisions for your own good is empowering, and the bravest decisions you will ever make. Take it from me.

APRIL 2018

DREAMS REALLY DO COME TRUE

The start of April was a total wash out. This led to the cancellation of my 'pre-event' due to waterlogging. They had done all they could, but it was terribly wet and there was more rain forecast in the days leading up to it. April showers huh! So, I decided to box up and head to Willow Banks for some jumping instead.

April 1st 2018

I'm alive!

So, tonight after yesterday's entry, Auntie Smurph and I took both boys (Pat and Jack) to Willow Banks for the unaffiliated show jumping. I had entered us both for the 80 and the 90cm classes.

Now, we have only been friends for 8 months but, in that time Smurph and I have got to know each other very well. She placates my nerves with funny chatter, and I push her out of her comfort zone and swear at her often in return. I think my nerves were in full swing by 2pm because out came a bottle of baileys left over from Christmas to soothe my trembling body!

Yet again I got to the yard and administered the calmer and soon we were ready for the off!

We walked the course, it looked very friendly for my out of practice brain to remember. I tacked up speedily and got on before: 1. It got busier and 2. I cried or followed through!

He warmed up a little sharper than Sunday's dressage but not scary sharp, just manageable and we popped a few warm up jumps! I felt okay, in fact I'd go as far to say that I felt like I was doing it okay. I wasn't hurling him at jumps or tensing last minute, I was just sitting and waiting, sitting and waiting until the jump arrived. Alien to me but I'm getting there! I like to faff you see and this is where it all goes wrong.

So, with no faffing, we went in. The buzzer went, and I got in my rhythm. The first fence jumped awkwardly as the sun was beaming on it, but he did everything I asked, when I asked. He got a bit forward from 3 to 4 but nothing a tickle on the reins didn't fix.

We came out beaming for a super clear round!

Auntie Smurph was next up and felt a bit lacking in zoom but jumped everything clear with a very unfortunate 4 faults for an impromptu circle!

We didn't really gun it round but, in a big class my nippy little lamb came 3rd with 2 ponies pipping him to the red!

Next was Smurph's first ever round at 90cms and I tell you what fellas... she rode for her life! She was amazing and had just a couple of unlucky rubs, but I was so proud of them!

Pat was in straight after them and he bloody soared the first 6 jumps, he was very careful and gave each one a good bit of room. Then the jump off. The timer started ticking from just before number 7 so I bloody went for it!

I'm no showjumper and my lines and turns were none of finesse, but we flew round for ANOTHER CHUFFING CLEAR!

I cannot tell you how magnificent he felt tonight, like we've picked up where we left off last season and it's all still there, ingrained, and happy!

So, waiting on the scores in another huge class... I just got pipped to first place right at the very last rider! But who gives a fat rats ass? NOT ME!

What a bloody horse! He's not jumped much of late, and he just came out there like a frigging legend! WE WERE IN THE FRILLIES AGAIN! 2nd place and £20 prize money too.

Gold stars all round.

HUGE love and appreciation for my wonderful horse, he is without doubt or hesitation, the most wonderful soul and I couldn't love him more if I tried.

You know those times where you are just so happy and filled up to the brim with love that you feel like your heart is going to burst open... It might seem daft to most people but, I adore my horse so much, I don't care if we don't jump the biggest jumps or get the best marks for our medium trot, I wouldn't give two hairy balls if I never did another show ever again.

I love his big dark eyes, the little white fluffy fluffle on his lip. I love how from a distance his star makes him look like a Cyclopes. I adore the sound he makes for his food bowl and how he lips up a whole carrot like you're posting it in a slot! He makes my heart burst the way he's so timid yet would follow me through the gates of hell if I asked him to.

He is mine, mine to respect, mine to cherish and mine to love for ever.

I'd been having lessons you see. For the first time in a long time I was have monthly jumping lessons to try and help me work out how to stand more chance of going clear in the phase that I find the hardest. The lady that has been giving me lessons is so good, she understands my nerves and pushes me just far enough out of my comfort zone to get the best out of us both. And isn't that the best feeling, achieving something you didn't think you could.

I was absolutely delighted with our show jumping improvements and that wasn't even the best part of this first week of April. I realise what I am about to write might make you sick to your stomach if all you have ever dreamed of is your own horse transport. I had, and I was about to realise how much that actually meant.

A few days before my 32nd birthday on Easter bank holiday weekend, we made a 7.5hour round trip to meet the loveliest family and bring home the best birthday present I could have ever wished for!

A little blue horse van, a Renault Master built in 1994, with exceptionally low mileage (70k) and a lovely interior with sliding storage and a good solid body with barely a sniff of rust. I had been hiring lorries or sharing lifts for the last 10 years and finally, finally I had my OWN van.

I drove him back 170 miles from Essex to Lincolnshire singing along to his radio at the top of my lungs! And for 3 days afterwards I had to keep going outside and checking that it wasn't all a dream! Huge love and thanks go to my irreplaceable Carrot, for the best birthday present in the world. If there were a 'best husband EVER' contest, he'd be right up there. Dreams really do come true, and I was now free, independent, and able to go out whenever the mood took us. And with my first event only a week away, this was almost certainly the start of something great!

5th April 2018

Today is Thursday 5th April 2018, it is also exactly 32 years since I arrived into the world.

In 32 years, I have been to 2 schools, 2 universities, lived in over 10 houses, owned 16 animals, ridden over 500 different horses, I have drunk more than my body weight in New Zealand Sauvignon Blanc and fallen in love at least twice. I have seen death and birth, I have saved lives, I have loved and laughed so much I can't really remember ever being sad.

So today, I am taking this moment to sit back and realise how lucky I am to be alive, to be healthy and happy. To have good friends, family and love surrounding my life. To appreciate myself and how I have grown into the person I am right now.

It is SO important to love yourself for who you are, don't try to be more like anyone but you. You are unique, you are the only one like you, so make sure you realise just how extraordinary you can be. Don't compare, don't look back with regret, be proud of who you are and feel excited about what you are going to bring to the world.

Thank you so very much for your endless support and love, you are part of me and who I am now, and without being able to raise up other people, I know I wouldn't be so happy in myself.

I would love it if you could do me a MEGA favour today, please go and look in the mirror, look at your scraggly un-brushed hair and tell yourself 'I LOVE ME for ME!' and then tell one other person in your life how much you love them too.

Mend the silly arguments, build people up who feel sad and don't let anyone tell you you're not good enough, you are, because I said so.

Lots of love on this special day

Vic xxx

~

Another few days of heavy downpours led to another cancelled event. Nothing was running up and down the country. The whole of April and now most of May were written off for us in Affiliated competitions. Last season I had already done 4 events by the time this season has any chance of getting off the ground. I can't say that I felt that relieved either, I pay an annual fee to be a member of British Eventing, this was going to waste and I couldn't see me fitting more events in later on to compensate.

2018, the year of the non-starter! And yes, I started to get a bit flat and restless. Just as I got my little van, I had no-where to go! I turned my attention to an unaffiliated run at the end of April and booked a jumping lesson and a group pole work session to give me something to keep us on track.

I did, however, find it very hard to pull my finger out and get motivated with all this rain. If I have learnt anything about myself lately it is; even though eventing puts the fear of jimmy-o into me, I wouldn't be the same without it.

I was about to foolishly change my goal posts, easy enough when your armchair eventing! I didn't just want to feel confident jumping 80cms... I wanted to do the very best I could at being confident full stop.

I felt so determined, I had fire in my belly and I wanted to feel good again. I had felt off games because there were no games, and a bit lack lustre and down in the dumps. This can make you lazy, flat and not going anywhere. I vowed to change this starting 'tomorrow'.

LESSON NUMBER FIVE: TOMORROW NEVER COMES. If you wait until tomorrow to change things, you will always be the same. It's true, tomorrow NEVER arrives because when it is tomorrow, the next day will then be tomorrow... it really never comes!

Why are you putting it off? What's stopping you changing things RIGHT NOW? Changing your mind set in that moment will be enough, you can action the changes in the future, but change things NOW or don't bloody bother. Remain mediocre for the rest of your existence, see if I care...! But you have SO much potential to be so much more, why wouldn't you take that chance?

I hope you can see how much potential you have to achieve greatness. I want to help you to work out how to get somewhere you want to be.

Whether you feel unfulfilled at work, you want to be a better rider or win more rosettes. If you want to be a better wife or mother, go after something you have been too afraid of or try something you have never done before... you CAN do those things.

It might seem a million miles away right now but taking those first steps makes you at least half a million miles closer than someone not willing to try.

What is it that you want to do? What puts a fire in your belly? What gets you out of bed in a morning?

I'm not advising you all go out and quit your jobs today, but I am advising that you to never, ever settle for a mediocre life. We get one go at this life, just one. Make sure you haven't left the world with things you wished you'd done or wished you'd tried harder for.

Today, let's make a change, make a difference and be the brilliant people that we all could be with just a few small changes. Don't feel disheartened if your dreams are something no one else has succeeded at. Pave a way, following will only get you to the same place as someone else. Don't fear being different, because you are so unique, there is already no-one like you!

YOU have so much POWER and so much skill you might not even know about yet....

~

The week leading up to my first (unaffiliated) event of the season I felt so prepared. I had learnt and practiced my test quite far in advance, packed up MY lorry and, because of this, my nerves were almost under control. I was desperate to get out there and see what happened without any expectations, and also see how much we had forgotten since October. So here it is… NUMBER 1:

EPWORTH 80cms Unaffiliated Event

I awoke that morning to a terrible bout of nerves, a VERY unsettled tummy and the fear I had been waiting for... I was back to square one all over again. I felt a failure before arrival, how was I ever going to claw that back?!

I dragged my beloved in from the field and got him ready for our departure time of 12pm for a dressage of 13.50. Plaited, brushed and ready to go, we set off and arrived in plenty of time without soiling myself and without any fuss. Can I just say, how proud and lucky I felt turning up in my OWN lorry? I've never felt so appreciative of anything in my whole life, it's my independence and I am so grateful to finally have my own wheels.

Having yet to walk the course, I collected my number and visited the porta-loo before tacking up ready for dressage. It was a little walk down to the warm up, but this was a great thing, it meant I could settle him in a little bit without the company of too many others. Only a few salmon fish moments and he settled okay. I'd have liked another ten minutes, but we were called down to our arena quite speedily!

In the ring, I did my best with what I had on the day. He was still sharp and still threatened the snake head moves he knows I hate... we made it through with no balls ups and came out smiling but guessing at around a 33 score.

NOTE: In eventing dressage, the lowest score is the best. The test is marked as a percentage like normal, with a mark for each movement and then reversed to give you a point score. Hopefully this is in the twenties, usually it's in the 30's but sometimes disappointingly in the 40s.

Anyway, a two-hour gap until my show jumping meant a course walk for both courses. Now, I'm not that keen on walking the cross-country course on the day as I'm usually knackered from the riding bit, but today I felt ok and there was nothing too hideous on the course! Well, there was number 7 and 8, and I didn't like the water much... but 1-4 looked doable at least!

Back at the box, we dressed for show jumping and got mounted. I felt stupidly nervous now. I don't even know exactly why, we've done more show jumping lately than anything else, so I should feel okay, but the course wasn't riding very well and there were a lot of fillers.

Warmed up and ready to go in, I discreetly showed him a couple of fillers before the bell, he was not accepting of them. The round that ensued was an absolute bloody shambles.

He spooked, jinked, looked and generally made hard work of what should have been a breeze. I nearly came off between 5 and 6, lost my stirrup and flapped about around his neck for a minute... but I stayed on, the poles stayed up (to my absolute amazement) and we soared the last for a bloody clear round!

Now, at this point we knew our dressage was joint leader in the section, which meant going XC in contention of the win. This is the absolute WORST THING you can tell me before the off!

Dressed and down in the cross country warm up, it was now or never. I had to put out of my mind, all of the doubts and worries of not having jumped a solid fence since Norton Disney last season. I gunned round the warm up jumping not just the 80 ones but, the bigger ones too and it felt bloody amazing. Pat hadn't forgotten, and I wasn't a wobbling, crying sack of shit. I quickly went down to the start box before doubt had a chance to creep in.

Those famous last words of the cross country starter; "3....2...1.....Have a good ride!"

The first fence, a wooden barrel arrangement, came up far quicker than I had anticipated, I rode for it like it was about to set alight, we were ON FIRE!! Galloping to the second, a wooden house; he backed off but boy I wasn't letting anything slip just yet... I fired him at it and he soared in reply. The third; a chicken coop, obviously had brutally murdered chickens still screaming inside it.... he backed off so much we nearly ground to a stop. I seriously had to give it some welly, but he answered my arse kicking and flew it in the end.

A gallop down to a white arrow head at 4, which jumped much better than I thought it would (and much better than 3!!), down to a hay wagon at 5 clad with spooky bales! He backed right off again despite my encouragement... I thought, this is where we come unstuck. But bugger me! He jumped it from nearly a stand still!

6 was a set of rails that I gunned it for and got a confident and bold jump (at last!) 7a was a roll top, up a bank to 7b, a log pile and drop... I slowed up to trot for this b element. I'm glad I did because it was new for us and rather unseating.

8 was in the trees and actually jumped very nicely for a long gallop down to 9; a castle. I yipped, and he soared this. He was absolutely flying now and felt just like where we left off last year. I screamed with joy down to 10 and 11, so happy that we got our rhythm back, our hearts beating as one around this bold course.

Back to reality, 12 and 13 were very kind, solid and wide but not spooky and then 14; the water, straight in and out no bother! 15; a double of flower dressed pipes, he looked but I yipped and squealed, and he flew them on a lovely stride! Galloping down to the big carrot box to finish, we got a fantastic shot at the last and screamed through the finish line absolutely bloody delighted!

I cannot tell you what today felt like and what it meant to me. I thought our time was up in this sport, I thought my nerves couldn't take another season, but today I proved I can do it. I can be brave, I can ride like my life depends on it. I can, and I did. I gave everything I had today, and we finished up on 32.8, 2.8 time penalties (too fast!) to add to our dressage of 30.0, DOUBLE CLEAR!

We were laying in first place for a very long time, but those 2.8tf were expensive. First place was out of sight, but we weren't out of the prizes. We finished in 4th with a lovely numnah, fly spray and rosette as winnings!

I cannot tell you what it means to have this Wimpy outlet for my documentary, it really keeps me going. The support and wishes of good luck, knowing that there are so many people willing us round that course is the reason I ride for my life. Thank you with all the energy I have left.

What a day, what a bloody lion-hearted horse and what a way to start our season.

Huge, huge thanks to Auntie Smurph for grooming, to Daddy Carrot as chief photographer and to my sponsors for supporting us so kindly, and generously this year. Without them, and without you, I'd be nowhere near the rider I am.

Thank you

Love as always

Vic and Pat xxxxx

~

That was that! The start of my 2018 eventing season with a double clear, a confident run and a placing! Overcoming doubt, fear and not giving two shits what anyone thought of me, long may it continue.

MAY 2018

A NEW PERSPECTIVE

As regular as a pendulum on a grandfather clock, my elation over that first event didn't last for ever and anxiety started creeping back in. It's a funny thing; emotion. I have the busiest brain of anyone I know, and I'm never really satisfied with things, just the way they are. I spend so much time striving for something better, something more or something different, I forget to just breathe and enjoy the right now. That definitely comes at a cost. I get exhausted easily, and the bad days feel all-consuming while the good days get less often.

7th May 2018

Anxiety, a constant battle with that uncertain feeling.

Monday morning, 5.45am.

I'm awake over an hour before the alarm again but not because I can't wait to bounce out of bed and start an exciting day. But because I'm riddled with this sinking emotion.

It's not sadness exactly, I can hear birds singing, I'm not sad. It's not grief either, I haven't lost anything, or have I? It's worry, fear, guilt, self-loathing, and feeling lost in myself - and it eats me away inside.

I'm going through a period of change in my working life. My security blanket of my main income (30 hours a week) is being pulled from under me and I'm panicking. This is not a surprise; this was agreed months ago but I'm still not ready! I set up a business to attract new clients before this event, but because I was so desperately lacking in confidence when I did it, I haven't felt right pushing it or in fact charging people for my time!

Yesterday I slept, almost 16 hours out of 24. I wanted to not think about anything. I wanted to feel nothing; no stress, no doubt, no panic. Instead, I prolonged the inevitable.

It's the most debilitating feeling, not feeling good enough. I don't feel attractive, I'd go as far to say that I quite dislike myself. I don't feel as though my husband wants to be with me anymore, why would he? When I have nothing to offer.

Now, here's the thing, I am absolutely not looking for sympathy, I'm making it very clear that despite what an Instagram feed or Facebook page portray, behind it could be a broken mirror. People going through things that you couldn't even see until the cracks appear.

And on reasoning with myself, I think that it's okay to feel this way. It's okay to feel out of your depth and struggling to keep your head out of water long enough to take a breath. It's okay to not love yourself, to feel as though you don't belong.

LESSON NUMBER 6: THIS. IS. NOT. PERMANENT!

And I know this because I've felt this way before. I made changes, got my shit together and fought for a life I deserve.

I won't let this beat me; not now, not ever. I'm off to learn to love myself, to feel proud again and be the best version of me that I can.

Don't feel alone, you're not. I'm here.

And this too, did pass...

On reflection, I find a lot of this hard to read, just like you will. But I bet your life you've felt it too in some way. That feeling of inadequacy. Do you know what snaps me out of it the quickest?

Giving some time to myself.

I'm a very happy person in general but I give a lot of that to others. I would walk over hot coals if you told me that it would make you feel better, but I do have periods of low self-esteem and regularly feel a bit of an underdog in a lot of areas in my life.

I find that giving myself an easy few hours, putting on some makeup, riding my horse and then enjoy drinking wine with my husband after work makes everything instantly much better.

Why on earth wouldn't you take full advantage of being alive, of having choices, of having the freedom to live.

Don't wait for things to come to you, make something for yourself – start a plan. Don't wait for life to happen, make it your own, take hold of it by the reins and go out and get what you deserve.

Make yourself happy and don't wait... you are brilliant, just look deeper.

I think it's very important to look after ourselves mentally. Think about you, about how you woke up feeling. Waking up worried is not nice, particularly for weeks at a time.

I often feel like I have a lot on my plate, like work is getting left because of the books, I worry that this book isn't as I want it yet, the horses haven't been ridden since Friday and I'm worried about getting back on, THE LIST GOES ON! And Carrot and I haven't "done it" in ages and I'm worried I'm a crap wife! I worry about getting fat, I worry about people at work thinking I'm useless, I'm worried that I haven't got children yet, etc. I just fret all the time. But do you know something else, THIS IS VERY NORMAL!

It's VERY likely that you worry about worrying too, but what does it achieve? If there is nothing you can do right that second, why fret about it. You don't get anywhere on a rocking horse, and that's what worry is.

Just breathe. Take a step back, make a list of the things you have to deal with and turn them all into positives, and you'll soon realise how little you can affect each one...

Are you alive?

Are you looking forward to anything?

Are you going to grab whatever good comes your way and make the best of today?

The thing is, you might not see it right now, but you are just like me, we are all brilliant for something and sometimes we are worried about showing how brilliant we really are. Well b*llocks!! I'm going to be exactly that today, join me will you!!

Be the best you today, ride like it's your last ride, make a nice dinner, eat a cream cake, hug a friend, tell someone you love them, just make sure when you are in bed tonight that you can look back and smile.

I want you to see how special and brilliant you are.

Love yourself before anything else because it isn't just something that will affect your riding, it will affect your work, your relationships and most importantly, your health.

So, what is it that we need to do?

Essentially, we need to work at being proud, not feeling ashamed or embarrassed to blow your own trumpet, and not entertain that downward spiral of self-deprecating thoughts.

Day one is right now... Do something for me will you.

Write down 3 things that make you proud of yourself – RIGHT HERE. Physically write them down and put them somewhere you can see them at least three times a day.

And start believing them.

Thing Number 1.

Thing Number 2.

Thing Number 3.

Try it, I don't think I know anyone that ever gives themselves enough credit... bloody well love YOU a bit more.

With this self-loving in mind, I wanted to throw myself into a new challenge. One that was massively rewarding, if a little outside of my comfort zone. I made a deal with Auntie Smurph last year, that if she jumped the big rails out on our ride, I would start teaching again. She bloody jumped them, didn't she?! So, here I was fulfilling my side of the deal and agreeing to teach at a Nervous and Novice Confidence Day Camp for the local Riding Club!

17th May 2018

2 months ago I got a text from my dear friend Liz, asking if I fancied helping her out with a bit of "motivational instructing" at a Nervous and Novice camp in May... it seemed such a long way off, and I'm at the stage in life where I will literally do ANYTHING to help anyone, so I agreed!

The day came, Liz sent me my agenda with my groups (plural) that I would be allocated, and it turns out I was set to impart wisdom upon 5 groups of 4 riders over the course of the day.

I think I fretted just as much as I would before an event! It's been a long time, almost 10 years, since I was actively teaching people to feel less crap, less scared, and more empowered on their horses.

I work very much on the basis of 'what I would need to hear?', and my lovely groups were all made up of riders that lack confidence and self-belief, not necessarily ability, just like me.

The only thing I cared about was that I wanted them to leave my arena more confident about themselves than when they came in.

"Today, I don't give a shit about outline, engagement or learning about contact...!" I think I said this a lot! But all I cared about was their confidence, happiness and self-worth. This will make you as a rider long before getting your horses head down will.

My first group were lovely. I was a little nervous, but I just put myself in their shoes and realised I was the one to be afraid of! I bellowed at them, cheered them on and made them all gallop down the long side of the arena until they smiled the whole length! We played pony games and spent some time without stirrups. I explained how to drop from the hip, how to relax on a horse and learning to feel tension and how to roll it away.

I repeated this format for the next groups, they were responsive, they all tried really hard and one lady in particular who came in very upset after being bronched with whilst getting on, did so well. I felt so desperately proud seeing her in a forward seat cantering down the school!

At the end, I pulled them in and thanked them all. I confess to tearing up rather unprofessionally, but I was full to the brim with pride for what these ladies achieved. Tears of pride are the very best ones.

I am so glad I pushed myself out of my comfort zone to do this, it was a brilliant day and I couldn't have wished for a kinder and lovelier bunch of people to dust myself off in front of.

Thank you to Liz, who always has such kind things to say about me, she is such a lovely person and a very, very good teacher herself. Thank you to my husband too, who took me through my lessons the night before and tolerated my nerves yet again!

~

With my arse in gear, I decided to take inspiration from these ladies I taught and knuckle down in preparation for my next event in a weeks' time. Pat is always better at an event if I have managed to get him out somewhere in the days leading up to it. So that's what I did. Carrot, Pat and I hopped into the Wimpy Wagon and popped down to Hill House, our lovely, local venue. I busted out 2 Novice tests taking 2nd and 3rd place in a tight class. I was so happy to be out on a balmy evening with my boys, I didn't really care what the outcome was as long as it was non-death.

This led nicely into the first affiliated event of the season. A BE90 at Shelford, a venue I was familiar with after two of my events last season being held there. Should have put my mind at rest, right?!

EVENT NUMBER 2: Shelford BE90

So, my routine outing before the big day was complete with my dressage trip on Friday night, I gave him a little pop over some jumps in the field yesterday to round off our prep. I then went to my big brothers for a family barbecue, drank a bottle of wine to myself and got a crap night's sleep... brilliantly done you whopping sack of crap. Why did I do that? Why? Maybe to dull the nerves, maybe that's it? Either way, I am an idiot!

I woke up feeling like a turtle had deposited its innards into my skull and had no one to blame but myself!

My first AFFLIATED 90 of the season, only my second run out this year too. I was dressaging at 12.30pm with a two-hour gap before jumping at 3pm, so I left the course walk until the day and luckily didn't have to rush. We arrived in plenty of time, I began flushing my system with litres of water and went and checked in. I was nearly the last rider to go in my section and there were already some very competitive scores written down on the board.

Back at the box, I got tacked up and headed for the warm-up. He worked in well with not too many moments where I felt scared this time. I'd given him a calming cookie before we left home, so it was in full flow in time for my most dreaded part (the dressage warm up). I came out quite optimistic for a sub 30 but alas, a 33 was what we received. Bizarrely this is the 3rd time I've been to Shelford and each time his scores have been 3 – 4 marks worse than anywhere else. I haven't seen my sheet yet to learn how to improve, I guess he was a bit behind the leg at times. I've done much worse tests for better marks, it's all a learning game.

NOTE: Behind the leg – is where, no matter how much you think you're travelling forwards, it's not enough. If you took the frantically kicking leg away, would the horse stop? If yes, he is almost certainly 'behind the leg'.

We were lying around 8th going into the show jumping though so I'll take that.

The cross country course walk was not ideal, not a disaster by any stretch, but definitely not ideal. There were a few I didn't like; the skinny house at 4, the feed bags in front of number 9 and the size of the hedge at 13… but aside from that, it wasn't horrendous.

Into the show jumping warm up and the calmer had almost definitely worn off, Pat was salmon fishing, squeaking, and ballooning after every jump. I was not having a nice time AT ALL. He was thoroughly enjoying himself whilst my white knuckles clung on for grim death. He felt strong but not in a confident way, more in a 'leg it back to the lorry' kind of way, and this was not funny.

In the ring, I felt totally out of my comfort zone, normally my quite easy to manoeuvre horse felt like steering a double decker bus through soft butter. He was strong, and I didn't like it. The jumps felt small, there was nothing to back him off and I'll admit it; I needed a bigger fence today. I never thought I'd say that, but he was running on and I was not enjoying it! But despite his exuberance, we just rolled one rail where I over checked and only had 4 to add to our dressage score!

Now, I will just add that this time last year I would have been thrilled with that, but I've been working so hard to ride him better, I can't help but pick holes. I had the handbrake on, I needed more power, it was totally my error and I will fix it! MUST enjoy going fast.

A quick change of clothes and we were turning a very lovely shade of green walking to the XC warm up. I don't think I've been this nervous for a long time. I walked for a good 20 minutes before the chest tightness subsided, I stopped blubbering and I got my shit together! We sailed a few practice jumps and went into the Start box of Doom....

It really is now or never when you hear "you've got 30 seconds" call out. What the fuck can you do about it then...? NOTHING! Sweet FA, so you may as well give it everything you've got!

3, 2, 1.... we flew out of the start box and galloped down to the first; a log shared with the BE80 course, phew...! A nice easer-inner and it jumped nicely which always gives me extra beans. A short gallop to the second, which was a wooden upright shared with the BE100... excellent! But I gave it some power and shouted "GO GOOOOO GOOOOOOOOO...." and go he did! Soaring over it with room to spare, and onto number 3.

Three hadn't looked much when I walked it, but he bloody backed off it a treat (wasurk!) so I had to ride for my life here, long before I had anticipated. It wasn't pretty...but we got over it! Down to the skinny house at 4, I shortened the canter and rode through the invisible funnel with nice short reins and a firm leg, and he pinged out over it like a bloody pro!

A gallop down to 5; a trailer dressed with two (obviously, life threatening) wooden acorns. He looked, looked again, thought about stopping but I caught him, picked him up and carried him over with a lot of vocal encouragement. I'm so used to his backing off now, I know if I want it enough, he goes! Into the woods for a palisade at six and a set of ladders at seven, both jumped really nicely after the killer acorns.

8 was a double of plastic pipes and he was so busy spooking at the jump judge we almost didn't lock on, but we got there, Pop! Pop! By now I have a few things running through my head;

- Ecstatic delirium
- Holding back the tears of joy
- How likely is it that a human being can cough up an actual lung?

If I have learnt anything from today, it's that I'm not fit enough for this part, that's for sure!

9 was the bags of feed... he backed off, but I was seriously ready for him and kicked his arse so royally over those bags that he galloped like the clappers over a log and drop for 10a and b into the trees. I grabbed a lot of mane down the bank and good job because 11; a log out of the woods, left me a little unseated, but he really did help me out there!

12 was a step up which was no bother for his Nibs, then a gallop down to the whopping hedge at 13, probably the best jump I got all day. It felt amazing... soaring through the air, squealing with

joy! 14 was on an angle back into the woods again and was catching a lot of people out, I pulled back to a strong trot just for the turn and cantered the last few strides.. ping! We nailed it! Out over the palisade at 15 and a nice gallop down to another hedge before the water!

In we splashed and out over the yellow pipes, soaring and squealing down the home straight to fly over the last and through those wonderful finish flags....

Huge pats and squeals all round! Pat came bucking and leaping, full of beans through the finish. He genuinely felt the happiness I felt. He was having the time of his life today, I could just feel it bursting out of him!

The love I have for that tiny boy, I don't care that he's not the bravest or the most careful or that we haven't won one yet. All I care about is how we gel together, how we are a team. We know each other inside out and that's worth more than any rosette could ever be.

So, that was it; inside the optimum time too for a finishing score of 37 leaving us in 11th place. Not bad at all for our first affiliated run and lots to take from it too. I'm happy, he's happy, that's what it all boils down to.

Thank you to my Carrot for being the best groom and chief photographer and for his never-ending support.

Also, a big thank you to everyone that came and said hello today. You guys are the reason I'm doing this, you keep me going and you've built up my fragile confidence and given me hope. So, thank you with everything I have left.

Good night, God bless and so much love, as always

Vic and Pat

Xxxxxxx

~

I was so pleased to have got back out at an affiliated event and not to have ballsed it up too much. Eventing brings with it all kinds of emotion; the preparation, planning, fitness, the stuff you have to buy just to even get there. It's not easy, it's hard work and you have to enjoy it otherwise it's an awful lot of heartache. The feeling I get afterwards is the best feeling ever, that invincibility that lasts for days. I expect the top riders feel it too, only on a much higher scale! We are a rare breed us 'Horse People' and deep down we are all the same. I want to share with you a few of the things that unite us and bring us together, the reasons I love being part of this madness;

First up…There is no other sport in the world that sees even the tiniest human masterfully control what was once a wild animal, and guide it through a dance routine, through flags and over death defying obstacles with total finesse. Those tiny racing jockeys who go so fast on these cherished beasts that they have to wear goggles so that their eyeballs don't fly out – you, my friends, are like no-one on earth, you are AMAZING. Number one, has to be a love for a sport like no other.

Number two - It doesn't matter whether you are 92 or 12, being 'pony mad' and having a phone cover with your beloved horse on it, is perfectly acceptable at any age. You can re-live your youth well into those twilight years and no-one will think you have early onset Alzheimer's. This includes clicking your tongue to get someone to move rather than saying 'excuse me please!'. Reason two; being marginally insane but in very good company.

Number three - The overall appearance. Being on public transport, in a supermarket, at the dentist, in the office, etc. post-yard/pre-shower and mouthing to the cashier; 'Sorry, I've come straight from RIDING MY HORSE!' is deemed acceptable in our circles. Wearing odd and often brightly coloured socks over too tight (sometimes stained) breeches and carrying foliage around in our un-brushed hair is certainly not a problem for us, we see it as time saving, making us PERFECT marriage material! Reason three; WE ARE UNIQUE and marching to the beat of our own drum!

Number four - The etiquette. Where else will you learn that a.) Your needs/feelings will NEVER come first. Stop thinking they will, your horses' needs come first! b.) That you should always pass wide and slow and drive with caution, making you the perfect road user! c.) That when pushing a supermarket trolley, regardless of cucumber location, you pass left hand to left hand. So many other things 'non-equestrians' are missing out on... Reason four; you can guarantee we've been dragged up in terrific style.

Essentially, being an equestrian affiliates you to a not-so-secret club, one that you will always be a part of whether you own a horse or not; 'For the Love of the Horse Club'. We are all united, we all shared something in common, we all LOVE horses.

We must stop tearing strips off one another, we have all smelt of piss, have had hay in our hair and have tasted a mouthful of soil after a fall. We all have the ability to put our beautiful horses before ourselves so there is absolutely no reason why we shouldn't support a fellow horse lover for doing the same.

You should feel proud to be an equestrian, I do.

JUNE 2018

THE HIGHS AND LOWS OF EVENTING

3rd June 2018

So, a last minute entry into the 90cms Show-cross at Epworth Equestrian saw us power trotting around our regular hacking route last night in an attempt to tire out my keener that usual pony ready for the big day. Normally I like to get out somewhere but with time being tight, a decent hack would have to do.

NOTE: Show-Cross is like eventing, only cheaper and with no dressage – just show jumping and cross country elements.

Now, Pat was super forward at Shelford last week. He was jumping out of his skin and it frightened me a little bit. I wanted him to be a bit sluggish so I could manoeuvre him around a bit more with confidence before our next BE at Speetley on the 10th.

We walked the course that afternoon and whilst it was super big and bold with a lot of fences shared with the 100, I didn't feel too frightened and was ready to take the challenge on. After a good sweaty hack, I gave him a lovely bath, loaded the lorry and felt very ready for our event today. For once, I felt ready. Yes, nervous. Yes, plagued with loose bowels and frequent toilet visits, but I was ready.

My times were 2.16pm and straight out on the XC at 2.45pm

Carrot and I loaded up at 12pm ready to arrive in lots of time to hopefully catch Auntie Smurph storm her first clear cross country, but alas, it was not to be.

The sound of my lorry was not how I left it. Carrot "borrowed" the Wimpy Wagon to pick up a new motorbike one evening last week and thought it sensible not to tell me that the speedo had stuck and that the noises coming from his under-carriage were not normal. He wouldn't have known but, there was an upset tummy in there somewhere.

I didn't push him, just drove him at my usual Sunday driver speed and 10 minutes away from home, I lost all power. In fact, not just power, it became apparent that Wimpy's innards had spilled out underneath his sexual body and were scraping along the tarmac.

FUUUUUUUUUUUUUUUCK!!!

PANIC set in, I indicated and luckily pulled in at a local dairy farm just off the main road. My heart was in shreds, my nerves frayed and with tears stinging my eyes we phoned roadside assistance. My beloved Wimpy Wagon parked up with his innards on show for all to see. And in 25 degrees, my sweating pony was on the back.

This is where karma repays you dividends. My lovely friend Kate and her Mum were driving to the same show and were 2 minutes from us. They stopped in and even though fate was trying to delay my run today, I unloaded my boy and hopped him up onto Kate's lovely lorry along with my essentials leaving Carrot at the Wimpy Wagon waiting for the recovery.

On arrival, I felt ridiculously out of sorts. I was dribbling about, disorganised and with no grasp on time, found myself flapping about at the last minute. Not great! I warmed up and normally, the calmer syringe distributed on departure ready for the sharpness in the dressage warmup was almost certainly a mistake. He felt flat, lumpy and not very forward. I didn't feel scared though, which is a silver lining of course.

I've never had a smooth show jumping round at Epworth, they have a lot to look at in the way of fillers and banners, and Pat is always a spooky little sh*t there. Today was NO different.

We went in, I got my canter WAY too late and managed to scrape over the first 3 fine, I turned left to the double at 4, put my leg on as he backed off (standard) and the little b*stard slammed the anchors on for the second part of a one stride double. This hasn't happened in 6 years... he's never just said no. But I watched the video back; I was up his neck, not really in a position of determination and I deserved it. It has definitely taught me to sit the hell up after a fence.

I circled and represented for him to try again, he jumped the first part and went to drop the anchors again, but this time I was cross. I rode that jump and the rest of the course like it was the last thing I was ever going to do. Determined, leg on, no second chances and we got round with a score of 12.

By Jove, I was exhausted and not feeling overly confident going cross country after that.

I put my medical arm band on, offered Captain Spookerson a drink and off we went to warm up for the death phase.

I jumped a couple of practice fences and went straight through to the start. I hadn't studded up for this and what a massive mistake. He skidded a little into the first fence, looking at it like a turd. He jumped it, but it felt horrid. The second wasn't much better; a roll top, he looked and thought about backing off but I nailed his arse and we scraped over.

Round a right hand bend to 3; a hedge and 4; the upturned boat, both jumped much better than I thought they would. A gallop down to the castle at 5 and he felt heavy, I also felt exceptionally out of breath and tight in the chest. I toyed with pulling up, there was still so much of the course to go, I just didn't feel like I could get around.

I wanted to cry. I felt shit.

I don't know quite what made me decide to carry on, but I found something from somewhere and came to the roll top and coffin at 6 and with grit and a good kick, we sailed both and galloped down to the biggest fence on course, a big grey table. I hit a duff stride because of him backing off, again. But he jumped it, just a bit backwards.

Now, I rarely ever smack this horse, but we weren't going to get round safely unless something changed. I thwacked him twice on the bottom and he pricked up down to the wishing well. 3 strides out he clocked the water which was straight after this fence and I screamed at him "help me out lad"... annoyed at being smacked, I obviously didn't deserve his help and he stopped.... STOPPED, DEAD.

I smacked his bottom again. It was stupid, it was my fault, I was massively on the defensive and I asked for his help. No... that's not the way it works! He asks me for help, that's our deal, not the other way around. I deserved that stop 100% and put it right behind me and kicked on, sailing it on the second attempt.

Over the big carrot table and up a bank to fly over some pipes and run back down, all rode fine. Then up over a wooden house to my only worry on the course, a log off a step with 4 strides to a skinny... well, I needn't have worried. I did what I set out to, ignored the log, locked us on to the next fence and we flew them both, no bother.

A gallop down to the wagon one from home and I really chased him in for a good confident finish, he sailed the last and we were home. Finally, home, safe and well.

Now, on paper it was the worst fucking day I think I've had out competing EVER! My lorry exhaust somewhere on the A15, my Carrot stranded with the van, my disastrous show jumping fails and a stop on the cross country course. But I felt elated with another beefy 90 under our belts. So what, we made some boo boo's, we're alive and well!

Something didn't feel right though, I didn't feel right, I felt weak and lacking in muscular fitness. My brain wasn't engaged, and my stirrups were set 3 holes lower than normal by mistake. I felt like a wet weekend in Bognor Regis and it showed in my results.

Not every day can be brilliant, not every run can be smooth, but it's these testing ones that we learn the most from. I will NEVER ride like that again as long as I live, I will never let him down or smack him for my failings.

Today was a day for learning, AGAIN.

Thank you so much to Kate and her mum for being there to pick us up and for being so kind. To my dear Smurph who stormed around her first 80 like she's been doing it forever (I'm so proud of them) and to my poor Carrot who I'm sure would have loved a hot dog at the show far more than waiting for a recovery man on the road side.

Now I need to get a new exhaust before Saturday and rest my drained body before dusting off and knuckling down in hope of picking up a Regional final ticket!

Thank you all for your endless support as always, sorry to have let you down today.

Love as always

Vic and Pat xxxxx

~

Possibly the cruddiest start to June I could have had but we were both safe and the van could be mended, it would all be fine. I felt really bloody flat about how I rode him on the cross country though and I wished I hadn't smacked him. He was obviously feeling out of sorts too. I didn't have long to get sorted for Speetley and this was a bit of the unknown for me. A venue I had never been to. I was really hoping to get a Regional final ticket for Badminton Grassroots but to do that you need to be in the top 10% of your section and the way things were going, this wasn't look that great!

I spent the week preparing my test and felt confident that I could get a good one bashed out on the day. Even if I was losing a few marks here and there, he was consistently in the low

30's which would just be enough if I could keep all the poles in the cups! To test this theory, I popped down to Willow Banks this week too and bloody nailed two clear rounds. The training is definitely paying off!! But it wasn't long until the day arrived, and with the Wimpy Wagon back on the road (and me £300 lighter), we were set and ready to go!

EVENT NUMBER 3 : Speetley BE90

So, Here it is... my 2nd BE event of the season.

As you will have read, I had a total knock in every sense last Sunday at Epworth with a refusal in the show jumping and another out on course... It was a day for learning not to ride like a sack of shit but it was also a BIG wake up call to how fragile confidence really is.

I went out and boxed away my show jumping demons at Willow Banks on Wednesday night with TWO clears at 80 and 90cms to put some wind back in our sails for today.

Yesterday evening I ran through our test again and he was so lovely and worked so hard that I slept quite well (after a few cheeky whites in the pub afterwards!)

I wasn't on until 13.36 for dressage and with the venue only 1.5hours away, I didn't have to leave until 11am. Good and bad having afternoon times, as you get all morning to empty your pride into the loo but you also don't have to rush around or wake your husband up too early.

I sent the usual message to Daddy Carrot, who was out for an early fishing trip saying; "I don't think I want to go today..." STANDARD wet fish!

We arrived in good time, stopped on the way for fuel and a McDonalds (... that's right, I ate something for the first time ever on the morning of an event, 4 and a half "chicken" McNuggets) and once parked up, went and got my number and registered my attendance.

I didn't have much time to fret and got him ready and mounted for my dressage time. He warmed up the best he has EVER done. I'm trialling a new bit to attempt to get a bit more consistency in the contact and what a difference this has made in just a few sessions! He's forward and not blocked in front, much more rideable and I thoroughly enjoyed our warm up today. In the arena he spooked at everything down one side and I thought there would be a lot of marks reflecting that tension, but alas, with some good marks for the not so tense parts, we managed to score 30, a top 5 score in our section.

Next up, the course walk. Holy Mother of Christmas.... the Hedge oxer was bloody gigantic!! I mean, seriously large. I think if I had walked the course yesterday, I would have bailed.

The show jumping was also causing problems and had LOADS of fillers. Not great after our recent stoppage experience at all.

I got back on and went down to the warm up, a few things I changed today. Number 1. The bit, Number 2. I put a fly veil on him and 3. I didn't just sit there like a wet fart on a hot day. I jumped 5 or 6 practice jumps and we elected to go in before our time for the first time ever!

In the ring, he was having a good look, but I tried to keep the rhythm, I brought him back to change a canter lead and other than number 7 that he gawped at and got a big kick, he jumped a fantastic CLEAR ROUND! I cried with utter joy when I left the arena, but lucky for me waiting to go in was the nicest young lad Ben, who hugged me (both still on horseback) and sent me on my very merry way.

So, I didn't know my dressage score yet and I didn't want to. We got ready and walked down to the death phase feeling a little green. It was very quiet, in fact there was only me in there warming up and the course didn't have a single rider out on it, so I jumped 2 or 3 warm up jumps and went to the box.

3....2....1.... Out the start box like a bullet we flew, pounding up to the flower box at one. I kept my leg on firm and he sailed over for a confident start. A gallop uphill back towards the lorries and he was giving it great guns until 3 strides out, I snapped out of wet fart mode and smacked him on the bottom. It was a risk, but he replied with a lovely jump over the 2nd; a milk churn under a rail. Around the corner to three; a bloody fruit and veg stand. No-one is in the market for a pound of plums in that situation, I'm sure. He eyeballed it, but I wasn't letting him stop. I got an awful shot at it, but we cleared it. Putting it behind us, we soared down to the next fence.

A gallop to 4; a roll top of sorts. He didn't look at it much because I was driving like Jenson Button on acid. Down to the double at 5; another roll top, which jumped really well on a great forward stride, to a rail with a flower box in the hedge line. He dropped the anchors and we ground to a snail pace, but my heart had sailed over long before then and by some miracle, my body and my horse made it to the other side too! 6 was another open rail with a left turn and gallop to the HEDGE OF DEATH! I kicked like never before, I growled, I shouted obscenities that would have been heard in all neighbouring counties, and we bloody soared like a pink and blue eagle over that big hedge!

Down to the water at 8; a jump before the moisture, was very aptly named the 'PUNT' (replace one letter if you will!) that was causing a few problems for others. I brought him back to a more balanced canter and growled like an old fish wife and we were over it. Splish splashed through the pond and out over a fallen branch! BOOM... HALF WAY!

9; a wooden table jumped nicely, to 10; a chair. Again, he backed off but got a firm leg on and we made it to the other side! Back up the hill to a hay-feeder at 11, one of my better efforts on the course and over a coffin and rail out at 12.

13; a house, I got a good shot at and we had a confident stride down to the rails and skinny nearing the end of the course. I rode the skinny like I meant business, nice short reins, closed leg... straight as a die, we soared it ... BLOODY GOOD BOY!

The next one I had doubts about but collected him up and nailed the skinny blue roll top on a dog leg to a corner. I got my line, tapped his shoulder with the stick and we flew them both. A gallop to the last, sailing over it and through the finish to come home 21 seconds under the time... 2.4 penalties to add to our dressage finishing on a 32.4!

WHAT A FUCKING HORSE... What a bloody tremendous result. Out of 43 in the section we came 3rd, got our Regional Final ticket and jumped another bloody DOUBLE CLEAR!

I literally cannot put into words how much today meant to me, how that bond we have that gets me so choked up, has conquered another outing in the most rewarding way. My horse is not easy to ride, he is by no means a confidence giver and all of his training is 7 years of putting up with my chubby arse guiding him through.

Today we proved that you don't have to be technically skilled or have a big bold jumping horse to go out an earn that placing. I feel I deserved it, I've been working hard, and I didn't let my jelly legs and last week's balls up get the better of me.

So, so much love for that little horse that will do anything for me, who answers my (sometimes, very vague) questions and makes my heart burst with love. I owe everything to him.

Massive thanks to Daddy Carrot for grooming and videoing. Thank you to you for your endless support and a big thank you to all the lovely people I met at Speetley today.

I cannot tell you how happy I am right now.... It'll be a few days before I hit the floor again that's for sure!

Love as always

Vic and Pat

Xxxx

~

Upping our game was going so well, preparing to succeed was also working for us rather than setting myself up to fail. I booked a jumping lesson the following week to keep my eye in and ended up pushing my limits once again. I was confidently jumping around a course, away from home, around 1.05m/1.10m and it didn't feel terrifying. This is the same horse and rider that didn't dare jump 60cms only two years ago. If ever you need proof that this is possible, you've got it right here. It is possible if you want it enough and boy, did I want it! I wasn't giving up and I was seriously going for it.

With this mindset, I entered my next event at Eland Lodge; another unfamiliar venue for us. But, Speetley had gone so well that I wasn't too afraid of the unknown anymore.

Only a few days had passed but these were days spent working away from home again, I was feeling really low for the first time in ages. I felt homesick and very run down and with anxiety never too far away, I lingered in this place of sadness and needed a kick up the arse.

The sads...

Five things to remember when you're feeling sad, when you feel beaten, when life doesn't seem to give you a break.

First thing, this too shall pass. It is not forever unless you choose for it to be. You have the power, you have the control, you can decide. You might need a hand out of the dirt, but that's why I'm here. It's just temporary, you won't be sad forever I promise.

Secondly, having the power... doesn't that feel great? You have the power; the right, the choice, to inhale, to wiggle your nose, to grab someone's bum (careful who you grab though, I don't want you on a sexual assault charge), you have the power. The choice to turn things around, to remove whatever it is making you sad, to deal with grief, to move forward... it might take time, it might not be instant, but YOU ARE IN CONTROL OF YOU.

Thirdly, find something positive to look forward to. Have a reason to smile, to get excited or to get out of bed. Have a passion, something you dare to dream about. Focus on it. Personally, I'm looking forward to being able to get shopping delivered from Morrison's now they've expanded their delivery zone, but you know... yours could be something much more brilliant.

Fourth, and perhaps most importantly, don't you dare linger on the negatives. Don't think twice about your grey hairs, cellulite or wrinkles... fuck that shit! Stop worrying about things you cannot control, don't stress about the little things. Scrunch those things up into a ball and toss them out like a leaf in the wind. You are bloody brilliant; can you just take a second to make sure you know it!

Lastly, don't let other people stamp their dirty footprints on your life. You are wonderful, be true to who you are. People will respect you more for truth and honesty over lies and backstabbing any day. Don't compare yourself to anyone, you are so unique and so wonderful, you have greatness in you, we all do... let it out.

And there I was, at the end of another month, royally kicking my own arse. But it was too little, too late and I withdrew my entry from Eland.

29th June 2018

I've made the decision to withdraw from Saturday's event at Eland. It's going to be so hot, the ground will be firm, and I haven't ridden much this week. Pat doesn't jump well in the heat or on hard ground (roll back to Rackham last year) and a knock in confidence is not worth any amount of entry fee! My boy means the absolute world to me and that's what I keep in mind

~

In honesty, I had panic entered Eland as a last ditch attempt to get a Regional Final ticket and now that I got one at Speetley, I took the pressure off us. The ground **was** hard and those people that did run confirmed it for me. I made the right choice for us and I wasn't disappointed in myself for that. You need to do what's right for you and your horse and I have learnt that more than ever this year.

With no events planned for a few weeks, Carrot and I decided it was high time we had a little break away. Neither of us have down time very often, and with limited funds a holiday seemed like a luxury we could ill afford, but it was almost certainly worth it.

We flew to Spain, hired a car and stayed in a cheap B&B for a week in the sun. Something was different for us, I felt different. I felt content and happy and full of love. I also felt bloated, swollen in the breasts and adamant I was harbouring a bun in my oven.

This was the happiest I have been in such a long time, I had secretly pined to be pregnant for ages and I was beginning to worry that it might not happen for us. But, there I was in Spain for a whole week, refraining from too much alcohol and looking forward to getting home and doing a test to confirm what I was already so sure of.

JULY 2018

The Moment of Truth

I didn't even get as far as the plane doors when the worst thing imaginable happened. I just popped to the loo one last time before we left the hotel for home and there it was, the moment that my week of ridiculous happiness came careering down around my ears. I got my period. The swollen boobs, bloating and contentment was just pre-menstrual symptoms, and having not had those during my years of long term contraception, I had convinced myself I was pregnant.

I hadn't just convinced myself though, I was so happy about it too. And I don't think I have ever felt so much disappointment as I did sitting on the toilet that day. I didn't even tell Carrot about my initial suspicions, so it meant I also had to hide my state of crippling sadness and anguish from him too. I felt fucking horrible. And I got so pissed on the plane on the way home that I slept the whole car journey back!

Horrible, horrible bloody female body trickery. My mind was all over the place and I certainly didn't feel nice and rested. Just anxious and back to convincing myself I had a defective womb! Great!

You shouldn't miss what you never had. But I did. Box it away Vic, come on!

Back to throwing myself into competing, I guess!

So, I trundled out and went for a lesson with an old friend to try and get my missing mojo back.

19th July 2018

Do you ever just take a step back and think, look and evaluate?

Today, I drove my horse, in MY little, slightly rusty horsebox through town and all the traffic (which would have scared me shitless before) for a lesson with one of my best friends.

Tonight, I have just showered and changed after my lesson in her beautiful home, and right now she's cooking me dinner. I don't have half the facilities, the beautifully soft White Company furnishings or impeccable taste that she has. Nor do I have quite the eye for a horse or the riding ability, but we are the best of friends and it makes anything tangible invisible.

She had taught me so much today. Not just about my riding but about how lucky we all are in so many ways. In my lesson we barely scratched the surface, but a true friend can give you very honest feedback without you taking offence. A true friend wants you to succeed as much as you want it.

This particular friend highlighted pivotal balance issues and tension in my thigh which is almost certainly the reason why I feel so scared. Being out of balance and grabbing hold of my horse makes him panic, which makes me panic, which makes me grab and grip... vicious circle huh?!

Now I know what the problems and areas of weakness are, I can work hard to fix them.

Tonight, I am grateful for good horses, for good wine and for very good friends.

~

You need times like this to get your perspective back and true friends like these don't come around that often. If you have these people in your life, cherish them. Message them often just asking how they are, be there for them and they will be there for you in return.

LESSON 6: YOU NEED GOOD PEOPLE. I think I've said it once before... Surround yourself with people that either couldn't give a shit, ones that would give their last shit to see you succeed, or the ones that don't know what shit you're doing. Forget about the ones that drag you down and give all your time and energy to the ones that make you feel as brilliant as you really are.

~

If I'm totally honest, July went so fast. I was away with work again and my heart was battered. I felt like hibernating, but I had entered Frickley BE at the end of the month, so I kept slogging forwards. It came up so quickly and I'm not sure my heart was really in it looking back;

EVENT NUMBER 4 : Frickley Park BE90

So, only my 3rd affiliated event of the season (can't quite believe I'm saying this when it's nearly August!) happened yesterday at Frickley Park!

I've been consciously trying to lighten up about things and try to enjoy having fun with my horse instead of piling on pressure and being a miserable cockwomble. This was the one and only aim of yesterday... no wobbles allowed!

Daddy Carrot had to work with it being a Friday so Auntie Smurph, who is a teacher and on school holidays stepped in as chief in charge of calming my nerves and helping me out.

We arrived in plenty of time for my 9.48am dressage (NEWSFLASH: no toilet happenings!) and with a 3 hour gap between that and show jumping, in almost 30 degrees, I'd packed plenty of water for Pat and stupidly decided that would be a good time to walk the cross country.

I collected my number and plaited (still no toilet happenings!) feeling remarkably calm and actually enjoying the day. At this point, time tends to just slip away so quickly and by the time I got on, I only had 20 minutes until I was in the ring!

Now, on the way we had rain, a miracle really, but it meant the hard ground was then lined with a film of dampness. I put in medium pointy studs on advice of my friend Kathryn who is very experienced, and that seemed to do the job of keeping him upright.

For anyone that doesn't know, the dressage warm up is my biggest fear. The time when he's usually fresh as a badger's arse, most likely to throw some killer shapes and send me flying through the air onto my head and potentially leaving in an ambulance. Today though, he was seriously awesome!

I didn't take up a contact AT ALL until I had to go down to ring, I let him lollop about and I just enjoyed it... WHAT A BLOODY DIFFERENCE!

I went into the test calm and happy, I felt like it deserved one of our better marks. He was forward, on the aids, happy and so was

I! I was enjoying cantering my last 20m circle so much that I forgot to trot resulting in a beep from the judge and 2 marks added but I couldn't have cared less!

I was absolutely over the moon to not feel frightened at an event, I could have gone home happy there and then!

On seeing the course photos the night before, I knew what I was in for and because we've done this event twice before, my course walk was purely to check the going. The organisers had worked so hard to water as much as possible, but the first section of the course wasn't filling me with joy.

It got better though, and I decided to see how he jumped in the show jumping as to whether I would run him cross country.

By the time I jumped at 1pm, it was unbelievably hot, and Pat was really trying his best. He has never jumped that well on hard ground, but I think the course was on the best going of the whole show ground! In the ring, fences came and went like they were nothing and 1-5 jumped really well off a beautiful big stride. We had an unfortunate rail at the back of the double at 5 and sadly, I took the shittest line known to human kind around a bend to 6. He slipped a bit, lost his footing and I just took my leg off on the turn to ease out of it. But the jump was upon us and with no leg on, the little bugger stopped. I couldn't get cross, it was entirely my fault and we came around a second time no problem.

The wheels fell off a little bit, having the next fence down but we finished over the last two brilliantly.

I came out of the ring happy and that's all that mattered to us.

16 to add to our dressage which was an unusually high 36 (reflective of the section, as we were in the top 10 dressage scores), on paper the crappest day we've had, but I didn't feel disappointed.

Now, with the heat and the way he lost a bit of confidence in the show lumping, I went and withdrew. Bailed out, lost my bottle, stormed off because of a bad score... or, quit while I was ahead! We had achieved everything I set out to in the first 20 minutes of our dressage warm up, so I would have left happy regardless.

My little horse has nothing to prove, we didn't need to gallop on hard ground for 10 minutes on a hot day. There's always another day but, my goodness; there's no other horse like him.

We left much cooler than we would have been, and we left happy. That's what's important.

I had the best day and I know to some I might have failed, but inside my head and my heart and the legs of my horse, we won today.

Here's to rain, moving forward and our next outing!!

~

And that was it, another month over. A massive disappointing non-pregnancy, a hugely expensive combined training show and nothing much to show for July at all. I felt a bit flat and kept dwelling on how much I came on last season compared to this one. Something had to change, and I was going to have to make it happen!

AUGUST 2018

Time Flies!

5th August 2018

Yesterday we ventured back to Epworth Equestrian for their Combined Training show. For anyone not familiar with this term, it's just like Eventing only much less expensive and no death phase (cross country) to worry about!

After bailing out at Frickley last Monday, I figured I might just take up knitting or cross stitch. But with Pat still lounging about in the field and some irritating fire for eventing in my groin, I knuckled down to setting things straight!

I actually sought advice of the Internet first, just like I would for illness diagnosis, and I received some excellent advice from one lady in particular. I learnt that to get consistent low-mid 20s dressage scores, I need to:

Have much more pizzazz and the trot needs more power!

The canter needs to be uphill and forward

Pat needs to be in front of the vertical

I need to look like I'm doing much less (ie STOP NAGGING!!)

Maintain accuracy of all the movements

Ride the centre line like you mean business

Improve the halt

Basically, improve EVERYTHING!! But above all of this, and no one in particular pointed it out, I've got to stop riding for survival and ride for the win. Up until now I have only gone to a show expecting to come home in one piece. That's not enough anymore if you actually would like to do well, which I think I do!

So yesterday I made some very drastic mental and physical changes. It was a turning point for us both.

First thing, I learnt the test and actually bothered to hire an arena and practice it! I also put spurs on (in practice too) because I often find that I'm nagging all the time with my big fat legs which are as useful as a wasp in my wine. The spurs helped me keep stiller and ask once rather than a hundred nags!

I carried my hands up and forwards but kept a shorter rein, kicking him up into that uphill feeling hand means his nose doesn't dip behind the bridle and he's rarely ever on the forehand!! Winner!

I prepared movements better, I also pushed the canter out of my rocking horse, "going nowhere" pace that I love to sit to, but that doesn't score points!! Having the shorter rein and better connection meant it wasn't too unbalanced either!

I will also add that I've stripped him of the calmer. Yep, I've said it out loud now! No more calmer, not the powder in his tea or show day syringes! If I want pizzazz, you can't piss on the spark, and I've spent 2 years pissing on those sparks for fear of the flames getting out of hand! Time to grow a pair!

I rode the best test I feel like I've ever ridden. It was BE92 (my upcoming RF test). My halt could be better, and my accuracy could improve, but the 74% it received meant these changes worked and would have meant a 26, reflective of the day because out of about 40 competitors we were the highest of all of them by a decent margin!

A quick change and down to the jumping, the course was long and winding but luckily, I chose to jump 80cms after recent stopping at both Frickley and the disaster last time we came to Epworth. It was a day for confidence and trying new techniques not for proof that we can jump big jumps!

We jumped clear after a lucky knock of number two that didn't fall... We went clear, which felt AMAZING!

He won the class by almost 10 points and I felt, and still feel, absolutely elated. Hard work, practice and knowing when and how to take and use advice has meant WINNING!

I've been riding for 25 years on hundreds of different horses (no exaggeration). I have experience, feel, knowledge and a very capable horse to ride BUT if you don't have the capacity to learn, to be humble and to hold your hands up when you hit a wall, that experience and ability is worth jack shit.

This week has been enlightening, my red rosette is one of my proudest yet and I will keep on trying in the same way.

Thank you all so, so much for your endless support and help. For being there for me and Pat, to those people that popped over for a chat and a cheeky cigarette, thank you all.

Love as always, Vic and Pat

Xxxx

~

What a difference these little changes can make. I learnt so much about how differently things could go if you actually go out with the intention of doing well. I feel ridiculous and as though I'm pointing out the obvious, but if you want to win; you can. You just have to want to, and change things in order to make that happen.

Things on the non-horsey (pregnancy) front were definitely not following the same pattern. I wanted that more than I've ever wanted any bloody red rosette and all I had was red visitor of a different kind. It was beginning to affect me more than I realised.

I was longing with all my heart to conceive and it wasn't happening.

9th August 2018

November marks a year of "not, not trying", calling it that seems much less threatening, and part of me thought it would have happened long before now. Yes, I am aware that just 10 months "clean" after 13 years of medicinal contraception is absolutely nothing, but I can't help the way I feel.

I am soon to be 33 and very happily married to my second husband, we are *coughs* active in that way too and both know the timing is right.

Every month when my boobs are sore and twice the size, and my body teases me by throwing my cycle out one or two days, I feel elated, hopeful and so happy. Then, just a day later, totally bloody shattered when I get my period that I don't fucking want. They don't call it 'the curse' for nothing!

I want to be fucking pregnant. But this is the trouble, I want it too much. I want it more than a spin around Badminton or possibly the end to world hunger… and that's totally fucking selfish too!

I'm sure there are people that will read this who have been 'not, not trying' for much longer or can't have their own babies, and all I have learnt so far is, I can quite imagine how you feel. You are amazing though, in your own right, with or without a baby. You are wonderful and don't ever forget it. Don't lose hope, please don't. You never know what life will bring, you never know what is around the corner. Don't plan too far ahead, live for now and be the happiest you can every single day.

~

And for once, I took my own advice! I stopped fretting as soon as I wrote this down in my diary. The power of a diary, I will keep one for as long as I live.

Back to business! With my Regional Final only 2 weeks away I decided we probably needed another run before hand to keep our eye in, and so I entered an unaffiliated event back at Epworth, just a nice local one to give us a spin out.

NUMBER 5: Epworth Unaffiliated 80cms

Now, for anyone wondering. Yes, I have my BE90 Regional Final at Shelford in 2 weeks and yes, I know I did the 80cm class today but I want my horse's confidence to blossom, I want him happy and keen and I also want to enjoy it too. Epworth was a challenging track last time, so I decided that instead of fearing the full up 90, I would have much more fun jumping 80 and letting him have a go at finding some balls too!

I've been quite slack this week on the riding front, mainly because the ground is rock hard and also because my lorry broke down on Thursday, pre-jumping lesson! (It's fixed...sort of!!) I had a quick run through of my test, but I gave him yesterday off and a pretty easy week all things considered.

We set off, (Wimpy Wagon started up like a peach) arriving in plenty of time to let Pat chill his beans and for Carrot and me to walk the course.

Within two minutes of course walking my belly burst out of my breeches through a zip fly which apparently, could no longer contain my sizeable gut!! Lucky, I had a pin spare! It was a nice course however, and the guys at Epworth have some excellent covered going!! I was happy!

Without calmer syringing or his daily powder, I was surprised that when I plaited and tacked up ready for dressage and walked down to the warm up, he was so chilled. He was lazy if anything, but we were having FUN! We were enjoying the dressage warm up! I didn't spoil it by picking him up too much and in the ring and it showed. He did a sweet test and got the second best mark of the whole class for a 30.3, it could have had more spark, but I was thrilled regardless.

Back at the box and a quick change for show jumping. I was really happy, content even. No nerves, no grizzly old baggage, I was even nice to my husband. I watched a few go, learnt the course and warmed up.

There were not many people going clear, and Epworth is renowned for having a spooky jumping arena (we've had a few disasters here too). I walked him in like we owned the joint, no flapping, no rushing, just mooching about like we were on a trip to Skegness having chips on the sea front. Popped up into canter and lolloped our way around the first few and he started TAKING CONTROL! My horse; that spooky, backward thinking fella, picked up the bit and started taking ME to the jumps! I nearly soiled myself; out of shock, not fear this time! It was sensational, I've wanted him to pull me into a jump for 6 years and today was his day. It was his day to start a journey and what a magnificent one it will be.

So, with only one unlucky rub of a shady jump at number 6. We headed out of the ring smiling our biggest smiles EVER!

Getting ready for cross country, the nerves were there, but manageable. I got us both ready and we set off to pop a few practice jumps. The lovely starter man said we could go straight through, but knowing how excited Pat gets in the start box of doom, I asked the man if I could settle him in there as good practice before he sent us away. I settled him and away we went!

Determined not to gun it too fast, I let the rhythm just come as he felt comfortable, like a medium to fast canter I suppose. The first fence was a bit sticky, he wasn't going to stop but he did hesitate, and I kept a firm leg on to number two; a box fence with holes in it. He looked but again I was right there to catch him, soaring it and cantering away round the sweeping turn to 3;

a table and 4 and 5; two log piles. I let him take the lead, he decided to go himself... HE TOOK ME IN!

I wiped tears of joy from my eyes before number 6a&b, two narrower jumps, b being quite gappy and bright... he nailed it! Bang on stride like an absolute pro! Crikey I need to stop pride making my eyes leak when I'm going around!

Next, a house which he also took on all guns blazing, and onto the carrot table which, never getting complacent, he needed my help at. I just put a bit of extra leg on and we sailed it.

Round the back of the woods and over three more jumps on a new track none of which a problem, and back out into the field to 11, he was back to being in charge! Pulled me in and I loved it, whooping and cheering to the next! 12; a pipe and flowers jumped well, onto the water which he usually likes to come back to trot for. Not today my friends! He cantered through it and out over a previously problematic wishing well like it was nothing!

A leg stretch up to the top of the field over 15; a roll top and bounding off the drop, he soared 16 like it wasn't even there! Through the woods I began tiring, I need to get fitter! We steadied up a little bit but out the trees and two from home, we both whooped with joy!!!

The last two fences came and went as we burst over the finish line of the most amazing round and day out eventing I have EVER had.

Turns out we went over 30 secs too fast! Giving us a penalty of 8.8tf to add. We still finished 5th in our section and got the most amazing PINK rosette!

Placings, numbers, prizes and records mean absolutely Jack sh*t if you're not out there having the absolute time of your life. It's all meaningless if there's no passion, no love for the sport or appreciation of anything other than the win.

For us, it's not about winning.

For us, it's being the best team we can be.

Today, we were the best, Pat was the best and he continues to surprise me with his big lion heart. Growing his confidence is more rewarding than anything I've ever done.

Thank you to my wonderful support team, my darling Daddy Carrot and to you, for your encouragement and love, it means a lot.

Love as always, Vic & Pat

Xxx

~

I don't think my pre Regional Final run could have gone much better than that. I was determined to not let the nerves get to me like last year's version of events. But for some reason I wasn't as in control as I'd have liked. Throughout the season you get to pick up qualifying results (approx top 3 in your section) which mean you collect 'tickets' that deem you eligible for a RF at that level. At the final you must come in the top 20% to get through to the championship held at Badminton alongside the main international event there in May. And as I am the LEAST competitive person EVER, I started to feel very uneasy about this. The lead up wasn't what I hoped for and nor did the day go how I thought it would in my head. So many times, I visualised how I would feel getting that Badminton place. Much like I visualise what I would do with the lottery jackpot. But the reality is, I'm still skint and I'm not going to Badminton... not yet anyway!

MITSUBISHI MOTORS CUP – REGIONAL FINAL

Unfortunately, my usual preparation in the run up to an event was scuppered because I had to stay away for work Monday to Wednesday last week. It also marked my job handover and official unemployment, so I expect my mind and nerves weren't helped by this pressure either.

Saturday, I walked the course with one of my Team Wimpy chums, Becki and I felt comfortable that there was nothing on the course that was dressed with flowers or seemed to be too scary! Result! That also meant the fight for a Badminton slot would rest solely on the other two phases! Heading home I was riddled by palpitations but not feeling too horrible. I got everything ready, rode through my test one last time and got an early (non booze filled) night!

I woke up to my 4.45am alarm and got out the house by 5.20am. With no time for bowel emptying or feeling too scared, we set off.

15 minutes into the journey, the nerves came. I used to feel them the month before, then just the week before, this year I've narrowed the time spent panicking down to the last few hours. I'm hoping to eventually get rid of them all together one day! But today, I had the WORST nerves I think I have EVER felt in my whole life.

Worse than waiting for my divorce to be accepted, worse than when Pat got cast and injured at Talland; the worst nerves of my life hit me like a train.

We pulled over, so I could use the toilet and eventually made it to Shelford and their line of portaloos. My body was a mess, it was making me physically sick which I don't think has ever happened before. I felt cold, shivery and light headed. My hands struggled to do up my tack and the tightness in my chest was making me panic. I wanted to cry and not just out of nerves, I felt desperately sad about how I felt. I thought after Epworth, we had turned a huge corner but the pressure of having to be competitive was making me feel this awful fear of disappointment.

I got on and warmed up, he was so lovely, not a single spook or salmon fish impression. In the test he was far lazier than I'd have liked, and I have learnt that this is penalised heavily in eventing. But I kept him out in the frame just like I'd been practicing, I thought it deserved around a 35 so guess what... I actually breathed for the first time all morning! I had resigned myself to never getting through on that score, you'd need sub 30 to be in with a chance and I was so happy.

The pressure was off, I laughed all the way back to the box at how stupid I'd been! I hugged Pat and apologised to Daddy Carrot and proceeded to enjoy the morning eventing as much as I could!

I went show jumping with the biggest grin on my face! We warmed up and chatted away to a load of lovely people, and in the ring, I just breathed and had FUN! He never jumps well in the ring at Shelford and he did have a couple of spooks! He was giving the fences a lot of room which made some of the distances quite short and deep resulting in rolling 3 poles, but I didn't care one bit! He was bouncing, and I was so happy to be out there having fun!

I also learnt that my dressage score was a 35 but not at all that bad looking at the other scores, definitely top half but certainly not what we are actually capable of on our best day.

Down in the XC warm up I was feeling excited to get going! I decided to test out wearing my stopwatch today too! And here we were, popping the practice jumps with no spooking, just me and my boy having fun!

In the box, I got counted down and actually remembered to start the speedo!! A short run to a kind log at number 1 which he boinged over no bother, to number 2; a box with milk churns on, he looked but I was there to catch him, and we bounded down to the step up at 3. We rounded the corner before it in a steady canter, probably not as bouncy as it should have been and then it happened...

He fell.

He misjudged the height, scrambled and stumbled and eventually scraped his way up. He's so good at steps that I just usually hold the mane and wait, but today he was left a bit sore and feeling very frightened. I trotted a few strides and he felt ok so popped him back up to canter for the chair at 4.

He stopped.

He was frightened after the step, and I don't blame him. But I needed to show him it was okay. We circled, I gave him a big pat and we flew over it, cantering our way down to a brush at 5 and a little log, number 6. Both of these we had a sticky jump, but I knew I had the rest of the course to make him realise it was okay again.

7; a roll top, he started to get a bit more confidence, splashing through the water and over the log at 8, he lost momentum but WHAT A HORSE! He pinged over it and galloped down to 9 and 10 two sets of rails in the hedge lines, ping ping!!! He was flying now, back in his stride!

Down at the double of pipes for 11 and into the woods, we were screaming with joy! He was pulling me into the palisade at 12 and we were flying once more!

The jump I got at 13, the straw bale pheasant feeder... was one of the best jumps I've ever had! He took me in and I sobbed with pride! 14 was a skinny house which he jumped well and onto the brush going back into the woods. No problem for him, he was heading home now, and he felt full of beans!

Pop pop! Out over the yellow pipes in the woods and down a step which I steadied him up for. A long gallop to the final brush and log which he was seriously keen for and through the finish flags!

I couldn't have been happier with how we finished our day, I was and still am, absolutely ecstatic. He was amazing and grew in confidence with every jump after his fall. I helped him, and he actually responded and what a feeling that is. Better than a Badminton qualification or rosette that's for sure!

He did manage to take a good bit of fur and skin off a hind leg, but I washed it really well and put some antiseptic cream on it before we took him home.

I grabbed a burger, my dressage sheet and my photos and headed home, so stupidly happy for what it might look like on paper.

Our dressage of 35 wouldn't have been enough anyway, 33 would have but that's hindsight. With 12 jumping penalties to add, a stop XC and a few time faults we ended the day at the very bottom of the most elite of 90 sections. And guess what? I was probably as happy (if not more) than those people that qualified.

It's not about winning for us, I say it often, but it really isn't. I don't want to be a disappointment and that's what got to me this morning. I have sponsors and all you amazing people that I want to do well for. But the truth is; I can't consistently do well, it's not reality and anyone that thinks they can are deluded. I want you all to know that you can win even if you aren't placed first. I've never felt like such a winner than I do having my horse bounding into a jump on his own accord and that's what matters.

I could blame the hideous weather, the comments on my sheet not being accurate, I could have ridden for the clear show jumping or walloped him over that chair from a standstill but that isn't us. We value smiles over prizes and points.

Massive huge thanks to all of you, who continue to support me even though our results might not be the best, my riding might not be perfect and without a string of top horses... you are all amazing. Thank you xxxxx

Here's to the next one!!

And that's the point isn't it? You are on your own path. If you want to jump small jumps, do that. If you want to jump big ones, that's fine too. If all you want is a hack to the pub, bloody well enjoy that. If dressage is for you, that's cool. Please don't feel you need to prove anything to anyone. **LESSON 7: MAKE YOUR OWN RULES**. It's your life, your horse and your sanity... do what makes YOU happy.

I wasn't massively pleased with my progression this year when I compared it to last year. But what hope did I have, the ground was too wet, then it was too hard, then I got pissed, the lorry broke down, I got nervous again... seriously, no wonder I hadn't stepped back up to jumping 1m classes. I was being too hard on myself and decided enough was enough. It was just fun, fun, fun from this point onwards!

September 2018

Falling into place

My next event was at Frickley Park again and this time it wasn't too hot, hard or wet! In fact, the going was great, I knew the challenges on the course and with Daddy Carrot coming along to kick my back side into shape, we got on with the job!

NUMBER 7: Frickley Park BE90

So, here we are again... on the eve of an event and having just walked the course, I didn't feel horrendous. Certainly, nowhere near as bad as my last event at Shelford. I put so much pressure on myself there and I didn't enjoy a single bit of that feeling.

Frickley was all about having FUN as a priority.

My dressage was at 8.18am and I was set to be finished all three phases by 10.30, so only two small gins in the pub on our traditional Friday night drink and we were home and in bed by 10pm all set for our 4.30am alarm!

The feeling that usually hits me "how easy would it be to just withdraw?" when the alarm sounds wasn't there today. I sprung out of bed and hopped into my breeches and out the door feeling almost excited for the first time in ages! We loaded Pat and set off on our 1hr45 journey. Made a pit stop for coffee and toilet necessities, and after a short directional malfunction we were parked up at Frickley albeit running a little behind schedule! I plaited in record time (about 3 and a half minutes!) and got ready whilst Daddy Carrot trotted off to get my number and pay the start fee. Minutes later we were heading down to dressage with only 20 minutes to go before I was in!

I stupidly gave him a bit of the calmer syringe when we stopped at the services, just like in times gone by. I thought it would help me with our recent show jumping stops but alas, it just confirmed what I already knew; that it just can't be relied upon and sometimes creates more tension and excitement in him (and was probably the cause of my last two years of fear to mount at shows)!

He was a total dick; buzzy, wired and I was back feeling scared again. I will happily admit that the calmer was a big mistake on my part and one I will not make again. Settled and in the test, the same one I've done pretty much all season, I went bloody wrong! I got the sodding horn of shame, I knew instantly what I'd done by cantering in the wrong place, but I gathered myself, redid the bit I screwed up and finished the test.

Walking back to change for jumping, the rain fell heavier and heavier... I felt anxious about slipping and skidding about in the ring and when I finally got my act together and got back on, my legs had turned to wiggly tentacles of uselessness!

We only had a few to go before us so I popped a couple of cross poles, knocked down an upright or two and saw a crappy stride to an oxer and we were in!

He spooked at the first fence, but we made it, despite having studs in, he had a little skid in front of the second and just ground to a stop! BOLLOCKSSSSS! I forgot to do anything again, I sat there like a wet fish on a soggy day... I did NOTHING! Dickhead Vic, you really, really are!

I circled and rode like I actually wanted him to do it and guess what... he did it! I then got my arse in gear and rode my very best hunting style round, growling and shouting and kicking like stink. It was not pretty but he was jumping so well! We actually came out with only 1 time penalty thanks to my forward riding so that was 5 to add to our dressage score and left us sitting in the top 3!

A quick change and we were in the XC warm up with 20 minutes! I was just aiming for getting around, building his confidence back up at the steps after his fall at Shelford and if we made it to the end, well that would have been a bonus!

The starter man was so nice, but his 3...2...1, still made me want to set him on fire and chuck him in a bush!

The first fence came up really quickly, barely 100 yards from the box; it was kind and we sailed it confidently and galloped I'm up to a wooden flower wall at number 2. He backed off and we hit a duff stride, but we were over it and it made me buck my ideas up a bit!

There was a roll top that I really had to ride him at, spooky little sod! Flying over that, I pulled out left and cornered into my planned line for a double of offset hedge-topped boxes. WOW! What a jump we got at those, he locked on and understood what I was asking! Result!

5 was the hedge and rails which he jumped so big, it felt like we were in the air forever, such an amazing feeling! I wish I'd got a picture of that, I was seriously beaming! 6a&b; a wooden box jump and down quite a large step, he pinged the jump and

confidently flew off the step pulling me down the hill towards 7! He was loving it, and so was I!

7 was a white house which jumped fine, to 8; the trakehener. I pushed for a big bold stride to that, so he wouldn't look into the bottom and it worked, eyes up, legs on and we soared! 9 was up a bank and just one stride down to and a wooden palisade, pinging over like a little dear, my first question on the course was looming so I shortened him up ready for a skinny log and step up for 10.

He came back to me well and popped the log, I held the mane and kept the rhythm and this time he pinged up the step no bother at all! Huge big squeal and pat on the neck and we were off!

Over the rail at 11 and a lovely wall at 12, my only two let up fences on the course. We hooked right into the woods, left and right again to a military style rail with hessian sacks under it. He backed right off it, ground to what was almost a stop and I had to think fast. I growled, kicked and waggled my whip and he hopped over it like a little stag! Bloody spooky sh*t bag! And complacent jockey! This did not bode well for the double of skinny offset logs at 14a&b.

I brought the canter right back and made it VERY obvious what the question was, he answered correctly and nailed both parts! I've never screamed as loud or felt such pride, I apologise to the spectators for my monster scream of "You are a Fucking GOOD BOY", what a bloody horse though!

Into the water at a trot because I literally didn't care about anything other than how amazing he was! We popped out over the roll top and bounced down to that hideous green and white corner! I collected, steered and he thought about running out, but there was nowhere for him to go. I held fast, and he jumped it bang on! A hard left turn to the flower box skinny that he's always had a look at and just like before, I held him securely together and true as a die, he pinged over it!

At this point I thought it had felt quite a fast round so I let him cruise a bit over the last two fences. We flew the flowered wall and saw a duff stride at the last, but we were clear and through the flags, screaming with pride! I hopped off and undid his girth and nosebands and hugged him so tight! We did it, we did it!

He was so unbelievably amazing, just the ability for him to understand what I ask and agree with what I'm telling him to do. I've taught him to jump these jumps, I've made mistakes too don't get me wrong, but what a feeling it is when it's right. Having a horse understand what is required at each testing obstacle and do exactly what is asked; it's just amazing. I will never take for granted how magnificent my horse is, how brave he and I can be when we are working as a team. We have something so special and I adore every little inch of him.

Back at the box, we washed him down and settled him back on the van with a big haynet and plenty of polos and sugar lumps. We went to buy photos and peeped in to find that I had actually gone a bit too slow and should I have not "cruised" home on the XC, we would have been in the top 5! Alas, 11th place for us but who gives a fat rats ass?! Not me!! My horse makes me feel like a winner every time!

Here's to the next one, the final one of 2018!

"You always look so happy when you're riding...."

I hear this without fail at least once a month sometimes more than once a day. I don't edit out the pictures that show my gurning, scared shitless face either. The truth is, I am happy and more to the point, why does that surprise people?

Despite how elated I was when I came back down to earth after Frickley, nothing was going to come close to how happy I was about to be.

You see, this doesn't start massively jovial because I was down in West Sussex for a few days to hand over my main income to a new in-house employee. Now, I had been with this group of companies for over 3 years and built this job roll up from nothing. The brands were mine, the websites were mine and I felt very out of sorts handing all of it over to a new lady who, with a background in law and professional services, didn't really seem fit for the very outgoing role. It was out of my hands, but I left with a heavy heart, nonetheless. I had become very fond and possessive of my position there and I didn't like the thought of them managing without me either.

Throughout my marketing career spanning the last ten years, I have had some great jobs. But none have got under my skin like this one did. I was obsessed. I think it's the main reason I wanted to start my own company, I wanted to feel ownership of something that was actually mine! But let me tell you; it's not the same when it's yours!

Anyway, I was down in West Sussex doing the final handover and as always on my trips down south, I like to try and catch up with my local friends. This trip was no different, I met up with my friend Linda for dinner.

Linda and I first met at a riding club training day in 2012. I took Pat there for the first time when I joined my new club Wey Valley RC. Linda ran the training there and she was so welcoming. At the time, I was riding and schooling a few horses for people for extra cash, recently Pat had gone out on loan because of my shitty financial situation and I was chatting to Linda about this when the subject first came up.

Linda had a horse in sales livery. This horse; a full thoroughbred mare, was costing far more per month on livery than she was hoping to get for selling her. So, what did I do? I offered to take her on the same arrangement but with no sales livery fee and went to have a look at her!

I remember going into the barn and seeing this little black horse, she wasn't really anything flashy and full thoroughbred, so naturally on the thin and stressy side! But, my goodness I love a thoroughbred and after everything Linda had told me about her, I thought she would be fun to have around. 2 weeks later, she turned up!

Her name was Pea. And she filled the huge Pat shaped hole in my heart far quicker than I could have wished for. She was ballsy, determined and knew her own mind, but she was also insanely loyal, with the biggest trusting heart I'd ever known.

Linda covered all of her costs and I did the work. Win win. I had her jumping courses, took her to shows and cross country schooling. I did all the Riding Club team events and qualified for the Festival of the Horse and the show jumping championships. She jumped clear so many times I lost count and brought me so much happiness when I needed it the most.

I vividly recall our first and only affiliated event. The rain pelted for days beforehand making trenches in the dressage arena, particularly down the centre line. She wasn't keen on this part at all never mind in the trenches with it pissing rain into her face! We had an unfortunate pole down in the show jumping and headed for cross country sodden, but really up for it! She flew out of the start box and tackled everything I asked of her, including THE WRONG FENCES! I jumped a fence that was part of the novice class the next day. I thought it felt big, but she didn't think so and cleared it by a mile! Sadly, we learnt of our elimination crossing the finish line and really didn't care either! She was AMAZING!!

I never felt nervous on her, not once. She taught me to trust a horse again and taught me to love riding just like I used to. I was totally smitten. She absolutely hated being stabled and regularly pulled a fast once pretending to have colic… see me dashing like lightening to the yard only for her to make a miraculous recovery as soon as I arrived! Minx! I could never really get her that round and soft on the flat either, but I didn't care! We were having so much fun.

When Pat came back under his naughty cloud from being out on loan, and having Pea there to restore my confidence, I was torn between them. Pea was so good, even Carrot rode her. But I was struggling for time and Pat was always left at home, with me choosing to ride Pea over him anywhere I went. He frightened me, and she didn't, it was a no-brainer. But he was my horse, she wasn't. It was him I should have sold, it was him that made me cry at night, not her, not my lovely little Pea. But alas I was drowning in it all, I had the conversation with Linda about finding her a new home and we did just that.

A friend of a friend tried her and a week later took her on full loan. Just like that, it was Pat and I on our own again. This was good for Linda as there were now no costs involved and the lady seemed nice, so I was happy (ish) too!

That was the last I heard from Pea for over two years. I felt guilty asking after her, I'm not sure why. I did get wind of her having problems with soundness and sore back problems, followed by ulcers and treatment for them. You never really know what goes on when you just Facebook stalk instead of actually asking! But I knew Pea wasn't right. I also knew Linda took her back at some point too. And there she stayed, feral in the field for the next two years!

Linda did try and ride her a couple of times and had a physio fella out to look at her a few times too, but she is such a strong-willed mare. Pea knows exactly how to tell you something isn't right and so she was just kept as a pet by Linda, who would feed her horses over herself any day!

Now, roll forward to our evening in West Sussex (September 2018). We sat having dinner and amongst other conversations; Linda explains that she is no longer in a position to keep Pea as a costly field ornament. She didn't have the time, the money or much hope that she would ever come sound enough to ride and aside from finding her a home as a companion (that doesn't like being on her own, weaves like Billy-o and fakes colic), the option of her being put to sleep, flashed across both of our faces.

It really was the easiest decision I have ever had to make.

"I'll take her."

There wasn't any question in the matter.

I messaged Carrot, he was happy too. We were both absolutely delighted to be getting her home. Both babies reunited. I was happier than I had been for many, many years that night.

OCTOBER 2018

WHEN ONE DOOR CLOSES...

In order to end my mismatched season on the best note possible, I decided to go out at 80cms and have an absolute ball with my horse on our last run.

I didn't feel embarrassed or ashamed about dropping down a level, he wouldn't notice, and I would just feel a little bit more confident ending my season this way. I've spent more money on lessons this year than events and I feel like our show jumping has come on so much because of that. I also feel more capable in this area and now the weaknesses are shining through in other places that I need to work on!

I had also driven the 200mile round trip to meet Linda half way from West Sussex with Pea, and she was out in the field with Pat looking very content indeed. I booked her feet in to be done, had my lovely physio booked to take a look and felt very happy to love two horses so much.

It was having Pea in the field with Pat that made me realise just how wrong it was with Bender. Although I loved him, he really didn't fit in with our very laid-back life here. My horses live outdoors 24/7 and I'm not sure Sir Bentley was up for that. You have to listen to them, be able to read what they are trying to tell you. Bender is very happy on a bigger yard with hustle and bustle. Pat fits in with most situations as long as I'm around (and food is around) and Pea is definitely an outdoorsy girl. Routine and having them happy and content are so important to me.

Once Pea had had the once over, I waited with bated breath for a couple of days before popping her on the lunge to see how level she was.

To my utter amazement, she looked totally fine! So, I started leading out off Pat for a few rides to get her strength up before I sat my chubby arse on her tiny body!

But, back to his Nibs… We were there, the time had come, it was the last event of the season already, I was determined to make it a fun one, but as always, things never turn out quite how you want them to!

THE FINAL ONE: Norton Disney BE80.

This is most certainly the hardest event report I've had to write all season. Even now, the morning after, I'm still so emotional about it.... it's a sport, a hobby damn it! Deep breath, here goes....

We spent the week hacking, running through my test and the usual. Nothing out of the ordinary and as we had stepped down to the 80 as a last confidence building run of the season, I didn't stress too much that we hadn't got out for a jump anywhere.

Now, I also entered the 80 because I am teaching all day today (Saturday) and Sunday's I can't really do (nerves, husband commitments), so it was either the 80 or the 100 on the Friday! Daddy Carrot took the day off and we trundled down to Norton Disney for our 1pm dressage and to walk the course beforehand.

The course was fine, we had loads of time too. We sat in the sunshine, just the three of us, drank tins of pop and I reflected on how lucky I felt... It really was lovely, but the nerves were lingering there somewhere.

I warmed up with the most awful pain in my nether regions. That one you get when you're greeted by a sodding period the day before a show, the one that not only reminds you that you're still not pregnant but also the one that means beige breeches are risking dark red leakage!

The pain was from a very unfortunately positioned string, one that I couldn't fix whilst on a horse and one that rubbed my skin so raw it felt like I'd been massaged by a cheese grater... anyway.... *ahem*!

I got on with it and in the arena, he was a total tit. I struggled to get him down towards the judges' car and the struggled to hold him together as he wanted to run from it! Either way, I wasn't thrilled with the outcome and thought I deserved about a 33.

With the string issue resolved, I changed tack and warmed up for the jumping. This has been my absolute weakest area for years and whilst I can't afford loads of training or many jumps to have at home, I've worked hard in my monthly lessons and practiced getting a good canter on the flat too.

In the warmup he felt a bit flat, but I like that, "flat-Pat" doesn't scare the living shit out of me like "buzzy-in-the-ring-Pat" does.

In we went, and he brightened up somewhat. Instead of soiling myself and clinging on, I used the energy to push forward and he was flying. A positive canter makes the world of difference for us and it certainly did today... WE WENT FUCKING CLEAR!

I properly welled up and felt seriously proud. My husband looked at me with that admiration I can't even put into words. That, right there, that was the proudest moment of my 2018 season.

We also learnt that in a section of dressage scores in the late 30's, by some miracle I was on a 29! Putting us in first place.... by a solid margin after that wonderful clear round.

No pressure!

Warming up for XC I didn't feel too bad, looking back maybe I was a tad complacent but as with horses, you very quickly get reminded that you need to wake up and smell the roses.

He wouldn't go down to the start box, Carrot pretty much had to lead him. I nearly soiled myself right there.

But stop watch set off and we were away.

Not too bad a jump at the first, a wooden palisade shared with the 90. Down to another plain upright at two which he jumped ok too. I was very mindful of not going too fast, at this level we would be heavily penalised for our usual speed. Number 3 was the smallest log you've ever seen, he looked and nearly stopped so I really got after him! Dick! And that's where the wheels started to fall off.

He spooked at all the other jumps leading down to ours fences, some spooks were so exaggerated that I was left hanging half off. He got to fence 4 on the duffest stride because of looking at everything else and we nearly parted company. Fence 5 was a rail with a banner alongside and thank goodness I've had a banner up in the field at home because this was actually okay!

We had a massive spook on the way down to number 6; a roll top just before a mound with number 7; a skinny hanging log on top. I focused on the three strides up to 7 in my approach, thinking ahead and being a good and well prepared rider.

He put in the dirtiest stop ever at 6. The fucking simple rolltop, it was sod all to look at. I tried to kick him over, desperate not to have a 20 to add. I kicked, growled, heaved, but it was over, it was all over.

20 penalties, I represented and of course he jumped it like it was nothing! I'm so disappointed. That was my win, I wanted it so

much, I've never been bothered about a placing but today I felt utterly awful.

7 the hanging log jumped fine, he got a smack into 7b because I was gutted and because he was being a spooky little knob. In hindsight, I should have done that earlier because he jumped round the rest of the course like it was nothing! The bank at 10, hedge at 11, in the water and out of a skinny at 15/16... he answered every question right.

He spooked horribly at the last fence and I came through the finish with tears in my eyes. These were not tears of pride. They were tears of frustration, of disappointment, of all the hard work I've done to get his confidence up, all for nothing. I felt drained, I still do. My husband's face... he felt it too.

We walked back, washed him off and went to the scoreboard for a bit more torture. I'd have had a win; clear by nearly 10 points. I just wanted to go home.

Now in reflection, I feel stupid. I took my eye off the ball, I planned too far ahead, I didn't do all I could have done. It was MY fault. It was not bad luck, it was bad judgment and bad reactions.

This sport can be won or lost in a split second and for everything to come together on one day is a pure miracle but...

We are progressing, we are getting better, we are still learning and I'm not disappointed anymore. He isn't a push button pony and anyone else would struggle to get him round the dressage for a sub 40 let alone a sub 30 or in the start box!! He is sharp, tricky and you have to make him think it's all his idea... but that's what I love him so much.

He's not easy, but my word is he rewarding. We might have lost our first red one today, but it was never really ours to start with and I will never think that way again, you don't win just by getting the best marks. That might determine what colour piece of folded satin and cardboard you go home with but winning is empathy, understanding and education, and that's all that really matters.

Horses are not machines, yet we use them for our enjoyment, what right do I have to be angry when he doesn't act perfectly?

I also thought people would laugh at me for doing the 80 and not being up there in the placings too. But that's another thing I need to stop thinking about!

Lots of love as always

Vic and Pat xxxx

~

And there it was, my educational 2018. Ending the season as we started; still lacking in confidence and still only jumping 80cms. But look at the lessons we've learnt and how much different those things will make 2019 and the rest of our lives together. I am more determined than I have ever been in my whole life.

I have stopped worrying for the most part, about what other people think of me. I have embraced the feeling of only having myself to disappoint and I will come out next year ready to succeed. I want to win far more than I did before, but not a red rosette. I want to win the trust of my beautiful horses, I want to win the admiration of my devoted husband and more than anything, I want to win a smile over every single finish line I cross.

THE FINAL LESSON: It is absolutely NOT about the placing, the fancy show jacket, the shininess of your lorry or the price you paid for your horse. It is about the empathy, love and understanding that you give to your animals, it's about what you take from each experience; good or bad. Don't think you can't turn a bad day on paper into the best day you've ever had, because I know you can. You get to decide how things turn out, you have that power. Why wouldn't you use it?

What are you waiting for? Make today amazing – you deserve it.

Until next time…

EDITORS FOOTNOTE.

Ending this book in 2018 and picking up the reworking of it 5 years on, SO much has changed. I am more experienced now, with more advance skills of the literary kind. I wanted to polish the trilogy so that it felt more 'finished' and less rushed.

The world has changed very much since 2018. I didn't get pregnant that year. I worried about it more than I let on. Thinking back to how I felt then, how vulnerable and insecure, it makes me realise how much stronger I am now.

I found editing some of this really hard, I really wish I could give 2018 Vic a massive hug and tell her it'll all be ok. Feeling how I do now, I just cannot believe *she* is me.

A worldwide pandemic, a lockdown baby, a heartbreaking miscarriage, a rainbow after the storm, 15 Wimpy Weekender Camps, and the devastating final goodbye to my best friend in the entre world…

There's so much more to tell you. – I can't see for the tears filling my eyes; I better start writing.

TO BE CONTINUED….

Printed in Great Britain
by Amazon